BLACK ENGLISH
A Seminar

BLACK ENGLISH
A Seminar

Edited by

DEBORAH SEARS HARRISON
University of Kansas

TOM TRABASSO
Princeton University

 LAWRENCE ERLBAUM ASSOCIATES, PUBLISHERS

1976   Hillsdale, New Jersey

DISTRIBUTED BY THE HALSTED PRESS DIVISION OF

JOHN WILEY & SONS

New York   Toronto   London   Sydney

Lawrence Erlbaum Associates, Inc., Publishers
62 Maria Drive
Hillsdale, New Jersey 07642

Distributed solely by Halsted Press Division
John Wiley & Sons, Inc., New York

Library of Congress Cataloging in Publication Data

Main entry under title:

Black English.

  Includes bibliographies and indexes.
  1. Black English—Addresses, essays, lectures.
I. Harrison, Deborah Sears.   II. Trabasso, Tom.
PE3102.N42B6   301.2'1   75-38897
ISBN 0-470-01395-8

Printed in the United States of America

To:

Joe and *Christine Sears*
    and
Susan Trabasso

Contents

Preface

Why *Black English: A Seminar?* The reasons are several, the simplest and most direct of which is that the editors conducted such a seminar at Princeton University during the fall semester of 1973, and we felt that the content should reach a larger audience than the sixteen of us who partook of the seminar as students.

The seminar, entitled Psychology 410. A Senior Seminar on The Cultural Context of Language and Thought: Black English, grew out of a meeting held the previous year between 18 Black undergraduate concentrators in Psychology and the members of the faculty of that Department. Following four years of increased enrollments of Black students at the University, the students were concerned about "legitimatizing" courses of direct relevance to Black Americans. They, rightfully, were concerned about the quality of their education and they, equally rightfully, were concerned that topics such as racism, Black personality, the history of slavery, Black culture, Black writers etc. should receive serious academic consideration. As students, they argued compellingly that any topic of scholastic interest should be determined by the academic community and that if a sufficient number of scholars in that community wished to study a given subject, they should be allowed to do so (within financial and other limits). While there was a successful Afro-American program on the campus, they recognized the fact that no "traditional" academic department was offering courses on topics directly of interest to Black students.

In response to this meeting, various faculty members made suggestions on courses that might be of interest and for which there was already a growing literature and knowledge base. Among these suggestions, three were realized as courses: racism, Black personality, and Black English.

Some events that happened in the course of proposing the seminar and after its inception are revealing of the attitudes and lack of knowledge about the language and culture of Black Americans by White Americans. They would be amusing except that their implications are ominous and reflect a continued unwillingness on the part of Whites to acknowledge the existence of a distinct and vital Black culture.

During the spring of 1973, the Psychology Department proposed to the Committee on The Course of Study, for recommendation to the Faculty of the University, a senior seminar (an experimental course) with the above indicated title, accompanied by five pages of rationale, need, course outline, topics, and references. During the review, we received some information that leaked out of the Committee's discussion, and alarmed us. Two quotes from these "deliberations" are revealing. One Committee member was quoted as saying, in argument against the course, "Why don't they offer a course on left-handed, bald-headed men?" Another member was purported to have argued, "This course is nothing but a sellout to Black students!" Fortunately, cooler heads and more open minds prevailed, and our subsequent conversations with the Committee Chairman revealed that these views were not representative of the Committee as a whole. The fact that they were said by members of the Faculty at Princeton University was sad enough.

A second incident occurred during the first week of classes in the fall of 1973, when the editor of a conservative alumni magazine, known for its attempts to discredit the current University administration's policies on student admissions (minorities and female students) as well as other liberal policies, called for an appointment with T. Trabasso, the faculty member in charge. The editor submitted a list of questions for the interview. Among these were such questions as, "Do you approve of students speaking *incorrect* (italics ours) English?," "Do you think that Black students are happy at Princeton?," "Are Black students as good academically as Whites?," "Do you favor a more homogeneous student body?," and "What is Black English, anyway?"

The problem of definition seemed reasonable and when the editor called upon the instructor, some pains were taken to provide him with a schedule of seminar speakers, reading lists as well as the difference between prescriptive and descriptive approaches to language. After about ten minutes of discussion, it became clear that the editor held prescriptive views, that is, there is only one way to speak correct English, and that he believed we were offering a seminar *in* Black English rather than *on* it. It was pointed out that this was not a foreign language course, that we were not holding language laboratory lessons on how to speak in the Black English vernacular, etc., etc. but that we were concerned with finding out what it was all about. Upon this revelation, he excused himself hurriedly and murmured something about calling back. He never did.

In addition to the reasons already advanced for the seminar, Dillard's excellent book on the historical origins of Black language, called *Black*

English, which first appeared in 1972, was generating a great deal of excitement and interest in the academic community. At the time it offered us probably the best single text on the subject and several of the seminar speakers, as you will read, were clearly influenced by it. In addition, we were aware of the Urban Language Series of The Center for Applied Linguistics in Washington, D.C. as well as of a few professional colleagues in psychology, linguistics, or sociolinguistics who had done research on aspects of Black language. Dr. William Hall and Dr. Ronald Williams were especially helpful in assisting us to identify and locate possible seminar participants. Through them and others, our list of contacts grew and we issued invitations to some twenty-five possible speakers, fifteen of whom were able to come and address the seminar. All but one of these has contributed a paper to this volume.

The expenses of bringing fifteen visitors to campus were generously underwritten by the Department of Psychology, the Office of The Dean of Student Affairs and Stevenson Hall, an undergraduate, nonresidential college. We are grateful to Dr. Leo Kamin, Chairman of the Department of Psychology at the time of the seminar, Dean Adele Simmons and Dr. Gerald Garvey, Master of Stevenson Hall, for their assistance, without which we could not have conducted the seminar.

The idea of the book came into being upon a suggestion by Dr. Klaus Riegel, one of the participants, and enthusiastic acceptance by Mr. Lawrence Erlbaum, our publisher. At the conclusion of the seminar, somewhat flushed with what we and the students considered to have been a very successful, rewarding and consciousness-raising experience, we asked each seminar participant to develop an essay on the seminar that he or she presented. In addition, we invited two students to develop chapters based upon their term projects.

The resulting contributions, we feel, reflect very well the content and spirit of the seminars. Unfortunately, the several excellent student discussions, presentations, debates, heated arguments, and personal revelations remain only in the memories of those of us who were present at the meetings. We would, however, like to acknowledge our students for their several contributions, not the least of which was their commitment to making the seminar a success: Vanessa Austin, Abner Boles, Beverly Canzater, Deborah Jordan, Melvin McCray, Verley O'Neal, Katrina Peters, Martin Schell, Deborah Scott, Beverly Shepard, Miriam Shustack, Danille Taylor, Saundra Weathers, and Danny Williams.

Pat Reed typed the voluminous correspondence and several of the manuscripts as well as our own contributions, and we thank her for her conscientious and cheerful support.

D. Harrison
T. Trabasso

BLACK ENGLISH
A Seminar

Introduction

Tom Trabasso
Deborah Sears Harrison

Princeton University

Seminars are usually on subjects that have not been well studied, and the idea is that all the participants advance in knowledge by pooling their resources to develop a subject. To organize a seminar, one usually first notes what information is available in published form (books, articles, preprints, talks, conferences etc.), contacts and draws up lists of resource persons ("experts" who have first-hand experience or are involved in the subject), lists tentative topics for presentation and discussion, assigns these to seminar leaders, adds new topics at their suggestion, and then lets the seminar run its course with readings, presentations and discussion. Seminars seldom turn out as anticipated. If one is fortunate, they take on a life of their own, evolve, grow, and expand in ways that enrich those participating in the group. From this, a new knowledge base emerges.

The organization and much of the material presented in what follows grew out of the seminar of the Fall Semester in 1973. Of course, the individual writers were responsible for the content then, but their ideas have evolved since that time and the present themes reflect what resulted from the bringing together of the students and resource people.

We have divided the chapters into four groups. Each group focuses on a different aspect of Black English: on its definition, on its historical origins, on its usage, and on its implications. The parts are not mutually exclusive but neither are they redundant.

They are not as complete or comprehensive as one would like for the treatment of so rich a subject. We hope, however, that the result serves as an introduction and guide to further study.

1

I. DEFINITION

"What is Black English?" is the most frequent question we have encountered since we first conceived of having a course on the subject. On the surface it seems to be a simple question which should have a simple answer. But attempts to answer it reveal that defining Black English is a complex and difficult task.

It is a personal question, asked not only by Blacks but by Whites who, through studying Black English, are becoming more aware of the many varieties of "White" English. It is a political question since language has served as an instrument of political and cultural control whenever two cultures meet. It is a social question since certain forms of speech are admired, prestigeful, codified and promulgated while others are accorded low esteem, stigmatized, ridiculed and avoided. It is an economic question since many feel that "speaking proper" or some variety of Standard English is required for success in middle-class America.

As Ron Williams points out, any definition of Black English is closely bound to the problems of defining the concept of "Blackness," and thus must be sensitive to the wide range of characteristics and experiences of *all* Blacks, from those in the street culture, to those in the middle class.

"What is Black English?" may be a psychological question. Riegel and Freedle theorize that there would be both cognitive and educational advantages in defining Black English as a structural system distinctly different from Standard English, and in treating Black English speakers as bilingual.

It is a linguistic question, but, as Gilbert Sprauve suggests, the efforts of those investigating Black English should not be diverted toward producing a rigorous definition of *language*. Rather, the emphasis should be on finding a functional definition that will facilitate "getting on" with the business at hand of studying and recording the language of Black people.

II. HISTORICAL ORIGINS

Language is a living, organic thing. It is not the codified set of rules of grammar and pronunciation which are stressed in school or modeled over television and radio by speakers who are, for the most part, reading aloud written language rather than engaging in natural, conversational speech. We need to make this distinction since there is much confusion about the *proscriptive nature* of language—that deemed "correct" by some subgroup within a society—and the *descriptive nature*—the attempt to study languages as they are used. As something that people use, language undergoes change through contact with people whose language differs from one's own, the necessity to create new words to reflect concepts which change with the expansion of one's experiences and discoveries, and for other, more immediate reasons, such as commerce, immigration, colonization or slavery, when the speakers from one culture must process or match the language used by the people from another culture.

Related to the definition of Black English are its historical origins and Dillard's (1972) book of the same title did much to remove or replace ethnocentric views held by nineteenth century linguists that Black English had its origins in East Anglia rather than Africa. There are many varieties of English spoken by Blacks, not only in the United States but wherever Black peoples settled as a result of the slave trade or colonization. The forcible uprooting of diverse peoples from their African homes forced major changes in languages and speeded the process of evolution. The changes a language undergoes from *lingua franca* to pidgin to a creole to a codified language are discussed by Elizabeth Traugott, with examples from West African and New World pidgins and creoles.

Ivan Van Sertima explores the still-surviving African traditions that are shared by the Blacks in Guiana, South America, and the Black inhabitants of the Sea Islands off the coast of South Carolina and Georgia. According to Van Sertima, the Sea Islanders maintained a massive Black presence throughout their history, absorbed and Africanized the Europeans rather than being absorbed and Europeanized by them. The language of the Sea Islanders has affected not only the language of the Blacks in the southern United States, but that of the Whites also.

This points out another ethnocentric tendency among Western linguists, namely, that language influence is a one-way process. In his chapter, Ernest Dunn dismisses the theories of linguists who assert that the slaves transplanted here from Africa were only capable of speaking an unintelligible, savage gibberish, and that the language they acquired was an improper, semiacceptable mimicry of the language of the white man, totally unaffected by prior linguistic experience or expertise. Dunn reminds us of the large family of languages (500–600 languages) spoken by the tribes from which slaves were taken. Angela Gilliam explores the influence that blacks had on European languages in South America, using lexicon and syntax other than that which Whites had taught them.

III.   USAGE

Language is realized most often in its natural form: speech. We use speech as a means of communication, and, according to some, a tool for thought. In order to appreciate speech, we need a means of depicting it graphically that transcends, and at the same time allows us to appreciate, the properties of particular dialects or lects (using Traugott's preferred term). Thus, early on in the seminar, William Moulton gave a brief introduction to phonology—the study of the sounds of language—and illustrated this introduction with examples of Black English noted by sociolinguists such as William Labov. Moulton's contribution helps remove the study of the phonology of Black English from the realm of the "exotic" by showing us that many of the terms used to describe it are also used to describe all varieties of English. For instance, "r-lessness" does not imply a structural deficiency, but is a point on a continuum of "r-ness" which linguists find useful in describing any dialect of English.

Important parts of communication are reading and writing and much conjecture exists on the relation of speaking (and listening) to these activities. O'Neal and Trabasso examine how readers of Black English might spell words differently (and thereby decode written material differently) than speakers of Standard English. If there is a relation between how one speaks (phonology) and how one spells (orthography), then Black English speakers, being bilingual, may be at a disadvantage, especially if conventional rules for spelling are closer to basic forms of Standard English.

Are speakers of Black English bilingual? Can they effectively switch codes between two lects? According to William Hall, Black children appear to be more skilled than White children at understanding and producing utterances in both Black English and Standard English. He suggests that this skill at code-switching is learned as a result of the child's perception of the risks involved in speaking a nonstandard lect and the gains or benefits to be derived from speaking a standard one. This ability to switch codes in different situations creates problems for the linguist who tries to obtain good representative samples of the Black English vernacular as it is used in everyday life, as Harrison demonstrates.

Our focus thus far, on phonology and syntax, is decidedly limited. It does not address itself to the richer uses of language by Blacks, either in rhetoric, in the church, in literature, or in the oral tradition reminiscent of African societies. This range of topics was of great interest to the students in the seminar, and they, themselves, conducted sessions on nonverbal forms of communication among Blacks, slang, music as communication, and folklore. On the latter, we were fortunate in that Danille Taylor developed her term paper into a chapter for the book. Along with discussing the rich oral folklore tradition of Afro-Americans, she traces the evolution of expressions used among speakers of Black English (in-group expressions) to refer to and describe themselves.

IV.   IMPLICATIONS

The implications—social, economic, educational, psychological, political—of speaking a language that is different from the dominant form of a culture are considerable. In the early study of language of Blacks, which stemmed from an interest in, and later the failure of, Head Start, there existed a tendency on the part of the White researchers to commit the fallacy of the linguistic relativity, or Whorfian, hypothesis. That is, they falsely attributed speech to being thought and their faulty analysis of the speech led to erroneous conclusions about Black children being deficient in logic. For this reason, we asked John Carroll to lead a seminar on the Whorfian hypothesis. He provides us with an historical perspective of the idea and concludes that the categories of thought are universal among mankind, and are universally reflected in all languages and dialects, including Black English.

When, during the 1960s, the American educational system found it necessary to explain its failure in educating Black children, Eugene Wiggins explains how and why the finger of blame was pointed toward Black English and, indirectly, the Black child by cognitive deficit theorists. He also discusses the social, educational, economic, and political consequences resulting from this example of the tendency of the system to "blame the victim."

Teachers are probably the first major group of persons encountered outside of one's home. These initial encounters with representatives of the dominant culture can have lasting effects on the educational development of the child. Ann Covington illustrates how proficiency in Standard English can be one beneficial by-product of a teacher–pupil relationship based on respect and acceptance of the child's culture and the language he brings with him to the classroom. These positive attitudes on the part of the teacher are more important and effective, she feels, than any language intervention program.

Another instrument of oppression of the poor has been the test. Walter Wolfram examines several potential sources of bias built into standardized tests which may work against those from different cultural backgrounds and those who do not speak Standard English. It is, Wolfram asserts, through language that one can most easily bias a test against whole groups of persons.

REFERENCES

Dillard, J. *Black English: Its history and usage in the United States.* New York: •Random House, 1972.

Part I
DEFINITION

1

The Anguish of Definition:
Toward a New Concept
of Blackness

Ronald Williams

Federal City College

When I agreed to write a paper based on my remarks to the seminar, I immediately thought of two intriguing directions that the paper might take. The first alternative was rather simple in that it followed the oral presentation that I had already attempted, that is, to talk about the educational and political implications of the study and use of Black English. The topic suited my interests at that time and was scheduled opportunely in the semester so that previous speakers and reading assignments had given the students a background that might encourage discussion.

Thus, my original plan was to talk briefly about the past and present structure of Black English. It appeared to me that three major positions should be mentioned: the Anglicist, the Creolist, and the synchronic. The Anglicist claims that the lect is a holdover of linguistic features used by immigrants from Southern England who settled along the Eastern seaboard and the South during the colonial period. The Creolist position, on the other hand, maintains that Black English is derived from a prototype Creole, and the present lect is the result of a movement away from this plantation Creole toward Standard English—a movement that has been going over for over 400 years and has not yet ended. Thus, any effort to provide a linguistic description of the lect must assume a different deep structure from Standard English. In short, the lect's semantic and grammatical structure originated in a non-English language.

Last, the synchronic position does not enter into the debate over the origin of Black English. Regardless of the linguistic influences that may have produced this lect, the synchronic view maintains that its description can be accomplished without reference to its history. There is no need, according to this view, to posit a separate deep structure from Standard English to account for the different phonological and grammatical features found in Black English; it appears that all differences can be accounted for by surface structure changes. This view does not make a judgment about competing historical accounts of Black English; it simply states that an adequate description of a lect may be accomplished without drawing on its history.

Following a review of the historical development of Black English, I had planned to talk briefly about how some educators were viewing this variant of English. Rather than discussing the difference–deficit argument, it seemed more rewarding to look at public education as a rather successful institution that has succeeded in educating those persons for whom it was designed, primarily those of the middle class and primarily those who are White. Although the middle class might have many complaints about a system that is far from perfect, there is every indication that it does a rather commendable job for them. No one measure of this success would satisfy everyone, whether it was the number of young people from a class who enter college or the number who seem to do well on the various tests which are prerequisites for certain jobs or apprenticeships. Yet the poor and the minorities do fall significantly behind the middle class in all of these measures of achievement or aptitude. For that reason, if for no other, the public schools appear to prepare the middle-class youngster better than the poor and the minorities to succeed in college and in qualifying for skilled jobs, and this accomplishment is an important one.

The success of the public schools in educating the middle class has led many persons to conclude that if the poor and the non-White were not learning, something had to be wrong with them. After all, the system does work. This reasoning then makes the victim responsible for whatever is wrong; there is something wrong with the poor or the minorities that accounts for their being unable to learn.

Black English has been currently isolated as the flaw that causes Blacks to benefit so little from public education, especially the working-class and lower middle-class Blacks, who are the principal speakers of the lect. This point of view, whether espoused by those of liberal or racist minds, is guilty of dehumanizing Blacks by reducing their plight to a single cause, a simple-minded reductionism. Little is ever said about the failure of the public schools to educate the poor, regardless of race.

The oppression of racism means nothing and is seldom weighed in trying to understand why Black children seem impervious to all school efforts in their behalf. Life-styles and values that make for survival in the limited world etched out by poverty and racism conflict with those of the school. From the very beginning these two worlds, that of the schools and that of the poor and minorities, are in conflict. It is the children who are destroyed in this violent clash; the public schools continue developing programs and receiving monies from all sources to study that which the schools neither have understood nor have ever served effectively.

The failure of the schools to educate students is to be expected. After all, to reiterate, the public schools were not designed to teach the poor and the minorities. Their programs, materials, and books were prepared for the middle-class White child. The public schools, then, have been an extension of a class and a way of life that have always been foreign to the poor and non-White. Its teachers were prepared in training schools and colleges of education by persons who were devoted to their class and life-style. It therefore should not be a surprise to learn that there is an almost one-to-one relationship between success in school and socioeconomic class. Those who are most like the models for whom the system was prepared do best in the system. And racism has retarded the drive of racial minorities toward middle-class status.

Any attempt to account for the failure of Blacks in school will have numerous political implications. It will influence the funding of programs designed to give Blacks a head start in school, to disperse the poor among the more affluent, and to provide a different education for Blacks based on their alleged inherent inferiority. Today the argument centers around education, which is but one aspect of the central question. The central question continues to be the role Blacks will play in this society.

Had I followed this first direction for this contribution, the above points would be elaborated. But I feel there is another immediate and vital concern, and that is what it means to be Black. It seems that we are operating under an unstated but tyrannically demanding definition of Blackness into which everything has to be compressed.

The anguish of examining that definition became the second alternative, and the one that I have decided to follow. The problem was brought into clear focus after one of the seminar participants began describing what he did when speaking Black English. The particular characteristics of speech to which he drew attention are unimportant here, except to say that they were not among the features that linguists traditionally cite to define Black English. I pointed out to him, first, that I considered his description to be that of a Standard English speaker, and second, that the term Black English, as used by most linguists, refers to specific grammatical and phonological features. Some work has been done on prosody that seems to indicate that Black English speakers use intonation differently from Standard English speakers, but while this research is interesting, it is only suggestive and far from conclusive.

It was then mentioned, and correctly I believe, that my definition of language was too narrow, that much more was involved in Black English than those items that can be inventoried. That observation was correct. Yet one can make such a statement about any language. Unfortunately, our description of a language is limited to the tools and models of analysis available to us. All of these instruments of discovery are restrictive and hardly scratch the surface of all that language does.

Certainly if one wishes to talk about other aspects of language, such as its intention and even the view of the world that it projects, one has to struggle to identify and isolate categories that will make clear and meaningful what is merely suggested. What is involved here is not a failure to understand some rather crucial basics about language and scientific discovery. Regardless of the lect spoken, some people feel compelled to identify themselves as Black English speakers. Their behavior appears to be inextricably involved in their conception of and identification with Blackness; no amount of rationality would be able to withstand their intention to place themselves solidly on the side of Blackness. It makes little difference that the majority of the speakers of Black English, as defined here, are found among the working-class and lower middle-class Blacks. Indeed such a discovery makes it all the more important that some, for example Black students, identify with the speakers of this lect.

Often Blackness is identified with the life-style of the poor, putting an inordinately heavy emphasis on the street dude, the hustler. The critical criteria for Blackness include intimate knowledge of greens, chittlins, corn bread, and sweet potato pie. The profanity of the street has to punctuate phrases appropriately, and other words have to be manipulated to achieve the proper effect. Positive virtues are found in the high style of dress that distinguishes the lower classes. Since the majority of Blacks are of the working and nonworking classes, the effort is to embrace the Black masses, to affirm the stereotype and hoist it as a banner of pride and honor.

It is understandable why a people would embrace the very stereotypes used to denigrate them. The act itself certainly requires courage, to embrace with affection all that you have been taught to loathe in order to affirm your existence. And it is not an easy task nor one without its contradictions and deeply disturbing conflicts. The parents of many Blacks have and still do guide their children toward a life style that does not include the diet, language, and dress of the poor. Differences between classes are also found in religious expression, entertainment, and behavior. Indeed the Black middle class has much in common with the broader middle class.

When Blacks, especially those striving to make it economically, attempt to validate their Blackness, they manage to resolve their conflict by choosing to identify with the street brother on two rather complementary levels. One is the verbal level that allows them to affirm brotherhood and allegiance to the required attitudes and principles. Usually there is no challenge to the avowed sincerity and commitment. Since everyone may use words, since challenges from any source would threaten everyone, and since there are no strict definitions for brotherhood or any clear statement of principles, the ritual is available to all, and quite safe. I suspect that the language of brotherhood is tolerated by everyone because most everyone knows that certain words and attitudes are expected; the times demand them. Yet everyone also knows that he must base critical judgments upon more reliable information, such as knowledge of the person who is talking; otherwise it is just talk.

The second level moves from language to other forms of expression. The occasional soul dinner is one, resplendent with all of the traditional fare. Another is the style of dress, which takes many forms: the denim of the farmer or worker, various versions of African styles, and a wide range of current styles that manage to avoid the extremes of the street while capturing its flavor.

The lure of the street cultures seems to be strongest among those young Blacks whose parents have moved away from the ghetto to secure better housing, better schools, and in general a better way of life for their children. No matter how desperately they may try to romanticize the life of the poor, it persists in all of its stark harshness, deprivation, and brutality, unmoved by the politics of language. It is the obstinancy of poverty, its enduring cruelty that weighs heavily upon the more privileged Black. This may be the source of his guilt.

Often Blacks who do not live in poverty or even on the fringes of it reject the term *middle class;* they associate middle-class status not only with economic position but with a social position that is free from racism. The argument goes like this: as long as there is racism all Blacks are of the same class. There can be no rebuttal to the statement that all Blacks are victims of racism, for racism by definition means that a people are oppressed solely because of their race. Yet it is dishonest to pretend that there are no class differences among Blacks. Everyday reality tells us of these differences. Essentially the point is that the neighborhood in which you grow up makes a difference, that your parents' job and the amount of money they earn make a difference, and that environment and money usually heavily influence your view of yourself, your expectations, and your perception of the world. These appear to be rather obvious notions, hardly worth repeating. It becomes necessary to state them only when some deny that having money, position, and some power have not significantly changed them from those who are without money, without position, and without power.

A casual observation can discredit the position which denies class difference. Middle-class Blacks are almost as uncomfortable and fearful of the Black slums as their White counterparts. We all appear to share a universal fear of the poor, wherever they are found; we all feel vulnerable to them—whether justly or not is another question. We do not trust the poor, and they have never trusted us. Black skin does not dissipate this fear and distrust.

The assertion of a classless Black society was just one manifestation of the larger problem: how do you reconstruct Black history, depict current Black circumstances, and point toward a Black future without reference to or dependency in some part upon a history forged by Blacks and Whites? The intention is to condemn the American past as having been a totally White and worthless undertaking in which Blacks were *only* victims. It seems to say that nothing of substance happened to Blacks outside of their tragic encounter with Whites. A definition of Blackness based on such a narrow view of the past must of necessity be deformed. What has resulted is something approaching cultural schizophrenia. In a sense it has affirmed a racist myth that Blacks have never played a significant role in the development of this country. By extirpating themselves from American history, some Blacks have deprived themselves of the rich background and fertile soil they need to nurture the myths and possibilities necessary to discover themselves anew.

Yet by making American history their own, Blacks must face some rather unpleasant truths about themselves. Blacks may not have made domestic and foreign policy, but they certainly have helped to implement it. The Buffalo Soldiers, who were Black, crushed the last Indian resistance in the Southwest. The Black Ninth and Tenth Cavalry saved the Rough Riders at San Juan Hill, insuring victory in Cuba. However one might describe the outcome of the Vietnam war, a high percentage of Black soldiers were there.

Obviously I am not trying to make the case that Blacks have designed and initiated a policy of genocide, as in the case of the American Indian, or imperialism, as in the case of San Juan. And there are very good reasons why Blacks strove to distinguish themselves in the military, ranging from efforts to prove that they were as good as Whites to efforts to win by valor some measure of freedom and respect upon returning home, not to mention that the military for most was the best available job at the time. Whatever the reasons, it is clear that Blacks, as other men, have not always had virtue on their side. A sadder bit of instruction emerges once again: in the name of their own freedom, men will cause others to suffer the same fate that they are trying to escape.

At some future point when men render a final verdict on the American experience, their words, for good or bad, will include Black Americans. Black history cannot rise separate and above whatever the American experience has been. That is our fate, regardless of any feelings to the contrary.

The definition of Blackness that was supposed to liberate Blacks appears to have created much confusion, and more, it may prove to be just as restrictive and pernicious as racism. Whereas racist doctrine sees the Black man as coming from African savagery, contributing nothing of consequence to American growth and incapable of rising to White standards, a current definition of Blackness defines the street culture as the primary Black experience, sees the Black masses as undifferentiated in terms of economics or class, and attempts to chart a future which fails to take into account an American history and social system. Both views restrict. The former would deny Blacks all of the attributes that expand and enrich the possibilities of life. The latter does the same but may prove to be the most oppressive since it is self-imposed. Blacks think nothing of railing against White racism, but for them to oppose the loosely articulated strictures of Blackness creates guilt, especially for the Black middle class.

The irony is that it has been middle-class Blacks who have attempted to define the Black experience in terms of the Black street culture. It was they who romanticized the life-style of the dude and hustler and who pronounced it as the authentic experience from which all else must flow. Indeed whenever discussions of this kind are carried on, regardless of their merit, it is done so by the middle class or those aspiring to that class, seldom by the poor. The poor are usually overwhelmed by the struggle just to move from one day to the next. It is the middle class which has the leisure, the awareness, and the implicit belief that words can create the impetus for change; it struggles to articulate an understanding of the world and a way of coming to terms with it. In most places in the world, this kind of activity is seldom engaged in by the poor, even those of the street culture. Black Americans are no exception to the rule.

The absurdity of the situation is that the Black middle-class youth has defined Blackness in a way which would forever estrange him. He may as well have defined Blackness as Whiteness. All the language in the world, all of the romanticism and longed-for suffering will not transform a middle-class youth into a poor Black. The middle-class youth, after meeting countless frustrations with trying to become what he is not, will return to his middle-class community and job and may sometimes turn to reactionary politics. Unfortunately, he follows a pattern set by White middle-class youths over the last 50 years: they come every season, stay for awhile working for social change, then disappear into the great American mass, while the poor and their problems remain unchanged by these seasonal comings and goings.

You have to wonder just what motivated these Black youths to make so much of the street culture central to their definition of Blackness.

Could it have been an effort to identify with their notions about the Black masses of the people?

In the past, it has been Whites who have been drawn to the "fun" aspect of the Black experience. American literature is full of the comments by Whites about the happy, carefree Blacks. Many Southerners pointed to the abandoned ways and careless pleasures of enslaved Blacks as proof of their happiness in slavery, which, by contrast, served as evidence of the civilized and gentle ways of the White masters. The myth of the happy Blacks served many ends. To the rest of the world, it was evidence of the Southerner's guilt that allowed him to overcome the barbarism of a cruel and vile system, making his handling of it acceptable to other civilized people. The Southerner created a fantasy about slavery that allowed his fantasy about himself to remain intact, that he was genteel, cultured, kind, and gracious in all matters and dealings with his fellow man.

Likewise, some have a need to view the poor as being happy and deriving a mysterious fulfillment and joy from life that is forever denied their betters. Regardless of the mountains of statistical data showing that the poor have a higher incidence of infant mortality and are doomed to a shorter life expectancy, this viewpoint persists. How do you explain this need of some to find a silver lining in the misery of others? Perhaps it lies in the obvious: many do not seem to be able to shake the feeling that they are somehow responsible for the misfortunes of the poor; and if not responsible, they may feel, at times, linked to them in a terrifying way that haunts and reminds them in most inopportune moments that they are but a chance away from a similar fate.

There is also a smugness to this attitude that seems to assert that the more affluent are burdened down with the weight of the world by doing all of those responsible, correct chores from which even the poor benefit to some extent. Thus, the responsible citizen could enjoy himself as much as the poor if he were less than what he is. Naturally, the edge of this knife cuts to the irresponsibility and slovenliness of the poor, holding them accountable for their abjectness.

The majority of White Americans persist in seeing poor Blacks as being fundamentally different from themselves. While it is no longer in good taste to use racial epithets or to talk derisively of the poor, we have developed rather interesting code words to reflect our basic attitude about them, such as "welfare cheaters." Such language sets impossible standards for "acceptable poverty." You must be really and truly poor, which seems to mean that signs of advanced malnutrition must be evident, that your clothing must be threadbare but clean, and that your housing must not be much beyond a shack or a scrubbed and well-tended hovel. The honesty of poverty must be established. Somehow it must be proved that whatever ill fate has captured you it had nothing to do with your efforts to better yourself, that under normal circumstances you would have made it, just as *we* all did. As a final touch, your pride must make you fiercely resist any help, and once overcome by the good forces sent to help you, you must openly show the pain of your humiliation. Since there are few people who can meet these criteria for acceptable poverty, most poor people are suspect, even those deserving of help.

Mix the suspicion of the poor as being unworthy parasites with the guilt that comes from somehow feeling partially responsible for their plight; add a dash of knowing that all of these relationships are somewhat tenuous and quite susceptible to chance; then it follows that the nonpoor are in need of a simple easy way of extricating themselves from their ambivalent and terrorizing feelings about the poor. Two old shibboleths are resurrected and paraded out: the poor are happy, and the poor are satisfied. You cannot argue against happiness. After all, that is what it is all about. Their suffering masked over with these easy words, the majority can oppose giving any serious thought or help to the nonworking or working poor. Once more you do not need to question a system that seems to thrive in the face of suffering and injustice, for the imperfections are in the people, not in how society is ordered. We have found for the moment easy and satisfying answers to very intricate and disturbing problems, easy and satisfying answers that are as fallacious as they are old.

The middle-class Blacks who turned to the street culture for their model of Blackness were following a persistent trend in American thought and behavior to reduce the lives of Blacks to rather simplistic and grossly distorted notions. And much like the stereotypes of Whites, the definition of Blackness has not moved to liberate, to include the seething diversity among the poor, or to try to tap the source of strength that enables them to endure and, for some, even to prosper.

And perhaps there are very good reasons why the broader and more viable patterns of Black life are not captured or even given due consideration in the current definition of Blackness. Blackness, as defined and heralded, was supposed to identify the uniqueness of the Black experience. It was something that had flourished in America without, at the same time, being American in any fundamental way. Blackness was to stamp a particular life-style, running the gambit from music to mental processes, distinguishing Blacks from Whites.

Looking into the lives of the majority of working-class and middle-class Blacks, the Black middle-class young people found little to distinguish Blacks from other Americans. The strong church affiliation among them certainly was not helpful in making a distinction. Although there was little direct denunciation of the Christian church, many young Blacks viewed the church as a relic of the past. Besides, the church had too strong a link with the White community, which in itself made it suspect.

Most importantly, many of the youthful voices attempting to give new form and substance to Blackness had at one time been involved in the Civil Rights Movement of the 1960's which was either supported directly by the churches or affiliated in some way with them. When many Black young people deserted the Civil Rights Movement and proclaimed it ineffective for bringing about social change, the churches were equally condemned. At least intellectually, the Black movement that sought to distinguish Black life as a unique and independent experience tore itself away from the formal religious structure of the community.

There were other strains within the Black community that were equally repugnant to the makers of the new myth, strains that stood in stark opposition to the street culture. The desire to get ahead was one of these forces that accounted for many Black men working two jobs, wives working, and countless sacrifices being made to make a dream come true. Often the dream was a new house in a better neighborhood with better schools so that families could be reared away from the evils of the street, the pimp, the hustler, narcotics, the rackets, the ubiquitous taverns, and the fear of assault and robbery. It does not seem too farfetched to assume that many Blacks struggled against all of these odds because they believed in themselves and believed that they could make it. Implicit in this drive of Blacks to better themselves was the conviction that the system would allow it, and that if they only worked hard enough they could succeed. Naturally it meant that racism would have to be fought every step of the way. But there does not appear to be any doubt about the system, once purged of its racist practices, as a way of making it.

A concept of Blackness that excluded the church and rejected the Puritan ethic could hardly become popular with the majority of Blacks. The majority of Blacks would certainly sympathize with any movement that sought to eradicate racism. They would certainly adopt the slogans and manners of the new movement for liberation but that would be the extent of their commitment, for their abhorrence of the street culture, *the low life*, their involvement in the Black churches, and their commitments to the inherent possibilities within the economic system ran too deep to be shaken by a few words, regardless of how logically ordered or passionately uttered. The irony here is that, whatever it means to be an American, race and racism have not prevented Blacks from sharing with other Americans some rather fundamental notions about themselves, their country, and their possibilities within the country. These notions have endured in spite of racism. Whenever the question of race is settled or put aside, Blacks will be found to be indistinguishable from other Americans in terms of their aspirations and faith in the economic system.

The unresolved problem of race continues to fuel the tension between those who would make the street culture central to Blackness and those who are repelled by this life-style. The dilemma for most Blacks hinges on maintaining faith in a democratic system and on affirming pride in race and its unique gifts while at the same time opposing racism. This is not an easy task. It is one which over time seems to have required of Blacks an act of faith in the democratic system, undaunted by the inability of that system all too often to work effectively in their behalf. Perhaps hope and faith in the ideal, the moral stance, is the only tenable position for minority groups who are without power. While the American system has been slow to live up to its ideal, Blacks have been asked to understand and accept politics that have excluded them from power and wealth and to bear their plight with patience and faith when there was little reason to have either. It is this frustration inherent in the American democratic process that produced a definition of Blackness that attempted to deny Black participation in American history, producing a concept of Blackness that excised all that is White or thought to be derived from White values.

The failure of the street culturalist to attract a sizable following is not a condemnation of the effort to clarify the issues surrounding Blacks. If anything it points up the futility of trying to force a large number of people to embrace that which is repugnant to them. Although a people may be forced to do a number of things to survive, they realize instinctively that their acts, while insuring the moment out of desperation, are in the long run destructive, a fact which may explain why Blacks themselves despise so much of what the street culture represents.

The conflict between these two worlds within the Black community has been examined quite critically by Black playwrights and writers. In the play *The River Niger,* Joseph Walker presents a working-class Black family trying to survive amidst the frustrated ambitions of the father, amidst the explosive temptation of Black militancy, and amidst the son's failures and self-deceptions, which in the end cost the family dearly. The play affirms a family's struggles to remain "decent," while the father proudly proclaims his Blackness. For the playwright, the two positions seem compatible since they are not placed in dramatic conflict. *The River Niger,* which is the poem the father recites in the play, speaks with pride of Black history and emits a veiled warning to those who would deny this history and its people. Those who would threaten the family are handled mercilessly by the dramatist. For example, the three militants in the play are portrayed respectively as a necrophile, a dope addict, and a ne'er-do-well. Whatever had been its cause, whatever its virtue, the militant movement is unqualifiedly discredited from the moment its leaders and representatives are presented to the audience. And when the son, who at one time had been a member of the militant group, returns home from the service, he too turns his back on the group, not with a denunciation of its ideas or its failure to achieve its goals. Not at all. He had merely outgrown it. It was not the rejection of a political position but rather a turning away from the odious street, renouncing adolescence, if you will. The play leaves much to be resolved in the mind of the viewer, but it makes one point quite explicit: strength and virtue remain within the good, hard-working struggling family.

It is this working-class ethic or credo that rises victoriously in the play, an affirmation that life must be lived within the law by working hard and doing those things which make for success, while struggling to overcome the oppression of racism. What is not spelled out is just how racism is to be confronted within a Puritanical framework, which, it could be argued, contributes to racism. You must wonder what social protest resides in the poem beyond an ambiguous warning, when the times appear to demand something more forcefully and clearly stated. Aside from what the play does not do, it certainly does attempt to state the case for the majority of Blacks by placing their lives in stark opposition to the ways of the street. The play makes no distinction between the militant politics that often borrows the language and style of the street and the hustler. It lumps them together and soundly condemns both without hope of redemption.

On the other hand, James Alan McPherson, in "The Story of a Scar,"[1] structures his story around the class differences that exist among Blacks. The narrator of the story encounters a young woman who works in the post office. The narrator's language is almost unnaturally impeccable, pretentiously formal. The young woman's language is that of the working class: "You *cain't* be no married man," she observed. "A wife *ain't* worth that much." This device of presenting two distinctly different language patterns brings two people, two worlds, together in a manner in which communication or any real exchange is just about impossible. McPherson gives the reader much to ponder about these characters and their story.

"The Story of a Scar" vividly presents class distinctions that often separate people, even those of the same color. And although the narrator might be viewed as pompous and even artificial, his character becomes so only in contrast to the earthy manner and language of the young woman. No apology is made for these differences; each is vital. And it is just this point that makes "The Story of the Scar" relevant to this discussion. Class differences are presented clearly, even brutally. I do not mean to state that is all the story reveals, but for the sake of this discussion, that is the important point.

---

[1] *Atlantic Monthly,* December 1973.

The question of class is one that is never squarely faced and examined in America. Aside from studies in the social sciences, there is a tendency in everyday life to pass over class distinctions as though they did not exist or, if they are acknowledged, as if they are of little consequence. There are undoubtedly many reasons for minimizing class differences, not least of all is an economic arrangement that seems to imply that individual effort more than often leads to prosperity. Regardless of how few actually succeed and how many are lost in the struggle, most people believe in the efficacy of individual initiative, of being able to make it, and perhaps none so much as poor Blacks.

Blacks are just as ill equipped to handle these differences that separate groups along economic and social lines as most other Americans. For example, a few middle-class Blacks have attempted to give Blackness those attributes that are antithetical to middle-classness and that are characteristic of the street. Accumulated anger and frustration with racism undoubtedly spurred this effort to hang Blackness on something that was in direct conflict with the White world. But in the end, something quite American, quite "White," for the sake of this discussion, may have doomed the effort—the failure to take into account that class differences separate Blacks as they do other Americans. Such differences have caused middle-class Blacks to question their ability to achieve Blackness and has caused them to agonize over their full stomachs, their spacious and well-appointed houses, and their general affluence. The formula seems to be that the greater the distance in terms of affluence from the street culture, which embodies the "essence" of Blackness, the greater the need to identify with it. Since, as stated above, the middle-class Black is repelled by much that defines the street culture and the poor, his can become a state of unrelenting agony. It is this tension, this anguish, that some Black writers and playwrights are attempting to examine, to better understand what is happening among Blacks today. Out of this cauldron of ambivalences and emotional conflicts will come the wisdom that will determine the political direction of the race in the years ahead.

The question might easily be asked: Is a concept of Blackness worth the effort? Given the diversity among Black people, is this the time to attempt to define or give some kind of structure to a concept that separates and distinguishes them? Of course, there never can be a final answer to a question of this kind, and I do not propose one. But such questions do permit one to consider alternatives to past actions and even to contemplate a state in which people make no effort to say who they are. The latter condition is impossible for me to imagine, and few people, if any, have ever elected to take it.

• The problem arose not out of the effort to define Blackness, that is, to talk about those characteristics and experiences which Black people might share with humility and pride as being a fit description of what they have been in the past and what they wish to become in the future. The problem arose when the definition of Blackness excluded the people to whom the meaning of the word was most important and included people for whom it meant the least, for those in the street culture have often been propelled by survival based on the hustler's ethic, which has *shown* little interest in developing racial awareness and pride. Not much more would have been accomplished by using the poor as the exclusive model for Blackness, for poor Blacks, even the working poor, have been occupied with the struggle for survival, which often is endlessly brutal and demanding of their time and energy. They are usually unaware of other alternatives to what they are doing. As was said earlier, since it was the middle class that carried on about the meaning of words and their importance in men's lives, it was the middle class who needed a definition of Blackness that was acceptable to them, that would allow them to locate themselves in time and place and to stand tall on a past that reveals an attractive future.

The task then was to define Blackness in such a way that it liberated rather than constrained. Naturally, no one definition would satisfy all groups. Yet it does seem that if one seeks to set boundaries for Blackness that speak more broadly to the Black experience, much of the conflict inherent in the recent definition can be avoided. Blackness would embrace a history, primarily an Afro-American one, rich with diversity and ambiguities, as is the history of most people. In no sense can the Black community be seen or understood as a monolith. It seeths with diversity from art to politics, and although the street culture is a part of that community and its history, it by no means represents the dominant part or that part to which the community wishes to point with pride.

Herein may lie what is crucial to any definition: it must embrace not only what has been and what is, but also what is essential for the survival of the community. This is something that the current definition of Blackness does not do. The best within the Black community, found at all levels of the community, must be able to move toward fulfillment in the future. The best of all groups and of all political persuasions in the community must be included.

Perhaps what is being sought is an attitude about Blackness, rather than a formal definition that would restrict and exclude. It would be an attitude that would never cause a Black person to question his Blackness—it would be a given, not something earned, as manhood, womanhood, even personhood within the general American context. It would not be a state or condition that would be harnessed with success or acquisition or even performance in sports or sex. It would be inseparable from personhood; it would mantle existence. Of course it would say nothing about how one would use it. More importantly, such a mantle should inspire and raise the best in its people.

The attitude would surely not imply a political stance. Undoubtedly many political positions would flow from it. Any effort to link politics either explicitly or implicitly to Blackness would cause divisions within the Black community too deep for even time to heal, for the consequences would be that those failing to take the "true" Black position would be somehow less than other Black persons, even traitors to the community. A doctrinaire definition of Blackness would continue to provide simplistic descriptions and answers to a complex existence.

The first National Black Political Convention, held in Gary, Indiana in 1972, may have fallen victim to the practice of tying a political position to a definition of Blackness. The convention represented a wide range of political positions and leanings, some dating to the turn of the century. The challenge at Gary was to bring all of these groups together into a political force, such groups as the National Association for the Advancement of Colored People, the Urban League, Labor, and various Black Nationalist groups. These groups came from various parts of the country, representing differing histories and struggles that had to be understood and reconciled at Gary. Each was adamantly opposed to racism; each had a different notion as to how racism should be opposed. When certain groups walked out of the convention at Gary, groups representing a conservative position but perhaps also the Black mainstream, the chances of creating a strong Black political force were seriously weakened. The implication is certainly not that if all Blacks were to accept an attitude of Blackness, as has been suggested here, all conflicts would be eliminated. It would mean only that conflicts and disagreements would move to a different level; there would be one less area to disagree on, one that is fundamental to the experience of Blacks, for if there is one note that has been frequently sounded in this discussion, it is that the Black experience has been a complex one, open to many perceptions.

An inclusive attitude toward Blackness might eliminate the guilt of middle-class Blacks. The nonpoor would be just as authentic as the poor. The new approach would allow those who are moving from one economic status to another to retain their identity and feeling of being at one with their people, for to exclude the nonpoor would certainly be an inversion of values, giving the highest recognition to those who have been unable to achieve while holding those who do in suspicion. If a dominant drive of the poor is to acquire money, in pursuing this goal, they must also divest themselves of Blackness, since "becoming better off" would diminish their Blackness. The blatant silliness of this kind of reasoning hardly deserves comment. Luckily few of the poor have paid much attention to it.

With the issue of Blackness resolved, it might now be possible for students to view the Black experiences rigorously and critically without the need to romanticize and to identify in a personal way with every aspect of their inquiry. Black English, as currently defined by linguists, can be viewed as the lect of a large number of working- and nonworking-class Blacks. The Blacks who do not speak this lect are no less Black because they speak a different language variety. The lect that one speaks has nothing to do with race but everything to do with social environment. One speaks the language of one's immediate community. If Blackness were embraced as proposed here, it would enable Blacks to approach their experience fully prepared to discover ambiguities and confounding perplexities within it, which seem to be common to most human activity. The experiences of Blacks are no different, and their attempts to find solutions should not be needlessly encumbered.

2

What Does It Take
to Be Bilingual or Bidialectal?

Klaus F. Riegel

University of Michigan

Roy Freedle

Educational Testing Service

INTRODUCTION

In the following presentation we will consider Black English to be a structural system distinctly different from Standard English, and we will maintain this supposition regardless of whether we are considering spoken or written language and whether, in addition, we prefer to regard Northern, Southern, or British English as different language systems or not. As we hope to make clear, our concern will be exclusively with education and the technology of training strategies which relate to the conditions under which any two language systems are to be learned.

Provided that we understand Black English to be structurally different in phonology, syntax, and lexicon, there remains the additional question whether psychologically the dialects are unified, partially overlapping, or distinct cognitive systems. Labov (1972) has shown that structural rules which govern contraction and deletion of Standard English have a close relationship with structural rules of contraction and deletion in Black English. One must not be misled here into overgeneralizing the import of such a correspondence. Psychologically, a language user who knows both dialects may cognitively separate these two dialects as functional systems in spite of the demonstrated linguistic correspondences. Indeed, Hall and Freedle (1973) and Freedle and Hall (1975) have analyzed sentence imitation data obtained from Black and White children wherein both groups were presented with sentences representing Black English and Northern White English and found correlational patterns within and across the two dialects indicating that these dialects operate as coherent and somewhat separate systems. However, across dialects they detected either no influence (zero correlations), some positive overlap in the systems (positive correlations), or cognitive interference effects (negative correlations), depending upon the particular grammatical structures which were examined. One could not have deduced these psychological patterns from knowledge of Labov's rules of grammatical correspondence. Thus, issues need not be tied just to linguistic analyses and the topic of cognitive processing which is raised in the next sections has special import of its own for psycholinguists working in the area of subcultural sociolinguistics.

EARLIER RESEARCH

At the present time, minority groups of Blacks, Chicanos, Puerto Ricans, Orientals, and Native Americans represent the largest contingents of bilinguals in the United States. There exist, however, small groups of bilingual children from homes with relatively high educational and economic levels. These are the children of professionals who have emigrated to this country and found it advisable to raise their children under bilingual and often bicultural conditions. Needless to say, both groups of bilinguals are psychologically and sociologically far apart from one another. These differences have been brought about by unequal educational and economic opportunities.

In the past, notably during the 1930s, a considerable number of psychological investigations were conducted with bilingual children (see McCarthy, 1954). A few reports on the well-educated children of the latter group have provided insights into the compatibility of two linguistic systems and about some psychological problems in processing such information (Leopold, 1939–1949). The bulk of the research was conducted, however, on children from minority groups, mainly in New York, Philadelphia, Los Angeles, and Hawaii. It raised the possible interpretation that serious deficiencies existed not only in the *use* of language via middle-class norms, but in other psychological skills as well. In the interpretations, the sociolinguistic basis of psychological performance was rarely emphasized with sufficient strength. The research was all too often restricted to sets of purely psychological variables operating in a context-free vacuum and, subsequently, overgeneralized and misleading conclusions were drawn about the lack of motivation, ability, and intelligence of these children.

A more instructive and positive approach has been used and, subsequently, more positive results have been obtained in recent studies of French–English bilinguals in Canada by Lambert and his associates (Lambert, Havelka, & Crosby, 1958; Lambert, Tucker, & d'Anglejan, 1973). Although differences in educational and economic opportunities seem to exist between Canadian subgroups, these differences are not as large as those between the minority and majority groups in the United States.[1] Their results, briefly, indicated that the cultural conditions under which the two languages were learned affected the cognitive organization of these systems and this structural difference in turn affected psychological performance. Thus their work raised the possibility that differences were due to cultural–historical differences. Further below we will refer in greater detail to some of the studies of French–English bilingualism.

The work of Lambert and his colleagues supports the view (see Riegel & Riegel, 1972) that the consideration of psychological factors in a cultural–historical vacuum leads to fictitious constructions which are, by and large, of little value both for gaining knowledge in sciences as well as for helping children gain knowledge of their world. In the following presentation, we will emphasize that psychological operations stem from linguistic interactions in the physical–social environment. Before we can sketch this theory two major comments are necessary, the first addressed to the social basis of language, the second to the structural properties of the linguistic system to which the growing child is being exposed.

SOCIAL BASIS OF LANGUAGE

Languages do not exist as isolated entities such as in the form of a single grammar, but as *collections of repertoires* which have appropriate occasions (setting, topic, social status of the respective speakers and listeners) for their realization in speech or other communication modes (Ferguson, 1973). The speech community defines optional and obligatory modes of communication—each repertoire has its phonology, syntax, and semantics as well as psychosocial rules to observe to appropriately fulfill its special social functions. The study of the interconnection between a formal linguistic system and its realization in the social setting is sometimes referred to as the ethnography of communication (Gumperz & Hymes, 1972). Psycholinguists have yet to examine many of these psychosocial

[1] Moreover, French Canadians represent a relatively large contingent located in a geographically coherent area who can rely upon a well-recognized cultural–historical tradition which for many centuries has overshadowed the utilitarianism of the British–American world (Riegel, 1972).

variables in their construction of a relevant foundation for examining cognitive problems in the choice and use of various speech repertoires (Freedle, 1973). This contribution is an attempt to construct a theory which examines some cognitive consequences of a language user who must learn one or several dialects of the same basic "language" or must learn two languages (such as English and German).

Subcultures define different settings for language usage, i.e., select a dialect which is judged appropriate to the condition. The majority culture as distinct from its minority subcultures may define different settings for language usage. This difference is one possible source of a mismatch which can lead to misunderstandings. Such a mismatch can lead, for example, to the assignment of a "wrong" answer, as in a formal testing situation, when the majority culture "evaluates" a response of a member from one of the minority subcultures.

In addition to the differences in social setting which lead to a different selection from the speech repertoire, there is a difference in cognitive load across subcultures. Members of subcultures must usually learn two or more "distinct" dialects in carrying out their full range of communicative encounters within and outside of their community. Thus they may have a larger linguistic repertoire to learn and select from whereas members of the dominant culture need not learn an additional dialect. Moreover, long suppressed rage at the injustice suffered by the minorities will affect their willingness to achieve competence in the dialect used by the oppressors, and thus the cognitive load does not merely reflect the size and structure of the linguistic repertoire but also the emotional stress produced by the social forces operating in the exercise of speech choices. Subsequently, the concept of cognitive load implicates all prior issues—that of speech repertoire, speech community and appropriateness of choice, social matches and mismatches within and across speech communities, and operations which seek to resolve these forces when they arise.

PROPERTIES OF STRUCTURAL SYSTEMS

Structures are based upon relations; elements alone do not provide structure but mere conglomerates. Stronger yet, relations are prior to the elements which they connect. To use a simple example, we always transmit information about relations, never about elements alone. We will tell the child that "a rose is a flower," thereby implying the relationship of class inclusion, or we point at the picture of a rose and pronounce its name, thereby implying an extralingual relation between an object and a label.

Extralingual relations which are tying labels to objects (rose) or actions (run) or qualities and affects (good) provide the foundation for language and language development but do not allow for detailed elaborations of language structures. This is done through intralingual relations which connect different labels to one another. In most situations, we are not able to point at an object when we label it but explain it by saying, for example, "A rose is a flower with thorns and a beautiful smell." A structural analysis of such a statement (see Riegel, 1970a, b; Riegel, 1975) would propose that at least the following major intralingual relations are involved: ROSE → FLOWER; ROSE → THORNS; ROSE → SMELL; BEAUTIFUL → SMELL. The identification of the meaning of the word ROSE requires the listener to intersect these relations at their shared term (i.e., at ROSE but also at SMELL). Although many additional relations (and terms) will be brought to bear upon the structure of meanings, the simple network described by the relations mentioned above provides basic information for distinguishing roses from other flowers and other objects and events.

As the child hears statements like the one above and those describing, for example, other flowers, he will also learn to abstract classes from the relational information received. For example, he will recognize that not only roses but also tulips, dahlias, and carnations are flowers. The intersection of the relations ROSE → FLOWER; TULIP → FLOWER; DAHLIA → FLOWER and CARNATION → FLOWER represent the necessary, though by no means sufficient condition for the recognition of classes (linguistic and otherwise).

The identification of elements, such as words, and the abstraction of classes from the relational information given describe two of the most basic cognitive operations for language and language development. Perhaps caused by the preoccupation with the mechanistic notions of verbal learning and elements, such as the nonsense syllable, or by the intoxication with abstract linguistic conceptions, such as with Chomsky's syntactic structures, little attention has been given by psychologists to the acquisition of meanings in natural language communication in various psychological and social contexts. Belatedly and still insufficiently, these issues have been emphasized in the study of first language acquisition by Bloom (1970, 1973), Brown (1973), Schlesinger (1971), and in the study of learning and memory by Kintsch (1972) and Rumelhart, Lindsay, and Norman (1972). In addition there is some earlier work which has dealt with denotative meaning in general (Riegel & Riegel, 1963) and different strategies for the identification of words and semantic classes by children differing in age (Quarterman & Riegel, 1968; Zivian & Riegel, 1969).

Our semantic interpretation can be summarized by the schema of Fig. 1 showing the three terms serving to identify the word ROSE and the four

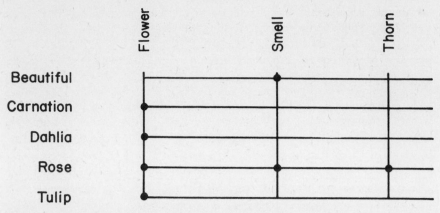

FIG. 1.   Schematic representation of four terms related to the class name FLOWER, three terms related to the word ROSE, and one term related to SMELL.

terms serving to abstract the class label FLOWER. According to the interpretation promoted here, the child acquires information represented by the cells of the matrix. Only after he has received a certain amount of such relational information is he able to move conceptually toward elements that designate the columns (or rows) of the matrix in order to identify individual words, explicate their meanings, and abstract semantic classes. In his own speech, the child will, of course, at first produce single word utterances, but this merely indicates limitations in his performance by which part of the intended relations remain suppressed. For example, the child will say the equivalent to MILK but from his actions and the surrounding circumstances we can safely infer that he experiences and intends to utter relational statements like THIS IS CALLED "MILK"; I WANT MILK; or I LIKE MILK. Recently, Bloom (1973) has called attention to the problems of the child's truncated expressions by pointing out that a single word utterance such as MILK can mean different things when it is uttered in different circumstances.

TYPES OF BILINGUALISM

In extending the relational matrix shown in Fig. 1, we can distinguish between at least two types of bilingualism with a third intermediate type between these extremes (see Fig. 2). Such a distinction is not new. A similar comparison has been proposed by Ervin and Osgood (1965). In contrast to earlier discussion, we emphasize exclusively the external sociological contingencies rather than intervening psychological conditions. It should also be noted at the outset that we attempt to describe idealized

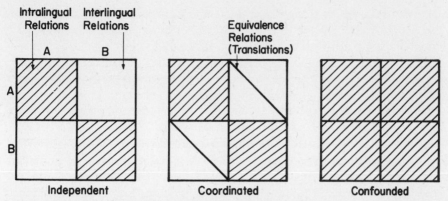

FIG. 2.   Three types of bilingualism.

and extreme bilingual types. Conditions that generate these types are not commonly found in natural social settings. Hopefully, contrastive comparisons of these types will enable us to conceptualize more clearly and to understand more fully the problems of bilingualism, including those of subcultural differences in language use. Questions of whether these types and the conditions which generate them "really" exist in our or any other society are irrelevant at the present moment. Eventually empirical explorations need to be made in order to determine the commonality of these types and conditions.

First, we think of a situation in which at a particular time a second language, such as Standard English, is introduced to a child who up to this point was exclusively exposed to another language, e.g., Spanish. In the extreme case, e.g., of a child who has lost his parents and is being brought up by another family in which his native language is not spoken, no provision for the transfer of his first language knowledge may be made. Because of the complete lack of practice, this knowledge is likely to be slowly lost. We will call the case in which both languages are introduced and used under different nonoverlapping conditions, i.e., in complete separation, the condition of *independent bilingualism*.

Second, a child might be exposed to conditions in which two languages are almost randomly mixed. In this case he does not only acquire two sets of intralingual relations, i.e., relations connecting different elements within either of the two languages, but also two sets of interlingual relations connecting elements from one language with those of the other. The latter occurs from crosslingual mixing within clauses such as "Give me the *Buch*" and "Gib mir das *book*." Intuitively it seems clear that such a condition, which we shall call *confounded bilingualism*, can not lead to an efficient acquisition of either the first or of the second language. If a child, during a given time period, can be exposed to and, subsequently, can acquire only a fixed amount of relational information, i.e., if we assume a fixed cognitive load represented by a small subsection or frame within the matrices of Fig. 2, the confounded bilingual child has to distribute his efforts over an area four times as large, and the independent bilingual child over an area twice as large as that presented to a monolingual child. Thus these children, especially the confounded bilinguals, are likely to receive less information in either of the two languages and it becomes unlikely that they will ever be able to compete successfully with their monolingual age mates.

Both conditions described so far represent extremes which are neither likely to occur in natural linguistic environments nor are they desirable for second language training.[2] The confounded condition overburdens the child with relational information too far scattered over the four quadrants of Fig. 2 and fails to assist him in separating the two languages. The independent condition, in separating the two languages too sharply, prevents the child from transferring his first language knowledge to his second language and, thereby, to facilitate its acquisition; both languages are acquired in complete separation. No wonder that many parents and teachers are applying a modified combination of second language training schedules which lead to what we will call *coordinate bilingualism*.

Under the simplest but by no means most efficient form of coordinate condition, the second language is introduced with the aid of equivalence relations or translation. Most conveniently, equivalence relations are listed along the main diagonal of the two interlingual matrices of Fig. 2, connecting each item in one language with its equivalent in the other. The use of equivalence relations allows for a limited transfer of first language knowledge to the second language but does not allow for sufficient explorations of the conceptual similarities between the two languages or for the performance of complex translations which rely on more than one-to-one equivalence relations between the items of the two languages.

While the use of equivalence relations represents a minimal degree of coordination, a maximum degree is attained under confounded contingencies where in theory, though by no means in practice, every item can

---

[2] Actually the problem is probably even more complex. Hall and Freedle (1975) report data which suggest that for dialect speakers of lower socioeconomic groups, preschoolers seem to have an overall positive correlation matrix across the two dialect systems (which may be likened to the confounded bilingual condition), but, after entry into school, these children without obvious "translation" equivalences provided them appear to partially separate the two systems so that across dialects sometimes negative correlations (suggesting cognitive interference effects), sometimes positive, and sometimes zero correlations can be observed. The real-world situation then seems to be much more complicated than our present theory can account for; our purpose though is to present simple paradigm conditions to help eventually in analyzing these more complex real-world cases.

be connected with every other item across the two languages. Optimal bilingual conditions are created through the use of an extended set of equivalence relations larger than that of the one-to-one translations but smaller than the total set of all interlingual relations. The main task for second language teachers is to find such an optimal set on the basis of educational intuition. One of the main goals of the present contribution is to delineate theoretically sets of equivalence relations which capture the conceptual and semantic properties of the two languages in a contrastive manner. More will be said about these issues in the section on interlingual relations.

As mentioned in the introductory section, children raised under favorable educational and economic conditions are commonly exposed to an efficient form of bilingual contingencies, i.e., those leading to coordinate bilingualism. For example, Leopold (1939–1949) exposed his daughter to one or the other language under distinct social conditions. Other investigators have advised parents in bilingual homes to use the two languages in distinctly different social settings, e.g., at the dinner table, in the playroom, outside the home, at the grandparents', etc. Thus, under coordinate conditions both languages are kept distinct, but the possibility for transfer of knowledge is also provided both by the use of extended equivalence systems and by reference to similar parts of nonlinguistic environments.

Children raised under poor economic conditions, on the other hand, are, it appears, commonly raised under the least favorable linguistic contingencies, i.e., either as monolinguals of the minority language or under contingencies leading to confounded bilingualism. Monolingual children of a minority language are forced to acquire the second language when they enter the school controlled by the majority or when they are looking for any better-paying job. Without equivalence relations provided to them, independent bilingualism can result (see Footnote 2). Children from the majority group, in contrast, do not need to learn the minority language when entering the school or the job market. As shown by Lambert *et al.* (1958) for French Canadians and by Hall and Freedle (1973) for Black American children, other members of the minority group, especially those who have attained a socioeconomic status which has made the use of the dominant language necessary, often expose their children to a mixture of the two languages. The more such a fusion has taken place, the greater the burden upon their children to acquire either of the two or both languages effectively and well. Not only is linguistic information spread out more widely and thinly, i.e., over all four quadrants of Fig. 2, but these children are also prevented from transferring knowledge in one language to the other because the two languages are not sufficiently separated. Subsequently they cannot possibly succeed as well as the independent or even coordinate bilingual in either one or both of the two languages. The first step to aid these children, we hypothesize, has to consist in accepting the two languages, e.g., Standard and Nonstandard English, as separate and equal. Such a segregation is the prerequisite for an intelligent transfer of knowledge, thus making an increased success in second language learning possible.

STAGES IN BILINGUAL DEVELOPMENT

The three bilingual types can be regarded as levels in developmental progression with the independent and coordinate types as early transitions and the confounded type as the terminal stage. In particular, we have proposed the following sequence (Riegel, 1968).

Stage I characterizes the very early steps in the acquisition of the first language during which parts of the lexicon A are provided by the social environment, most notably the caretaker, through the use of extralingual relations. Thus, the interconnections are of a special type, namely, between words and the objects, events, or qualities which they denote. The number of these extralingual relations, placed into the cells on the main diagonal of the upper left quadrant in Fig. 2, i.e., into the $A \times A$ matrix, is equal to or less than the numbers of words in the first language, i.e., A. At stage I no second language is acquired, thus the number of relations and words in the second language, B, equals zero.

At stage II various interconnections in language A will be presented to the child. In theory but, of course, not in practice every item could be connected with every other item and (as at stage I) with the object, event, or quality which it denotes. Thus, the whole upper left quadrant could be filled out and, therefore, the maximum number of relations equals A^2. At this stage, too, the number of words in the second language equals zero.

At stage III parts of a lexicon of language B are provided by parents and teachers through the use of equivalence relations. Equivalence relations appear on the main diagonals of the two interlingual quadrants of Fig. 2 and connect items in language A to their translations in language B and vice versa. Thus, the total lexicon of both languages could be as large as $A + B$. The total number of possible relations equals $A^2 + 2B$, whereby the first term refers to the set of intralingual relations in language A which can be as large as A^2, and has been acquired already at stage II. The second term refers to the equivalence relations $A \rightarrow B$ and $B \rightarrow A$, which can be as large as $2B$. The number of equivalence relations going in either direction may be unequal if the two languages differ in the size of their lexica.

Stage III resembles stage I and is important for the initiation of second language learning under coordinate conditions where items of the second language are introduced through the use of equivalence phrases, such as "In German, table is called Tisch." Under independent bilingual conditions the similarity between stage III and stage I is even stronger. Here lexicon items of the second language are introduced through the use of extralingual relations which connect their labels with the objects, events, or qualities which they denote, rather than with their translation equivalents in the first language. In this case, the total set of relations equals the set of intralingual relations in language A, i.e., A^2, plus the set of extralingual relations in language B, i.e., B.

At stage IV items in language B are also interconnected. The relations with A remain of the equivalence type for the coordinate bilinguals and of the extralingual type for the independent bilinguals. Thus, the total lexicon for the two languages equals $A + B$, and the total number of relations consists of those in language A, those in language B, and (at least for the coordinate bilinguals) of the equivalence relations $A \rightarrow B$ and $B \rightarrow A$, that is, $A^2 + B^2 + 2B$. The extralingual relations of the second language might be placed along the main diagonal of the quadrant for the second language, i.e., in the quadrant at the lower right of Fig. 2. Even if the extralingual relations are not presented to the learner, he may derive them in language B without further instructions on the basis of the extralingual relations in language A and the equivalence relations $A \rightarrow B$ and $B \rightarrow A$.

At stage V all items of both languages, potentially, can be interconnected. The lexicon remains $A + B$. The total number of relations equals $A^2 + B^2 + 2AB = (A + B)^2$, i.e., all four quadrants of Fig. 2 are now covered.

The major differences between the five stages have been summarized in Table 1. All stages must be regarded as transitional conditions in a process of continuous change. They overlap greatly. Thus, while an individual continues to be exposed to extralingual relations, he may already face intralingual relations between the different items of the first language. Also, while still being taught equivalence relations, he may be exposed already to intralingual relations within his second language or to other interlingual relations between the two languages.

The first four stages represent an idealized sequence of bilingual development, i.e., development as it "ought to be." The few children who may ever follow such a progression most likely belong to the culturally favored group of well-educated bilingual parents. In contrast, minority children are likely to be subjected to a reversal of this five-stage sequence. They enter a linguistic community that resembles the most complex stage of

TABLE 1
Qualitative Stages of Bilingual Development[a]

Stage	No. of relations	No. of elements
I	A	A
II	A^2	A
III	$A^2 + 2B$	$A + B$
IV	$A^2 + B^2 + 2B$	$A + B$
V	$A^2 + B^2 + 2AB$	$A + B$

[a] A = size of repertoire in first language; B = size of repertoire in second.

cognitive information, i.e., Stage V of confounded bilingualism, and then have to proceed backwards, most often left all on their own, in order to separate the two linguistic systems from one another as well as to apprehend the details of the transformation matrices of interlingual relations (see Footnote 2).

INTERLINGUAL RELATIONS

Undoubtedly, one-to-one equivalence relations are the exception rather than the rule in translations and occur among the most common terms only, such as TABLE ↔ TISCH and HORSE ↔ PFERD in English and German. In most instances equivalence has either to be established at *higher ranks*, e.g., at the level of sentence parts, phrases, or whole utterances; or equivalence has to be sought between *semantic classes* rather than between their elements, i.e., words.

The issue of equivalence at *higher ranks* touches upon differences between languages in syntactic organization. To give but one example, languages differ in their degrees of inflection. Since inflections are used for marking sentence parts, such as the subject, predicate, and predicate-object, word order can be varied more widely in inflected languages. Since inflected languages use different word orders for different types of sentences but noninflected languages do not, words will have to be shifted around in translation. Such operations tax heavily the memory of the translator and, in particular, rely on interlingual relations between various nonequivalent item. For example, Standard English, a language with a low degree of inflection, uses only one major order of sentence parts, i.e., subject (S), predicate (P), predicate-object (O), as in the sentence: The boy threw the ball. Highly inflected languages, such as German, Russian, or Latin, use different obligatory word orders to mark different sentence types. For example, the above declarative statement would use the same order of sentence parts in German as in English, i.e., S—P—O. However, when rewritten as a question, German would use the order P—S—O, and when used as a dependent clause, the order would have to be S—O—P. It is possible to make use of these rearrangements in inflected languages because sentence parts are sufficiently marked by specific endings. Since English does not allow for the clear identification of sentence parts by their endings, a fairly rigid word order has to be maintained. Differences in sentence types are indicated by auxiliary construction, such as the question word DO.

Lack of one-to-one equivalence between the terms of two languages has to be resolved by considering their organization in *semantic classes*. Membership in semantic classes is generally determined by asymmetric relations which group items together that, for instance, *do* similar things (predication), e.g., tools, vehicles, etc., have similar *parts* (attribution), e.g., animals, furniture items, etc., are found at similar *places* (location), e.g., food items, toys, etc., or are *logically* included in the same class (superordination), e.g., all of the above. Most languages seem to consist of similar kinds of classes, but they may differ in the range and distribution of items and, thereby, in their degree of topical specialization. For example, English and most European languages are known to be highly elaborated in their technical and scientific vocabularies and thus may provide greater variety in membership within some semantic classes and, perhaps, a greater variety of classes themselves. Far Eastern languages, on the other hand, provide a richer vocabulary of aesthetical, psychological, and philosophical terms.

The differences between these languages would, therefore, require that instead of simple one-to-one equivalency one-to-many or many-to-many relationships have to be explored in the translation process. In other words, translations can be achieved only by relying on semantic classes rather than single word equivalencies and/or at higher ranks, i.e., by rephrasing whole parts of sentences.

Although poorly understood at the present time, issues of semantic classes and organization make up the most significant topic for bilingual comparisons and for exploration of language development. During recent years, a few psychologists have directed their attention to these issues (Bloom, 1970, 1973; Brown, 1973; Kintsch, 1972; Riegel, 1968, 1970a, b; Riegel & Riegel, 1963; Schlesinger, 1971) but the complexity of the problem seems to have prevented the majority of behavioral scientists to apprehend the significance of this issue. No comprehensive studies and interpretations have been completed on subcultural differences in semantic organization. This topic ought to become a major task for further explorations which, as they progress, are bound to exert a strong influence upon our understanding of these differences, of educational praxis, and social equality.

ENVIRONMENTAL UTILITY

The three matrices shown in Fig. 2 represent three types of bilingual environmental conditions. The child's acquisition of the languages proceeds by receiving consecutive samples of relational information from the environment. Stated differently, the child, in the course of his daily activities, is skimming over the matrices of intra- and interlingual relations. His intake will be limited during a given time period to a certain amount of relational information which will be determined both by the type and the richness of the environment and by his processing capacity. The amount of intake might be visualized as a small subsection of the matrices shown in Fig. 2, bounded by a frame of a given size. The longer the child has been scanning one of the matrices, i.e., the longer he has lived, the more likely it becomes that he will encounter information which he has already received once or several times before. With advancing age the individual slowly depletes the set of general information provided; it becomes less likely that he discovers new semantic relations.

On the basis of such reasoning it is possible to generate a growth function in which the depletion of the outer linguistic contingencies is plotted against age. As academic as such an enterprise might seem, it opens important possibilities for evaluating the utility or efficiency of various bilingual conditions. Since the details of such models have been presented elsewhere (Riegel, 1968) we restrict our present discussion to some inferences concerning the conditions of the minority child.

Figure 3 shows two growth curves, (a) for independent and (b) for confounded bilingual development. In both instances the shift into bilingual contingencies occurs at the relatively late age of about 17.5 years; also in both cases the distribution between languages A and B is even, i.e., half of the time is devoted to the first language, the other half to the second language. The main purpose of models like ours is, of course, to vary both the time of shift and/or the proportions of exposures in order to study the efficiency of various bilingual conditions.

Detailed information on the utility of bilingual conditions can be obtained by using the monolingual curve as upper boundary and comparing the area below it with those below the different bilingual curves. The closer the monolingual curve is approximated by any of the other curves, the greater the utility of the bilingual condition. For example, in Fig. 3a figure the first bilingual curve approximates the monolingual curve much closer than in Fig. 3b. Thus, the utility of the independent bilingual condition (Fig. 3a) is greater than that of the confounded

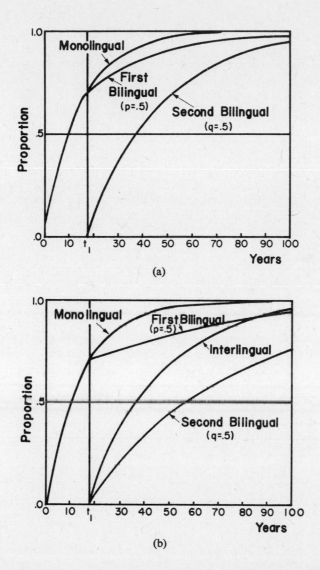

FIG. 3. Growth of the sets of relations provided in monolingual and bilingual environments as a function of independent (a) and confounded conditions (b). Proportion of time devoted to first language is p, whereas q is the proportion devoted to the second language; p and q both equal .50; age at which the two languages compete for time is 17.5 years; the monolingual spends 1.00 proportion of time on a single language.

condition (Fig. 3b). This result is due to the large efforts directed toward the interlingual relations under the latter condition. Under both conditions, the second language is less effectively mastered, i.e., approximates the monolingual curve less well than the first language. This is not surprising, since the second language is introduced relatively late in life, i.e., at an age of almost 17.5 years, and thus a good deal of "catching up" has to be accomplished.

Keeping the distribution of efforts between the two languages constant at 50%, the utility is a direct function of the time of the switch into the bilingual condition. If this switch occurs early in life, the acquisition curve for the first language will be depressed over an extended period of time; second language acquisition will make relatively quick advances, however. If the switch occurs late, the first language is less affected but the progress in the second language is retarded. Special inferences about shifts in dominance between the two languages can be made if the proportional distribution is varied in conjunction with the time of the switch. Although these comparisons are purely theoretical, they allow for more explicit conceptualizations about development and subsequently for the planning of optimal environmental, linguistic conditions.

CONCLUSIONS

We have stated at the beginning, and it has become evident throughout this presentation, that our analysis is predominantly theoretical. Moreover, there exists at the moment little evidence and few comparable interpretations directly concerned with subcultural differences in language and language development. In particular, we had to limit our discussion by regarding the two languages acquired by bilingual children as completely independent from one another. Undoubtedly, such an assumption is not very realistic. We know rather that all languages are interrelated, be it through common cultural–historical bonds or through the universality and equality of human beings. But before the interdependence of different languages and cultures can be seriously considered, and before behavioral and social scientists should rush into empirical investigations, a more rigorous conceptual framework is required on which such comparisons can be based. Our present contribution—it is hoped—will serve this purpose.

In spite of the limitations mentioned and in spite of the lack of empirical evidence, our discussion allows for rather concrete inferences regarding such issues as educational policy, social planning, and the ideological basis underlying both. The different conditions depicted in Fig. 2 coincide with and reflect different sociopolitical attitudes toward other cultural and, especially, subcultural groups.

At one extreme, we have, first, the monolingual situation. If a monolingual state were ever attained in modern society, no problems of the type discussed would arise.[3] It is obvious, however, that in the modern world such an isolation cannot persist. Rather people are dependent upon other people, nations upon nations, and cultures upon cultures. The communications and exchanges required make bilingualism and multiculturalism necessary. Not surprisingly, therefore, the majority of people in the world are bilinguals, including the large populations of the old civilizations in India and China. Not surprisingly either, narrow monolingualism is most rigidly preserved in colonial and imperialistic societies, the United States, the Soviet Union, England, France, Germany, and a few centuries ago, Spain, Portugal, and ancient Rome. Monolingualism, to a much more limited degree, is also preserved within isolated tribes of so-called underdeveloped countries, but in all of these cases recent political and economic developments have brought the future of these groups into grave doubt.

Second, the condition of independent bilingualism represents a sociopolitical arrangement which virtually prevents any exchange and communication, for example, between two subgroups of a society. In history such an arrangement has never succeeded for long. The only known and fairly successful case is that of Switzerland where, aided by geographic barriers, German, French, and Italian (not to mention the Rato-Romanch) communities have coexisted in harmony. In most other cases, however, and because language differences are commonly tied to cultural, economic, political, and, worst of all, religious frictions, few of these societies have persisted. The development either led to the domination of one group over the other (the British in Northern Ireland) or to the separation of both groups (the Greeks and Turks in Cyprus—similar problems continue to exist in Canada, Belgium, and Holland).

Third, opposite to independent bilingualism, we find at the other extreme the condition of confounded bilingualism. Like the former case, a true fusion between cultural and linguistic groups has rarely taken place in history. Most of the time, one group absorbed the other either

---

[3] It is useful to recall our earlier discussion of the impact of sociolinguistics upon psychological approaches to language. Since even monolingual speakers actually have a range of speech registers for various occasions, the theory presented here can be extended to encompass a cognitive theory of how information across the two or more language registers which a particular speaker may use comes to be acquired. The differences across register types in the monolingual speech community need not be lexical; instead if the differences are, for example, phonological, then our theory could be reconceptualized so that phonological translations are the main focus rather than lexical translations. The general conceptual power of our theory is therefore seen to transcend bilingual or bidialectal theories and can be applied to analyze the development and cognitive interpenetration of any two conceptual domains.

through violence or smoothly without any open frictions and conflicts. Nevertheless, the goal of fusing two cultures or languages into a new, "better," or "higher" system remains the ideal for many utopian movements. The promotion of Esperanto, Volapük, and other international languages, for example, represents attempts to generate a universal and unifying mode of communication. As long as these attempts fail to deal with the underlying social and political issues at the same time, their success is bound to remain rather limited. Nevertheless, a fusion of Standard and Black English, for example, accompanied by social and political awakening, might occur in the United States and provide a new basis for communication and exchanges.

Fourth, as long as the last possibility remains a remote ideal, the only concrete hope for solving cultural and linguistic conflicts consists in the development of coordinated or cooperative conditions. Such efforts have to depend first and foremost on mutual recognition and appreciation. Both languages have to be accepted as separate and equal. In regard to Black English, this goal is far from being attained and, therefore, we have emphasized throughout this presentation the need for a separation, as far as possible, of the two linguistic systems. Only after such recognition is achieved does it become possible to succeed in coordination and cooperation. In language this goal would be attained by comparing and contrasting the two semantic structures. At the present time little is known about this task. Our presentation—hopefully—has moved us a small step closer toward this goal.

SUMMARY

1. Although the burden upon bilingual children is heavy, they are advantaged in a higher sense because monolingualism is a true form of cultural deprivation. Since monolingualism provides restricted information in an effective manner, however, we ought to study monolingual development carefully in order to find the best route and methods for optimal progression in bilingual development.

2. Neither independent nor confounded bilingualism in their extremes constitute reasonable and efficient conditions of progression. A coordinated form is best which maximizes transfer and minimizes interferences. Such a form of bilingualism can only be established through detailed explorations of semantic interlingual structures or, what might be called, semantic–syntactic transformation matrices. At the present time, such explorations are lacking.

3. If raised under such conditions, the independent bilingual becomes able to transfer a large share of his first language knowledge to his second

language. The confounded bilingual is still not much assisted, however, because he has first to differentiate the two language systems from one another before such transfer can take place.

4. In returning to our introductory limitations, we request that regardless of whether Black and White English dialects are linguistically sufficiently distinct, for the benefit and well-being of many ghetto children living in a confounded linguistic environment, the two systems ought to be treated as such. Only after a clear separation is achieved can we expect the child to progress effectively in either or both of the two languages.

REFERENCES

Bloom, L. *Language development.* Cambridge, Massachusetts: MIT Press, 1970.

Bloom, L. *One word at a time: The use of single word utterances before syntax.* The Hague: Mouton, 1973.

Brown, R. *A first language.* Cambridge, Massachusetts: Harvard University Press, 1973.

Ervin, S. M., & Osgood, C. E. Second language learning and bilingualism. In C. E. Osgood & T. A. Sebeok (Eds.), *Psycholinguistics.* Bloomington, Indiana: Indiana University Press, 1965. Pp. 139–146.

Ferguson, C. Language problems of variation and repertoire. *Deadalus,* 1973, **102,** 37–46.

Freedle, R. The marriage of psycholinguistics and sociolinguistics. Paper presented at Georgetown University's Summer Institute in Linguistics, Georgetown, 1973.

Freedle, R., & Hall, W. S. An information processing approach to developmental sociolinguistics. In K. F. Riegel & J. A. Meacham (Eds.), *The developing individual in a changing world.* Vol. I: *Historical and cultural issues.* The Hague: Mouton, 1975. Pp. 384–395.

Gumperz, J., & Hymes, D. (Eds.) *Directions in sociolinguistics: The ethnography of communication.* New York: Holt, Rinehart & Winston, 1972.

Hall, W. S., & Freedle, R. O. A developmental investigation of standard and nonstandard English among black and white children. *Human Development,* 1973, **16,** 440–464.

Hall, W. S., & Freedle, R. O. *Culture and language: An essay on the black American experience.* Washington, D.C.: Hemisphere Press, 1975.

Kintsch, W. Notes on the structure of semantic memory. In E. Tulving & W. Donaldson (Eds.), *Organization of memory.* New York: Academic Press, 1972. Pp. 247–308.

Labov, W. *Sociolinguistic patterns.* Philadelphia: University of Pennsylvania Press, 1972.

Lambert, W. E., Havelka, J., & Crosby, C. The influence of language-acquisition contexts on bilingualism. *Journal of Abnormal and Social Psychology,* 1958, **56,** 239–244.

Lambert, W. E., Tucker, G. R., & d'Anglejan, A. Cognitive and attitudinal consequences of bilingual schooling. *Journal of Educational Psychology,* 1973, **65,** 141–159.

Leopold, W. F. *Speech development of a bilingual child.* Evanston, Illinois: North Western University Press, 1939–1949. 4 vols.

McCarthy, D. Language development in children. In L. Carmichael (Ed.), *Manual of child psychology*. New York: Wiley, 1954. Pp. 492–630.

Quarterman, C. J., & Riegel, K. F. Age differences in the identification of concepts of the natural language. *Journal of Experimental Child Psychology, 1968,* **6,** 501–509.

Riegel, K. F. Some theoretical considerations of bilingual development. *Psychological Bulletin,* 1968, **70,** 647–670.

Riegel, K. F. Relational interpretation of the language acquisition process. In G. B. Flores d'Arcais & W. J. Levelt (Eds.), *Advances in psycholinguistics*. Amsterdam: North-Holland Publ., 1970. Pp. 224–236.   (a)

Riegel, K. F. The language acquisition process: A reinterpretation of selected research findings. In L. R. Goulet & P. B. Baltes (Eds.), *Life-span developmental psychology: Research and theory*. New York: Academic Press, 1970. Pp. 357–399.   (b)

Riegel, K. F. Time and change in the development of the individual and society. In H. Reese (Ed.), *Advances in child development and behavior*. Vol. 7. New York: Academic Press, 1972. Pp. 81–113.

Riegel, K. F. Semantic basis of language: Language as labor. In K. F. Riegel & G. C. Rosenwald (Eds.), *Structure and transformation: Developmental and historical aspects*. New York: Wiley, 1975. Pp. 176–192.

Riegel, K. F., & Riegel, R. M. An investigation into denotative aspects of word meaning. *Language and Speech,* 1963, **6,** 5–21.

Riegel, K. F., & Riegel, R. M. Development, drop and death. *Developmental Psychology,* 1972, **6,** 306–319.

Rumelhart, D. E., Lindsay, P. H., & Norman, D. A. A process model for long-term memory. In E. Tulving & W. Donaldson (Eds.), *Organization of memory*. New York: Academic Press, 1972. Pp. 197–246.

Schlesinger, I. M. Production of utterances and language acquisition. In D. Slobin (Ed.), *The ontogenesis of grammar*. New York: Academic Press, 1971. Pp. 63–101.

Zivian, M. T., & Riegel, K. F. Word identification as a function of semantic clues and associative frequency. *Journal of Experimental Psychology,* 1969, **79,** 336–341.

3

Toward the Parameters
of Black English

Gilbert A. Sprauve

The College of the Virgin Islands

Perhaps. we can talk sensibly about the parameters of Black English only after at least one ground rule is stated. Namely, we shall suspend any excessive preoccupation with the question "What is language?" The language-free route can hardly be said to be a revolutionary approach. In fact, we should perhaps pause just a moment here to consider why the question is even raised concerning the definition of language when the subject happens to be Black English. (In my experience, this question is not uncommon when presentations on Black English—and Creoles—are made.)

Are investigators of Black English naturally constrained to produce a rigorous definition of language? No more than the biologist observing living cells in the lab should be required to hold forth on the definition of life, or the political scientist in the field on the concept of the nation. The philosophers of language have appropriated to themselves, codified, and regulated much of the discussion on the nature of language. And, as one who is interested in finding a functional definition of Black English, I say, "So be it!" Impatient as we are to see greater rigor and consistency enter the dialectic of Black English, we must not lose ourselves in the language philosophers' web of complex abstractions and explorations into matters like the logical form of grammers. In this respect, one is intrigued by the motives of those who would demonstrate to us that Black English has its logic!

Some traditional definitions of language can be quite neutral, that is, in the sense that they reflect neither cynicism nor malevolence vis-à-vis the specific enterprise of defining parameters of Black English. Sturtevant

(1947, p. 2) defines language as "a set of arbitrary vocal symbols by which members of a social group cooperate and interact." Two traditional definitions are cited by Labov (1972) in *Sociolinguistic Patterns*. Sweet (1900) defined language as "the expression of thought by means of speech sounds." This and the above definition can be lived with as far as the search for the essential properties of Black English is concerned. Hermann Paul's (1889) "rough mixture of the well-formed speech of individuals" is itself endowed with the mixed blessings of pragmatic accomodation and susceptibility to undesirable prescriptivism.

It should be obvious by now that we are working toward avoiding the pitfalls of definitions and terminologies that are charged with the biases of power. Recent strides made along these lines tend to be taken for granted. In truth, quite apart from the potentially substantial inputs to effective pedagogy that are evident in the Black English studies of Dillard (1972), Haskins and Butts (1973), Stewart (1969), and others, we are now in a position where we can examine the speech behavior of communities in the modern world with fewer prejudgments than ever before. (In the past, critical observation in the field and objective description in texts seem to have been extended almost exclusively to the so-called primitive or exotic languages.)

Considerations on Black English's integrity "as a language" suspended, we may now ask ourselves what the available workable definitions of the subject are. One would have thought that since Dillard's (1972) book is entitled *Black English* it would be the natural place to look for the definition we need. The fact is, Dillard does everything but to define the book's title. He probably never meant to, his approach being essentially an extension of the Herskovits' manner of compiling massive amounts of data on the diaspora and tracing within these data patterns of distribution and dispersion. One of the side benefits that accrue from this type of presentation is that the author need not go out on a limb. The data might be seen as "speaking for themselves." Unfortunately though, we are perhaps permitted to cite Dillard as one of several exemplary bases for the following observations:

> Research into Black English, until recently, has been neglected by linguists, and their findings remain fragmentary and incomplete. Final agreement on what Black English is, based on intensive research, seems far away. [Holt, 1972, p. 45].

William Labov, in an address at Rutgers (1972), utilized yet another method to circumvent the problem of defining Black English. He simply referred to the subject as "the vernacular." Implicit in Labov's approach to the larger issue of urban language, in any case, is the well-sustained viewpoint that meaningful language observation must take place within a social context. "Vernacular" can thus be viewed here as a practical term attached strictly to the earliest stages of research on Black English. This stage we would call observational, and we would recognize (from a theoretical perspective) the essential embedding of the observational stage of Black English research within the more advanced descriptive stage of urban language studies in social contexts. These methods are valid but unfortunately have not, to my knowledge, been explained anywhere.

Haskins and Butts (1973) have suggested yet another kind of approach to the parameters of Black English. While recognizing that each group of Blacks "reflects the dominant culture in which they were raised," and noting, accordingly, the initial strangeness of the West Indian when confronted with the culture of Harlem, they are disposed in earnest toward the philological approach whereby the origins of Black English are traced back to Creoles and Pidgins. It must be noted, however, that even the somewhat new philological orientation in Black English studies is not devoid of a substantial range of varying—and often contrasting—theories on origins (see Hancock, 1971). While Haskins and Butts do appear to declare themselves for the relexificationists explanation, they also recognize a significant ongoing cultural particularism that distinguished Black communities throughout the diaspora. This factor is susggestive of either tenuous links or of an early breakoff from the condition of common origins.

Where does this much place us with respect to the definition of Black English? We are perhaps in a better position to evaluate and inform at least one of a number of metrics currently being applied by sociolinguists and creolists in the organization of Black English and Creole data—and therefore, in one kind of definition. The specific device we shall describe has been utilized by Stewart (1962a) to describe the complex linguistic situation in Haiti. It involves a chart on which are plotted the features public versus private and formal versus informal. These features relate to social environments. As a descriptive tool this matrix facilitates the isolation of the Creole within the speech chain. It does this by simply sifting out telltale variables from the social contexts in which the language is used. On this simple matrix the context combinations are just four: private–formal, public–formal, public–informal, and private–informal. More recent work along these lines has tended toward such a high degree of sophistication, i.e., incorporating such a high number of variables, that links with the pioneering tradition are often overlooked. Nevertheless, it is safe to say that the path for implicational scale models, such as those used by DeCamp (1971), on Jamaican Creole, Bickerton (in press) on Guyana Creole, and certainly that for Midgett's study of St. Lucia sociolinguistics [possibly Fasold's margin of cruciality, as cited by Carrington (1971) and some of Labov's (1972) charts of variability] was opened by Stewart's (1962b) work on the Haitian speech community.

Whether simple or complex, these matrices cannot be said to have as their primary objective the *defining* of Black English or of a particular creole language. Rather, they represent a methodology for *survveying* speech communities. A somewhat abstract model of Black English or the Creole, each of which is designated the basilect (lower language), is a natural by-product of the analysis, since the overall speech community defines itself in terms of bipolar relationships, or a continuum, between the Standard, or acrolect, on the one hand, and the basilect on the other.

While the speech community can be seen as defining itself *naturally* in terms of a Standard-to-Creole continuum (and in the case of Black English, as a possible embedding of its current data—as was suggested earlier—within the sociolinguistic profile of the dominant speech community), the matrix model is basically paradoxical. It need not be so. The crucial applicability of sociolinguistic research in this area to the problems of effective pedagogy has already been mentioned. The primary consequence of the new sociolinguistic–educational liason, it appears, is the very casual conversion of an essentially descriptive device into a prescriptive one. The further consequence of this perversion of the model is the interference with the self-definition of Creoles and of Black English.

The problem is manifest primarily in the perennial policy consultations that take place between the new Black education spokesmen—in effect, relevance brokers—and the White power structure. The sociolinguistic grid we have been discussing, when viewed from another perspective, converts itself into a formidable horror chamber for linguistic policy-making, as can be seen in the following sketch:

Power structure

		deficit		legit
Relevance	deficit	4	←	3
brokers		↓		↑
	legit	1	→	2

The relationship between the public versus private, formal versus informal model and this "legit" versus deficit matrix is quite straightforward. What we are dealing with, in effect, is a model for rules of shifting or style selection. In this model recognition of power relationships is vital for the selection of appropriate linguistic behavior. (Certainly, if you were to grade the four strata in terms of prestige, success value, etc., the public–formal stratum, i.e., French, in the case of Haiti, would outstrip the other styles. Similarly, on the larger American speech scene, certainly where educational policy is concerned Blacks would be inclined to place a premium, not on the language or style of the Carolina or Georgia Guichee, but rather on something much closer to the Standard, presumably on the colorless model of much of the Northern Black upwardly mobile and middle class.)

Attitudinal dispositions—including negative perceptions of one's own language—are not to be overlooked by the field observer. On the other hand, they are dispositions. Above all, the policy-maker must not confound attitudinal matters with the language itself. Yet, such confusion is at the heart of the policy acrobatics discussed above. And in the end, the relevance brokers, while clamoring for Black English in the curriculum, have sowed the seeds of chaos wider on this already troubled terrain. Worst of all, just when it appeared that the process of self-defining for Black English was really making headway, we are confronted with the disruptive short circuit embodied in theories of deficit behavior. Self-consciously, it is explained that expediency and practical democratic considerations justify the intervention.

There are reasons why we need not despair completely at this state of affairs. For one thing, we may take as a healthy sign the fact that there is a full blown controversy under way among Black linguists on the questions of whether there is, and what is, Black English. Thus, trigger-happy educators notwithstanding, the book has not been closed on the definition of our subject. Second, we still have the option of cutting loose from the cycle of educational nonpolicy on Black English that seems to be going exactly nowhere.

Indeed, a quick and effective retreat from this cycle would result naturally from the realization that we are dealing here with a full language (whatever the latter might be!). Let us consider what happens when we do this. First, on the academic front, we will have secured for ourselves charges of sacrificing objective criteria and rational indications for strictly political considerations. No single charge has had a more debilitating effect on Black scholarship vis-à-vis the Black condition than this one. Let us therefore get this much straight: language is a political act. It is without a doubt the most powerful political tool that man commands. The very assertion and recognition of a speech system as a language is absolutely a political act.

While it may be true that languages don't just happen, one needs only consult the history of medieval nationalism to bring into perspective the political origins of many of the modern languages. Such a review, along with a perusal of policy deliberations of several modern speech communities, offers a number of convenient points of departure for the discussion of languages as capricious national or political entities. Modern Hebrew is a case in point (Blanc, 1968). And it is working! Moreover, with respect to Black rhetoric, it has been observed that "soul" seems to be a folk conception of the lower-class Black's own "national character" (Hannerz, 1972).

Reinecke (1969), despite a general heavy-handed treatment of canons of adequacy for "makeshift" languages—and a penchant for confounding attitudinal matters with factual claims—observed

> The Taal of the Boers was originally the despised colonial dialect of uneducated farmers, men who had neither subtle ideas nor the vocabulary to express them had they possessed any. Now, Afrikaans under the pressure of a new nationalism and widespread education has discovered new riches of expression, and its simplified syntax, at one time as condemned as the "pidgin" syntax of the Hawaiian schoolboy, is boasted as superior to the more complex structure of Holland Dutch [Reinecke, 1969, p. 146].

Certainly then, the notion is questionable—possibly, erroneous—that any speech community or vernacular group may not one day simply declare itself to be a *language* community.

Assuming we survived our detractors' irrational charges of "absurdity" and "lack of objectivity" for declaring Black English a language like any other, what would follow? Maybe nothing substantial within the language would change immediately, or ever. What should follow is the prompt removal of Black English from the zone of vulnerability to which it is now confined. The significant benefit to the Black linguist and social scientist of this withdrawal is that we would now find ourselves liberated from a contrived distraction that has so far managed to usurp too many of our vital energies. I refer to the specious language–intelligence dialectic.

Once we have declared Black English a full language the game of policy acrobatics—or legit versus deficit—goes. The practice of testing people's intelligence via a foreign language while commanding only a limited understanding of the native language is exposed for the sham that it really is. We can now turn our energies to investigating and recording the language of Black people.

What has been done so far along these lines is often primitive and deficient. These deficiencies stem primarily from two sources, and the latter are also heavily influenced by power relationships. They are namely (1) inadequacies in the recording devices and (2) the absence of native inputs at all levels of the analyses save at the very bottom. There are, of course, also field techniques that need to be radically different from those in current use.

Let us accept that our motivation in investigating and recording Black English is the moderately political desire to have available some authentic models of the language of Blacks in this country. Leaving aside for now any prescriptivism, particularly since it is not clear now why we should distrust the seemingly notoriously fluid parameters that characterize

Black English in the intuitions of Black folk, we would want only to initiate our investigations with a minimum of preconceptions. In this respect, Mitchell's (1972) outline of the features of Black English should be instructive:

> What then are the contrasting features which distinguish Black English from standard English? One is the slower rate of delivery. Another is Black sentence structure, which on the average is simpler than white middle-class sentence structure. Still other differences range all the way . . . to the peculiar tonal inflections characteristic of Southern Blacks. As I have said, no book about these speech features could teach one to use them effectively.... Only a healthily Black identity, born of acute exposure to the experience and of complete Black acceptance, can complete the process of lingual identification and implant Black language naturally on one's tongue [Mitchell, 1972, pp. 93–94].

As a definition Mitchell's statement poses a number of problems. I am not convinced, however, that the vagueness of it should be of primary concern here. I am more disturbed by its dependency on the Standard. Moreover, the prerequisites for the mastery of Black English are too powerful. Yet Mitchell's brief exposition represents a bold new step in the direction of defining—as opposed to surveying—Black English. At the very least, some hypotheses on the properties of our subject could now be tested.

In testing these hypotheses we would have attained the early stage of the optimal investigative methodology desirable for Black English. The elimination of preconceptions requires, among other things, an acute sensitivity to any intrusion of foreign abstractions in our initial recording device. The natural ramification to this achievement would be the high premium we would place on the native presence at every level of the investigations. This native presence would embody a respectable content of the Black experience, including sensitivity to attitudinal and other variable factors. We would be seeking to get as deep into the language of this community as possible, finding our way into it, as it were, by the antennae of our own sensitivity as natives.

Lorenzo Dow Turner's (1949) report on fieldwork among the Gullah tells us something about how this kind of immersion into the informant culture is accomplished. What passes for Black English studies of the past decade has failed to follow up on or refine this methodology. What our new sociolinguists have harvested from the urban communities instead is a plethora of graphs, scales, and maps on which are plotted factors like socioeconomic rank, level of education, occupational background, etc.

But where is the human dimension in all of this? Where are our elders, the tradition-invested, history-wise older people? Certainly when we start our new investigations we have to talk to these folk. More important, we have to listen to them. Perhaps, sophisticated recording equipment notwithstanding, we have to relearn the art of creative listening.

An informant of mine, a Princeton resident of 40 years standing, has provided me with some indications of the language of Savannah, Georgia Blacks of 80 years ago. It is interesting to note how close this language was to current Creole English of the West Indies. (Of similar interest is the fact that when I first went to Harlem from the Virgin Islands in the mid 1950's, Blacks from the South, upon hearing my speech, asked me if I was a Giuchee from South Carolina.)

My Princeton informant will inform you, even while using the palatalized /ky/ before /a/ and expressions like "it have" and "an t'ing," that *he* is not a Guichee, but that he did know some in his earlier days. Since he unloaded ships from different ports as a young man, and in this manner, made the acquaintance of West Indian sailors, he recognizes my speech immediately. It should be noted that this gentleman—for all intents and purposes just another Princeton Black senior citizen—is a uniquely informed source of information on a broad spectrum of Black English, quite a contrast to the two-dimensional informants that converge on the pages of urban language studies.

To effectively draw language information from my informant is to shift the dynamic of linguistic investigation to new heights of wisdom and sensitivity. We would take great pains to observe the informant's speech acts in a wide range of activities, including, for example, conversation and storytelling. We should seek to capture transfer of this older informant's speech to a younger generation.

The tools we have been using heretofore in transcribing may well prove inadequate for working with the "new" language. While the basic alphabet of the International Phonetic Association (IPA) is used everywhere for signaling surface level realizations, the symbolizations are already quite abstract. Adequate recordings, given this condition, would call for close attention to adjustment rules. When—and only when—we have shed all perverse and foreign prejudgments and substituted the necessary methodological and technical measures, then we can start thinking of capturing the real Black English.

The parameters of the language will define themselves from within. This is, to a large extent, what my Princeton informant was involved with when he (1) ordered my speech alongside West Indian as he knew it 50 years ago, (2) placed Guichee close to West Indian, and (3) positioned himself a distance from both and declared: /dɪ 'spik ɪn a 'dɪfrɛnt 'vain 'wi 'spik ɪn a 'dɪfrɛnt 'vain 'tu bʌt 'de spik 'dɪfrɛnt 'stɪl/.

Notice that this process of self-definition is by no means foreign to the methodologies we matter-of-factly utilize in setting up taxonomies of languages. Were we to encounter a Portuguese resident of a village adjacent to the border with Spain who conceived of his own language as Spanish, I doubt very much that we would dispute his judgment. Rather, automatically—and naturally—we should seek to elicit further judgments from such a unique informant on the linguistic conventions of the vicinity. "In general, how close is the language of village Z here to that of village A over there?" "And, what of villages Y and X here and B and C over there?" In any case, the thing we would probably expect least from such an informant is an impromptu exposition on the nature of language.

As regards Black English, some skeptics might ask: But, what source would the language draw on to enrich its vocabulary? I should respond that, first, it is not evident to me that the present lexicon is impoverished, earlier references to Reinecke (1969) on Afrikaans notwithstanding. Second, I should suggest that the fluid and flexible parameters of Black English, from the perspective of its lexicon, are as much a part of the current language itself as the syntactic or any other component.

As for policy matters such as (1) the teaching of the language—presumably to nonnatives—and (2) the coexistence of Black English with what we refer to as Standard English, these considerations fall somewhat outside the primary thrust of this presentation. Suffice it to note here that some of the investigations carried out during the last decade on what is generally called Negro Nonstandard English (NNE) could have some practical application as curriculum material. Imperfect they are, but useful, so long as the language learner would appreciate the fact that to gain a fair degree of competence in the language he would have to do the same thing that Americans, for example, do who have a serious intent to "master" French, Russian, or Portuguese.

Finally, the above, to the extent that it is built on the supposition and eventuality that conceivably one day Blacks in this country and parts of the Caribbean may entertain the thought of conscientiously and consciously "elevating" Black English to the status of a full language, attempts to set forth some modest political, methodological, and technical considerations that could advance the project.

And, if we chose not to intervene in Black English's development and status? We still have before us the serious business of investigating and recording the real Black English.

REFERENCES

Bickerton, D. On the nature of a Creole continuum. *Language,* in press.

Blanc, H. The Israeli Koiné as an emergent national standard. In J. Fishman, C. Ferguson and J. Das Gupta (Eds.), *Language problems of developing nations.* New York: Wiley, 1968.

Carrington, L. Implications of the nature of the Creole continuum for sequencing educational materials. Unpublished manuscript, 1971.

DeCamp, D. Toward a generative analysis of a post-Creole speech continuum. In D. Hymes (Ed.), *Pidginization and creolization of languages*. Cambridge, England: Cambridge University Press, 1971.

Dillard, J. L. *Black English*. New York: Random House, 1972.

Hancock, I. F. A provisional comparison of the English-derived Atlantic Creoles. In D. Hymes (Ed.), *Pidginization and creolization of languages*. Cambridge, England: Cambridge University Press, 1971.

Hannerz, U. The rhetoric of soul: Identification in negro society. In A. L. Smith (Ed.), *Language, communication and rhetoric in Black America*. New York: Harper & Row, 1972.

Haskins, J., & Butts, H. F. *The psychology of Black English*, New York: Harper & Row, 1973.

Holt, G. S. The ethno-linguistic approach to speech-language learning. In A. L. Smith (Ed.), *Language, communication and rhetoric in Black America*. New York: Harper & Row, 1972.

Herskovits, M. J. *The myth of the Negro past*. New York and London: Harper & Bros., 1941.

Labov, W. *Sociolinguistic patterns*. Philadelphia: University of Pennsylvania Press, 1972.

Midgett, D. Bilingualism and linguistic change in St. Lucia. *Anthropological Linguistics*, May, 1970.

Mitchell, H. H. Black English. In A. L. Smith (Ed.), *Language, communication and rhetoric in Black America*. New York: Harper & Row, 1972.

Paul, H. *Principles of the history of language*. (Translated by H. A. Strong.) New York: Macmillan, 1889. Cited by William Labov, *Sociolinguistic patterns*. Philadelphia: University of Pennsylvania Press, 1972.

Reinecke, J. E. *Language and dialect in Hawaii*. Honolulu: University of Hawaii Press, 1969.

Stewart, W. A. Creole languages in the Caribbean. In F. A. Rice (Ed.), *Study of the role of second languages in Asia, Africa and Latin America*. Washington, D.C.: Center for Applied Linguistics, 1962. (a)

Stewart, W. A. *The functional distribution of Creole and French in Haiti*. Georgetown University Monograph Series on Languages and Linguistics, No. 15, 1962. (b)

Stewart, W. A. On the use of negro dialect in the teaching of reading. In J. Baratz & R. Shuy (Eds.), *Teaching black children to read*. Washington, D.C.: Center for Applied Linguistics, 1969.

Sturtevant, E. H. *An introduction to linguistic science*. New Haven, Connecticut: Yale University Press, 1947.

Sweet, H. *The history of language*. London: J. M. Dent, 1900. Cited by William Labov, *Sociolinguistic patterns*. Philadelphia: University of Pennsylvania Press, 1972.

Turner, L. D. *Africanisms in the Gullah dialect*. Chicago: University of Chicago Press, 1949.

Part **II**

HISTORICAL ORIGINS

4

Pidgins, Creoles, and the Origins of Vernacular Black English

Elizabeth Closs Traugott

Stanford University

In the last few years a large number of descriptions of Black English have been given by various authors. These descriptions vary considerably, as would the study of any other language variety, according to the fineness of the distinctions made between lects,[1] and especially according to the criteria chosen for definition; significantly different results may be obtained if the varieties are defined socioeconomically rather than regionally. The study of Black English tends to be subject to more varying analyses than many other varieties of English since descriptions are made not purely for the purpose of characterizing the language, but for political, pedagogical, or other purposes. Inevitably, comparison with other varieties of English is made, usually with Standard English; sometimes comparison is made with written, idealized forms of English, and speech may then be confounded with writing. The differences are often expressed in terms of "absence" or "omission" of features present in Standard English. Consciously or unconsciously such terminology may contribute to the concept that Black English is somehow linguistically deficient.

[1] The term "lect" is used here in preference to "dialect" to designate any language variety, whether defined regionally or socially, without judgment of the "purity" of the variety in question. The term "dialect" is not used because some speakers associate it with regional varieties only, or with nonstandard varieties.

57

Extensive work still needs to be done on all varieties of English to establish suitable bases for comparison, including correlation with socio-economic status, job status, age, sex, geographic origin, style (for instance, degree of formality or informality), situation, and topic of discussion, but a substantial start has been made, especially in large urban areas like New York, Washington, Detroit, and Philadelphia. Arguments will probably continue for a long time about whether Black English, at least the varieties spoken in the ghettos and those least affected by Standard English, should best be treated as directly derivable from rules for English in general, or should be treated as an essentially different system which overlaps considerably with other varieties of English. Answers to these arguments may well depend on the purpose of the study. Pedagogically the transition from Black English to Standard English may be easier if Black English is considered on a continuum with other varieties of English. On the other hand, it can be argued that psychologically it may be preferable to treat Black English as a separate system, since separate treatment readily allows for linguistic and ethnic identity and tends to counterbalance the complex implications of the deficit theory. From a historical point of view there can be no question that Black English derives at least in part from a system rather different from English, although we do not yet and probably never will know exactly what this system was, since, having been a spoken rather than written language in the seventeenth and eighteenth centuries, it remained virtually unrecorded except in stereotyped scenes in the drama and fiction of the time. The evidence from such scant records, from the linguistic structure of contemporary Black English, and from the cultural and social history of the last three centuries strongly suggests Black English originated in creole and ultimately pidgin lects. It has become more and more assimilated into the large variety of lects that can loosely be characterized as "English." The assimilation has, of course, by no means been merely one way. Black English has been the source of borrowings in many other lects of English. This is particularly clear in the realm of vocabulary; many Black English words have been adopted into the mainstream of English, but not necessarily with the exact meaning that they had in Black English: *that's where it's at, cool, jive, rap,* and *bad* and *mean* in the positive sense of "powerful" and "exciting" represent just a miniscule example of a large number of such borrowings.

It is not my purpose here to attempt to answer the intricate question of how to handle the current but ever-changing status of Black lects vis-à-vis other spoken lects of English, but rather to explore the linguistic implications of the statement that Black English is derived from a creole and still has features that reflect that derivation. In doing so I will attempt to present descriptions that characterize the structures in question in positive terms relating to the system as a whole, rather than in the negative terms of omission and absence compared to other lects. Limitations of space prevent detailed discussion of the influence of languages spoken in West Africa and of varieties of British English, including Irish, on the development of Black English. It must always be borne in mind, however, that to speak of a creole means to speak of a contact language situation, and that British English as well as West African languages were essential ingredients in the language mix out of which Black English developed.

To put the problem in perspective, it is useful to characterize certain types of language with respect to their social function so that we may recognize features of Black English that are at least in part typologically determined. Some distinct types of language are pidgins, creoles, vernaculars, standard languages, classical languages, artificial languages, and so forth. These labels do not represent absolutely distinct categories, but define characteristics of language that tell us about ranges of use, social status, degree of homogeneity, and to some extent features of syntax and vocabulary. They are useful in considering arguments for or against the teaching of varieties of a language in school, in adopting specific languages or varieties of a language in newly independent countries, in recognizing the cultural heritage of a language, and in gaining insights into how language may change through time.

A pidgin may be broadly characterized as a language that is nobody's native language. It typically arises in situations where speakers of mutually unintelligible languages come together as social subordinates to a socially dominant group who speak yet another language; for example, slaves from different parts of Africa coming together on a plantation owned by a European, in a country foreign to them all. The socially dominant group may be in only marginal contact with the socially inferior one which is usually numerically a small minority. In such a situation speakers in the socially inferior position try to use the socially superior language, with or without direct input from that language. Reinforcement by attempts on the part of the socially superior group to communicate with the subordinate group may lead to the lengthy survival of a pidgin, sometimes over hundreds of years. The development of a pidgin is typical of trade situations. It is particularly common among maritime communities where social stratification is clear and where language barriers constantly have to be overcome in journeys to foreign lands. It is, however, by no means restricted to maritime communities. Indeed, it is possible that the branch of Indo-European called Germanic (including the ancestors of modern German, English, and Scandinavian) is the descendant of a pidgin which had developed along the overland trade routes from eastern Europe.

As might be expected, pidgins typically serve limited functions. In their simplest form they follow little more than the basic needs of communication. They identify social groupings (who is in and who is out), differentiate speech functions (for example, statement, question, command, request, and naming of trade objects and body parts), and specify immediate local contexts (trading post, ship, harbor, or road). They are often extensively supplemented by gesture. As a pidgin develops, increasingly subtle linguistic distinctions are made. These include modifications specifying quality or condition of objects, or temporal contours of events (events seen as moments without duration or as involving duration, events designated as completed or noncompleted, and so forth). The particular functions of the pidgin, whether used for bargaining, for work orders, or for communicating reports at the end of the day further determine what types of linguistic structure develop. Furthermore, the limitations of internal acquisitional linguistic processes also to some extent determine aspects of the structure of pidgin languages relatively independently of the contact languages in question and account for the tendency of pidgins to find expression for the most fundamental and general categories of language in fairly uniform ways.

In the situation in which pidgins thrive one would not expect complex sentence structure or extensive vocabulary, but rather ingenious use of limited structures to express complex relations. We must always remember that in normal cases speakers of pidgin bring with them in their own native languages internalized linguistic systems of enormous complexity. Their knowledge, albeit unconscious, of linguistic systems is as great as that of most speakers of any language; therefore complex relations may be understood, though not expressed. To this extent, pidgins are limited in function and surface representation, but not necessarily in cognitive complexity or "inner form." However, in some situations, such as slavery, the psychological ravagings of displacement and suffering may result in a temporary limitation of cognitive complexity. This is a psychological, not a linguistic, problem.

Pidgins typically have a vocabulary related to one or more of the languages of the dominant or "superstrate" group and a grammar more closely related to one or more socially subordinate or "substrate" languages. There is sometimes evidence of adoption of the vocabulary of one superstrate language, say Portuguese, and subsequent "relexification" or adoption of the vocabulary of another superstrate language, say Dutch, while the grammatical structure remains relatively unaffected. Such evidence for relexification comes especially from the presence in a wide number of maritime pidgins, including those with primarily English lexicons, of forms for "to be able, (to do something) habitually" (related to Portuguese *saber* "be able") and forms for "what" (related to Portuguese *cosa* "thing"), but in many languages such evidence is rather scant.

A pidgin may die out or continue in use, in modified form, for several centuries, as did Sabir, the Portuguese-related pidgin used in maritime communities in the Mediterranean from the twelfth to the early twentieth centuries. In special circumstances, such as in New Guinea where large numbers of native languages are spoken in a small geographic area, pidgin may come to be used in a wide variety of social situations, including political administration, and even pedagogy. A pidgin may also give rise to a creole in communities with relatively stable populations. This is happening right now in New Guinea. It happened in the eighteenth and nineteenth centuries in the Caribbean.

Unlike pidgins, creoles are typically native languages usually developed by the children of pidgin speakers. However, they may also develop as the regular home language of adults in situations of intermarriage. As a native or home language, a creole clearly has more linguistic functions than a pidgin and therefore is more varied in structure. More possibilities of subordination are present, and the vocabulary is greater. Various kinds of inflectional structures tend to arise, partly because as native languages creoles are spoken more rapidly and with an easier flow than most pidgins, which allows for contractions of elements that tend to be separate words or particles in pidgin languages. Creoles thrive where there is a large ethnic mix and clear social stratification such as existed during the colonial period in the Caribbean and many islands in the Pacific. When there is little access to the superstrate language, the creole will develop relatively independently. This was the case with Sranan, which despite only brief contact with English in the eighteenth century, nevertheless continued to be characterized by a heavily English-related vocabulary, but underwent minimal grammatical modification toward English. (Sranan has now become the national language of Surinam.) When access to the superstrate continues, however, we usually find progressive "decreolization," that is, modification in the direction of the socially superstrate language. Such decreolization is evidenced by Jamaican Creole. The decreolization process may operate so extensively that the creole eventually becomes largely assimilated into the superstrate language, as is the case with Black English. We may then speak of a "post-creole" continuum from varieties relatively far from the mainstream to varieties indistinguishable from it. Assimilation of the creole does not necessarily mean that all traces of the original creole are lost. On the contrary, as always happens in language change residues of the earlier structures remain and may become identifying features of particular varieties of the language, as will be discussed in relation to some Black English texts at the end of this chapter.

It is often said that pidgins and creoles are simplified languages. In the sense that they are limited in function, this is true. In the sense that they have small lexicons, and in the sense that they are inflectionally limited and tend to be syntactically coordinating rather than subordinating, this is also true with respect to the level of linguistic expression. However, what is not constrained by inflectional representation is constrained by word order and particles. That modifications are expressed coordinately and parenthetically rather than by relative clauses does not imply that the cognitive relation of modification is not known. "Simplicity" is a deceptive term. Insofar as it implies "economical" it is useful. Insofar as it implies "unsuitable for abstract thought" or for subtle manipulation of participants in a conversation, it is probably realistic. But insofar as it is assumed by some to imply cognitive deficit, it is clearly an inappropriate term.

Pidgins, creoles, and decreolized languages are traditionally regarded as representing a progression to freer and freer social communicative function. The terms, however, always imply some degree of social inadequacy. Vernacular forms of language, by contrast, are typically defined not socially but stylistically. They are primarily spoken forms of language, used in the street, at home, and in a wide number of informal situations. The vernacular, in other worls, is the language spoken by people in daily life. What characterizes vernaculars is that they do not necessarily involve extensive ethnic or linguistic heterogeneity, although such heterogeneity may and often does exist. Therefore, a vernacular may result from the adaptation of the creole into the mainstream of linguistic usage, but vernaculars need not necessarily have creole origins. Vernaculars tend not be codified (except by linguists) or to have widely accepted lexicons. They may have greater or lesser social acceptability, depending on who speaks them. Their salient characteristic is that they are spoken. By contrast, standard varieties of language are written as well as spoken; they are codified in grammars for pedagogical purposes or verification of stylistic propriety and have accepted lexicons, usually formalized in dictionaries. They are used as media for legal, pedagogical, and academic expression. They are likely to be the only accepted medium for the written language. Finally, they are widely regarded as norms.

One of the difficulties we encounter in dealing with notions of Standard English is that there are, broadly speaking, two views of what is a standard language. One is the view that Standard English is the norm used by educated people, especially those commanding local or national respect as leaders; that is, Standard English is defined descriptively, with reference to social and stylistic parameters; it is clearly not conceived as an absolute, but rather as the medium for the widest spectrum of communication, both spoken and written, in activities of social prestige. In this sense, speakers of Standard English are also speakers of the vernacular, at least in its more prestigious varieties, although the reverse may not be true. Standard English, so defined, is simply the variety of English spoken in the most formal situations or in certain situations such as the classroom. It is not fundamentally different from other less formal or prestigious varieties that conform to a greater or lesser extent to this codified variety, according to situation and topic of discussion. Given this view, it is reasonable to claim that there are a number of Standard Englishes, not only regional varieties such as British versus American, but also ethnic, as, for example, Anglo versus Black; there is considerable evidence that a Standard Black English is currently developing, as used by congressmen and writers, as well as by a large number of teachers. There is, however, also another very different view of Standard English which is essentially *prescriptive* rather than *descriptive* and which regards the standard language as an absolute and as a thing apart, recognizable primarily through the written form of language. This is the idea of a standard as an ideal rather than a norm, and as the repository of refinement in language. It underlies the function of legislative judgment on the language of works to be published, and on the acceptability or otherwise of new vocabulary items into the language. In this sense, standard and prestigious vernacular varieties are regarded not as overlapping, but as in opposition: the standard is a written norm, the prestigious vernacular a spoken norm in daily life.

The two concepts of Standard English are largely traceable to the rise of the middle class and to territorial expansion in the eighteenth century. The upper classes felt threatened in urban communities, especially London, by the growing importance of the middle class. At the beginning of the eighteenth century we find grammars that were essentially descriptions of the language spoken by educated people. These grammars were aimed primarily at "maintaining caste," that is, establishing for the upper classes a linguistic code based on their own behavior that would, along with moral and other codes, separate them from the threat of middle class "upstarts." By the end of the eighteenth century, however, we find a new kind of grammar, primarily prescriptive, codifying the language of the upper classes as models or ideals for the social betterment of the middle class. Such prescriptive grammars dominated thinking about language until this century when linguists' insistence on the importance of description in analyzing language led to greater interest in the schools in descriptive approaches to Standard English.

Having considered the broad functional characteristics of various types of language, we may now turn to look in more detail at some pidgins and creoles. The characteristics to be discussed and illustrated were selected specifically with the structure of Vernacular Black English in mind, especially the variety spoken in large urban areas. Since the history of Black English is largely unknown, the passages discussed do not represent specific stages of Black English. Rather they show forms of language which are typologically rather than genetically related. This typological relation is highlighted by an example of Neo-Melanesian (also called Tok Pisin). Obviously this language cannot be regarded as genetically related to Black English, but it does demonstrate remarkable typological similarities (and differences).

SYNTACTIC STRUCTURE

1. Clause structure

Sentence structures may be simple or complex. An example of a simple structure is *The slaves husked the corn*. Complex sentences may have coordinated clauses (sometimes called compound clauses), as in *The slaves husked the corn and their masters ate it*, or they may consist of a main clause and others subordinated to it, as in *The slaves husked the corn so that their masters could eat it. Although it was the slaves who husked the corn, it was their masters who ate it*. Pidgins show little evidence of subordination. This simplification is directly related to the communicative context. Here complex structures are difficult to understand and the limitations on expression favor juxtaposing clauses rather than hierarchizing them. Thus, events are mentioned in their order of occurrence, simply juxtaposed without connective, coordinated by *and,* or sequenced by *first, second,* or *then, afterwards*, but are rarely subordinated, as in *I bought shells before I bought incense*. Similarly, descriptions are juxtaposed, as in *I bought the shells. They were beautiful*, rather than subordinated by relative clause formation, as in *I bought the shells which were beautiful*. Greater use of subordination develops in creoles, where finer distinctions need to be made. (Notice the distinction between incidental description in *I bought the shells, which were beautiful,* and contrastive description in *I bought the shells which/that were beautiful* implying there were some I did not buy, presumably, those which were not beautiful.) However, subordination is in general not extensively evidenced by spoken forms of language. The visual medium of the written word allows more complexity than the auditory medium of the spoken language. The written word allows one to make a more permanent record of clause structures that are connected in complexly hierarchized ways, especially clauses within clauses, as in *The cat which ate the rat is my neighbor's.* Such sentences may be difficult to comprehend when spoken, since the utterance is relatively impermanent memory may become overtaxed.

2. Active versus Passive

The most frequent way of expressing an action performed by an actor on some goal is, in English and many other languages, by selecting the actor as the subject of the sentence, as in *Bill kissed Mary.* However, in some circumstances, for example, if Mary has been the topic of discussion up to that point, or if the actor is indefinite, the passive may be preferred, as in *Mary was kissed by Bill, Mary was kissed (by someone).* Among possible reasons for this is that there is a tendency in language to match order of event and order of mention, that is, for expression to be "iconic." The actor in most cases exists before the action, and the goal is typically affected after or during the action. In pidgins, sentences are always active. Indeed passive sentences seem to arise only during decreolization. Similarly, as indicated above, the principle: Order of mention matches order of event, is very important in pidgins and creoles; such structures as *Before I bought incense I bought shells,* where order of mention and order of event do not match, also develop during decreolization.

3. Repetition of Subject

Structures of the type *John he left* where the subject is repeated by a pronominal form abound in pidgins and creoles (however, the tense may not be marked; see Section 5b below), and are typical in spoken language of situations where attention needs to be drawn to the beginning of the sentence. These repetitions may be though of first as a kind of gesture for attracting the attention of the person addressed in a conversation; it later becomes generalized to sentences which do not open a discourse.

4. Nominal Phrases

By nominal phrase is meant a noun or demonstrative plus a noun, or a prepositional phrase including at least a preposition and a noun, as in *men, the men, for men, for the men;* such nominal phrases may function as subjects, objects, indirect objects, or adverbials.

(a) Nouns. In pidgins and creoles nouns are typically noninflected. Singular and plural are normally determined by extralinguistic context,

or else by quantifiers such as *onefela* "one," *twofela* "two." Possession is indicated in various ways, most often by position, as in *king he head* "king's head." The development of nominal inflections is a function of creolization, and especially decreolization, when the superstrate is inflectional.

(b) Pronouns. Pronouns distinguish person and number, that is, singular and plural [in some instances also dual (*we-two, you-two, they-two*)]. Otherwise, they tend to be invariant. Distinctions between preverbal and postverbal forms are not found; hence some form of either *I* or *me, he* or *him,* but not both, is found in all positions in the sentence. Male, female, and neutral are usually not distinguished for third person; hence *he* (or *him*) is equivalent to *he, she,* and *it.* It is important to notice that many languages, including Chinese, Finnish, Persian, Turkish, and several African languages, also do not distinguish gender in third person pronouns. The absence of a gender distinction is therefore not a function of pidgins and creoles as such.

(c) Prepositions. There are few distinct prepositions in pidgins and creoles. One preposition only may be found in some pidgins. Creoles develop more prepositions under the influence of the superstrate.

5. Verbal Phrases

By verbal phrase is meant a verb, with or without auxiliaries, and inflections for tense (present, past, etc.), mood (indicative, subjunctive, etc.), and aspect (the "time contour," such as completive, durative, iterative and so forth). English has a vestigial subjunctive as in *If I were you* (as opposed to *was*) and it distinguishes past, as in *I walked,* from non-past, as in *He walks.* Other tenses, aspects, and moods are expressed periphrastically by auxiliaries, as in *I'm going to go, I will go* (both future), *I have finished the job* (completive aspect), *I am finishing the job* (continuative aspect), *I would go if I could* (conditional mood).

(a) To be. The English copula verb *to be* serves a wide variety of functions, some of which may in other languages be expressed by different verbs, or even nothing at all. *Be* functions descriptively in *He is happy;* it expresses the relation of a member to a set in *She is a teacher;* and it expresses a temporary relationship, or one that has just come into being in *He is happy now.* (Compare also the descriptive *He is naughty* as opposed to the event-related *He is being naughty.*) Spanish is a well-known example of a language which distinguishes description of relatively permanent states from set-membership, or event-related states;

we find *Jacinta esta bonita* "J is pretty" (this is her characteristic), as against *Jacinta es bonita* "J is pretty" (she is a member of the set of pretty girls, she has just become pretty). A further distinction may be made between the functions of *be* as mentioned above and the function of/*be* as a locative or existential, as in *There is an oak/tree in my/garden*. In many languages, including Arabic, Aztec, Bengali, Hungarian, and Russian, nonexistential functions of *be* may remain unexpressed under certain circumstances in the present, but must be expressed in the past, while existential *be* must always be expressed. Similar distinctions between various functions of *be* may be found in pidgins and creoles. In particular, we often find that where English uses a present tense form of *be* in its nonexistential function, none is used in pidgins and creoles, while some verb expressing a *be* relation may be required for the past tense. We therefore may find *He happy*, but *He been happy*.

(b) Tense and aspect. There is a marked tendency in pidgins and creoles to subordinate the role of tense to that of aspect; in other words, it is often more significant to consider whether an action is completed or ongoing than to consider whether it is past or not. Like nouns, verbs are usually not inflected; tense and aspect, if expressed, are periphrastic, expressed either by verbs like *finish, done, been,* or by adverbials like *long time before, baimbai* "later" (from *by and by*). As is true of the nouns, periphrasis rather than inflection is not exclusive to pidgins and creoles; it is typical of languages like Chinese, and English itself is mainly periphrastic rather than inflectional.

It is essential to note that all characteristics just mentioned in this section (Syntactic Structure) can also be found in languages that function as vernaculars and standard languages. None of the features is necessarily pidgin or creole; however, a language is not a real pidgin or creole unless it has these features.

LEXICON

If no syntactic structure is restricted to pidgins and creoles, the nature of the lexicon can be a sure indicator at least of a pidgin. While it is certainly not true that pidgins consist of "only a few hundred words" as is sometimes thought, pidgins do not typically have vocabularies of over 3,000 or 4,000 words. By comparison, most standard languages average over 20,000 words. English, with some 40,000 words codified in Webster's Third International Dictionary, has one of the largest vocabularies of the world's languages (although much of it is rarely used), partly because it is used in so many parts of the world, and also partly because there has always been a tendency in English to borrow rather than reuse extant words for new meanings. Furthermore, English has been used for a large number of academic fields, including philosophy and theology, and for scientific and technical research, not just in the 20th century, as is the case with the languages of many of the Third World nations, but for several centuries. Whereas in Standard English subtle meaning distinctions are conveyed by different words, in pidgins and also to a considerable extent in creoles words are used with a great variety of meanings. Hence a familiar word may have quite a different meaning; in West African Pidgin English, for example, *morning* is a greeting used at any time of day. Words are often combined in novel ways to create periphrastic expressions for concepts expressed by one word in English, as, for example, *king-boy* for "prince," or *house sick* for "hospital" (perhaps reduced from *house for the sick*).

Another characteristic of pidgin and creole vocabulary is that it is mixed. All languages are, of course, to some extent mixed, and English especially so. However, in standard languages mixture is not usually extensively in evidence in the language of daily life, and especially not in the grammatical words of the language, such as prepositions and auxiliary verbs, and strata of borrowings are often identifiable with particular styles or topics of discussion (consider, for example, the preponderance of Latin and Greek borrowings into English in the language of science). By contrast, in pidgins and creoles the evidence for lexical mixture in everyday language is proportionately very high, while the formal and academic contextual conditions that elicit borrowed vocabulary in English do not apply.

PHONOLOGY

The phonology of pidgins and creoles varies extensively according to the languages in contact. However, it is possible to generalize that sounds which are common to all the languages in contact will form the core of the phonological system and that sounds that are relatively rare in the languages of the world such as the voiceless interdental [θ] as in *thin* and the voiced interdental [ð] as in *then* tend not to occur. In English-related pidgins and creoles, we find *t* in words corresponding to English words beginning with [θ], *t* or *f* in words corresponding to English words ending with [θ], and *d* in words corresponding to English words with [ð]; hence, *tin* for *thin*, *den* for *then*. Furthermore, most English-related pidgins and creoles are "*r*-less," that is, there is no *r* in words corresponding to English words with preconsonantal or word-final *r* (*ka* corresponds to *car*, *kad* to *card*). This may reflect contact with British rather than American English in the formative stages of the languages in question, as well as absence of *r* in similar positions in some of the substrate languages. The absence of preconsonantal or word-final *r* illustrates the way in which many features of pidgins and creoles may arise by reinforcement of a substrate structure by the superstrate.

Another reflection of substrate languages, particularly African languages and languages spoken in the Pacific, is the relative absence of consonant clusters, particularly in final position. This absence of consonant clusters may also reflect to some extent patterns of spoken English, where the second of two voiced or two voiceless consonants is often lost in final position; hence *ole* for *old*, *neks* or even *nek* for *next* (phonetically [nɛkst]), but *hunt*.

SAMPLE PASSAGES

As indicated above, the following passages have been chosen to show patterns typical of English-related pidgins and creoles and to demonstrate certain similarities to Black English. They were collected by different linguists at different times and are transcribed in different notations. The following vowel chart should provide approximate identification of the symbols used for simple vowels:

	Front	Central	Back
High	i		u
	ɪ		ʊ
Mid	e		o
	ɛ	ʌ/ə	ɔ
Low	æ	a	

Simple vowels
  i roughly as in *beat*
  ɪ roughly as in *bit*
  e roughly as in *bait*
  ɛ roughly as in *bet*
  æ roughly as in *bat*
  a roughly as in *father*
  ɔ roughly as in *bought, law*
  o roughly as in *boat*
  ʊ roughly as in *full*
  u roughly as in *boot*
  ʌ/ə roughly as in *but* (stressed vowel) and in *Rosa* (unstressed second syllable)

Diphthongs
  ai/ay/aj roughly as in *bite*
  au/aw roughly as in *bout*
  oi/oy roughly as in *boil*
Consonants
  Consonant symbols are fairly self-explanatory. Special symbols are:
  ŋ the final consonant in *ring*
  č the initial and final consonant in *church*
  ǰ the initial and final consonant in *judge*

WEST AFRICAN PIDGIN ENGLISH

West African Pidgin English (WAPE) is currently used as a medium of communication among Africans of different linguistic backgrounds, especially in the area of West Africa that was formerly British West Africa. The earliest period at which English was known in West Africa was ca. 1550. At that time it was used chiefly in nautical situations by sailors as well as slaves. Most sailors are known to have used a Portuguese-related pidgin at this period. There is therefore considerable argument about the origins of WAPE. Some argue that it is a relexification of the already established Portuguese pidgin, but others point out that a nautical English, characterized not so much by regional peculiarities as by the functional constraints on language in the maritime situation, may have been established independently of the Portuguese pidgin by the end of the sixteenth century, and that this may have been the origin of both WAPE and later Caribbean creoles. Considering its history of some 400 years, WAPE has undergone extensive linguistic expansion and shows regional variation. The text used here is representative of WAPE spoken in the West Cameroons; it was recorded and transcribed by Gilbert D. Schneider.

In the following passage [e] and [o] are transcribed as [ey] and [ow], while [ɛ] and [ɔ] are both transcribed as [e] and [o]; [ŋ] is transcribed as [ng].

SENSE PASS KING[2]

1. som   boi i   bin bi fo som fan kontri fo insai afrika,
   Some boy he Past be in some fine country in inside Africa,
   There once lived a very clever lad who lived in a beautiful part of Africa,
2. we   i   bin get plenti sens. i   pas king fo sens   sef,   sow
   where he Past get plenty sense. He pass king in wisdom self,   so
   where he got much wisdom.   He was smarter than the king himself, and so
3. i   neym bin bi sens-pas-king. king i   bin feks plenti, ha i bin hia sey,
   he name Past be Sense-pass-king. King he Past vex plenty, how he Past hear say,
   his name was Wiser-than-king.   The king was very annoyed, when he heard
4.   dis simol-boi i di   kas eni-man fo sens. sow
        this small boy he Continuative catch any-man for sense. So
   how this young boy was outwitting everyone.   He
5. king i   bin mimba sey,   i go kas i,   i   go win i   fo   sens.
   king he Past decide say/that, he go catch him, he go win himself with wit.
   decided to put the lad in his place with a few tricks of his own.
6. i   bin sen i masinja som dey, we   dem bin tok sey, meyk yu   kom fo
   He Past send his messenger one day, when they Past talk say make yourself come to
   One day the king sent a messenger to the young man and summoned him to come to

[2] From Gilbert D. Schneider, *West African Pidgin-English: A descriptive linguistic analysis with texts and glossary from the Cameroon area.* Athens, Ohio, 1966; pp. 177–179, by permission of the author.

7. king i   tong, na palaba i dey. sens-pas-king   i bin gow, i mas-fut fo
   king his town, and talk   in there. Sense-pass-king he Past go,   he makes for
   the palace for a discussion.   Wiser-than-king began his journey.

8.   rowt, waka trong   fo   hil, sowtey i rish   fo king
   (the) road, walks vigorously up-and-down hills, so that he reaches at king
                                 up and down the steep hills he went and so finally arrived at the

9. i tong.   king i tok sey, yu don   kom. meyk yu klin
   his town.   King he talks says, you Completive come. Make you klin (i.e. shave)
   king's palace. (Upon arrival) the king welcomed him   and aked the young man

10. ma het.   biabia i don   plenti tumos   fo ma het. sens-pas-king
    my head. Hair it Completive grow / too-much for my head. Sense-pass-king
    to cut his hair because it was too long.   Wiser-than-king

11. i bin don   gri sey, i gow bap king i het. i bigin   kot-am
    he Past Completive agree that he go   barb king his head. He began (to)[3] cut-them (i.e., hairs)
    agreed to cut the king's hair

12. bot ha i di   kot-am, i di   sowsow trowwey   simol kon
    but how he Continuative cut-them, he Continuative always throw-away small corn
    but as he was cutting   he was also throwing down a little corn for the

13. fo fawu, we   i dey fo king i domot.   king i aks i sey, ha yu di
    for fowl, which in there at king his courtyard. King he asks he says, how you Continuative
    chickens in the king's courtyard.   The king asked him, "Why are you

14. sowsow trow   kon? boi ansa   i sey,   na   lo fo   gif   chop
    always throw-away corn? Boy answers he says, (Is)there law against giv(ing) food
    always throwing down corn?" The lad answered,   "Is there a law against feeding

15. fo fawu?   simol-tam i don   finis i wok. king i het don
    to fowl?   Small-time he Completive finish his work. King his head Completive
    the chickens?" Soon he finished his task.   The king's head looked

16. nyan'ga bat.   king i bigin   hala, sey,   na   wati?
    look-fine very-much. King he begins (to) holler, say(ing), (Is)there what?
    very fine.   The king (then) began to shout, "What's going on here?

17. simol wowwow   pikin klin   het fo bik-man?   meyk yu
    Small good-for-nothing child clean/shave head for elder?   Make yourself
    Can a good-for-nothing youngster cut (shave) the hair of an elder? Put the hair

18. put bak ma biabia wan-tam.   a gow kil yu ifi yu now put-am!
    put back my hair immediately. I go kill you if you not put-them (back)!
    back in place immediately.   I'll kill you if you don't put them back."

19. sens-pas-king   tok sey, now keys.   a gri.   i bi dasow sey,
    Sense-pass-king talks says, No problem.   I agree. It is just that
    Wiser-than-king replied,   "It doesn't matter. I will gladly put your hair back,

20. meyk yu   gif bak ma kon bifo   a gow fiks yu biabia agen. king i now
    make yourself give back my corn before I go fix your hair   again. King he not
    if you return the corn I fed to your chickens."   The king was

21. sabi wati fo tok. i mof   don   lok. sens-pas-king   i di
    know what to say. His mouth Completive lock. Sense-pass-king he Continuative
    speechless.   He was dumbfounded.   Wiser-than-king went on his way

22. gow dasow.   man now fit fan i keys fo   dis wan.
    go that's-all. One not able find his case against this one.
    and no one was able to find fault with him.

---

[3] Glosses of words not in the original text have been parenthesized so as to maintain the literalness of the word-for-word translation.

COMMENTS

Syntactic structure

1. Note that the clauses are connected by *we* 'where,' *sow* 'so, there-fore,' which provide a loose subordination typical of narration. Particularly interesting is line 5–7. In this sentence *na,* the coordinator 'and,' is derived from the Bantu coordinator *na*; sequencing of events, specifying that the messenger went and then talked, is signaled by *we* 'where, when'; a distinct personal relativizer such as 'who' is conspicuously absent. Also, there are two instances of constructions closely resembling 'serial' or two-part verbs, such as are found in many African languages, notably *meyk yu kom* 'come, get yourself to come' (line 6) and *tok sey* 'say, talk say' (line 9). Phrases like the latter can be traced historically all the way to Vernacular Black English. In many pidgins and creoles, the *sey* functions not so much as a verb meaning 'say,' but rather more like the complementizer 'that'. There is some evidence that *sey,* as the second member of a serial construction, is approaching a complementizer in this particular passage, at least in some instances. Compare, for example, *tok sey* in line 9 where a direct quotation is introduced and the meaning 'say' is transparent, with *gri sey* in line 11, where an indirect quotation is introduced and the meaning 'say' is more opaque, and finally with *mimba sey* 'decide' (line 5), where the action of saying seems irrelevant. In any event, *sey* in a serial construction does not have the full meaning of an independent verb, as can be seen by contrast with *i aks i sey* 'he asks he says' (line 13) where two clauses are involved.

2. The number of actor–action–goal sentences is striking; subjects are regularly animate actors.

3. Subjects are typically iterated by a pronoun, as in *king i tok sey* 'king he said' (line 9).

4a. Possession is expressed by the formula: noun—third person pronoun—head noun, as in *king i het* 'king his head' (line 11).

4b. Only a few pronouns are attested in this passage: singular first person *a,* second person *yu,* third person singular *i,* and plural third person *dem.* WAPE does not distinguish gender in pronouns, but it does distinguish number for all persons (the plural second person is *una*), and it also has an emphatic form of the first and second singular pronouns, *mi* and *im,* which are sometimes also used nonemphatically in the object position. Emphatic stress seems to be a condition for the introduction of a variant pronoun form in many pidgins and creoles, with only subsequent extension of the form to either subject or object position.

4c. The preposition *fo* is a general localizer, functioning roughly like *at;* concepts like 'in' can be expressed periphrastically, as in *fo insai* (line 1).

5a. The copula is noticeably present in WAPE, unlike some other pidgins, both as a main verb and as an auxiliary in the present as well as the past. Therefore we find *sow i neym bin bi sens-pas-king* 'so his name was Wiser-than-King' (line 2–3) with a copula past tense *bin* and a descriptive *bi* (main verb), and *it bi dasow sey* 'It is just that' (line 19) with present tense main verb. Locatives and existentials can be differentiated from other copulas; if so they are expressed by the locative particle *na*, as in *na lo . . . ?* 'Is there a law?' (line 14), and *na wati?* 'There is what going on?/What's going on?' (line 16).

5b. Past tense, if expressed, is periphrastic: *king i bin feks plenti* 'king he was vexed plenty' (line 3); *bin* signals not mere past time, but rather emphasis on the past, sometimes a past which is relatively remote. Present tense or unemphatic past usually remains unexpressed: *king i aks i sey* 'King he asks he says/King he asked he said' (line 13). Aspects are represented in this passage by *don* (completive), as in *yu don kom* 'you have come' (line 9), and by *di* (noncompletive, continuative), as in *i di kot-am, i di sowsow trowwey simol kon fo fawu* 'he was cutting them, he was always throwing a little corn to the chickens' (line 12–13). *Di* and related forms (e.g., *de, də*) derive from West African languages like Ewe, Twi, and Wolof, where they express continuative action. They are also evidenced in Caribbean pidgins and creoles and in Gullah.

Lexicon

Palaba 'talk' (line 7), *pikin* 'small child' (line 17), and *sabi* 'know' (line 21) derive from Portuguese; *nyan'ga* 'very fine' (line 16) is related to Mende *nyanga* 'ostentation'. Extended use of English words is exemplified by, among others, *plenti* (adverb in line 3, verb in line 10), and *domot* (line 13), literally 'doormouth'.

Phonology

Note that there are few word-final consonant clusters; those there are end in *-s*: compare *fan* 'find' (line 22) with *feks* 'vex' (line 3). All word-final stops are voiceless, e.g., *bap*, corresponding to English 'barb' (line 11), *bat* 'bad(ly)' (i.e., 'very much') (line 16), *het* 'head' (line 10), *rowt* 'road' (line 8). The absence of a voice contrast in stops in final position is frequently to be found in the languages of the world; German is a well-known example among the European languages. In keeping with the sound patterning of many West African languages, initial and word-medial as well as final consonant clusters are rare [cf. *trong* 'strong' (line 8)]. Some English words that do not conform to the pattern of West

African languages have been remodeled, e.g., *simol* 'small' (line 17). [θ] and [ð] are remodeled as [t, f] and [d] as expected: *domot* 'doormouth' (line 13), *mof* 'mouth' (line 21), *dem* 'them' (line 6). *ng* [ŋ] for English [n] occurs in *ton* 'town'; this velarization of the nasal occurs in many pidgins and creoles, as we shall see.

NEO-MELANESIAN OR TOK PISIN

Neo-Melanesian Pidgin, more recently called Tok Pisin, is spoken in New Guinea and Papua. Geographically the area is mountainous, with deep valleys that have tended to separate linguistic communities; this separation has led over the centuries to the development of a large number of related yet considerably different languages. This linguistic diversity on the island has led to the development of Tok Pisin as a language of considerable status; it is used as an administrative language, and official documents are published in it.

Tok Pisin derives from Beach-la-Mar, which had wide currency among sailors, traders, and recruiters of indentured labor in the southwestern Pacific during the nineteenth century. The name of this pidgin derives from the sea cucumber (French *bêche-de-mer*) which was the chief object of trade. Basically English in vocabulary, it has French, Portuguese, Malay, Austronesian, Polynesian, and other elements. The influence of Austronesian is clear in the grammatical structure, especially in the verbal affixes (cf. Section 5b below), and in the personal pronoun system, which has singular, dual, trial, and plural distinctions, and also an inclusive–exclusive distinction in the plurals which differentiates, for example, between 'they and I' (inclusive) and 'they, not including me.'

The following passage, originally collected by Margaret Mead, ca. 1936, was transcribed by Robert A. Hall in 1942. It is from an autobiography told by a workboy and represents a relatively simple form of Tok Pisin. It is useful for the present study in that it illustrates a pidgin developed half-way round the world from West Africa, but probably with similar influences from maritime pidgins. The similarities to other English-related pidgins are striking.

ČAVI'S STORY[4]

1. naw mi stap rabawl. mi stap lɔŋ bɪglajn,   mi kətɪm   kopra.
   Then I   stayed Rabaul. I   stayed with workgroup, I   cut-object-marker copra.
   Then I stayed in Rabaul. I was in the work-group,   cutting copra.

---

[4] From Robert A. Hall, Jr., *Pidgin and creole languages*. Ithaca: Cornell University Press, 1966. Pp. 149–150, by permission of the author, with literal translation added.

2. naw wənfelə mastər bıləŋ kəmpəni ɛm i-kıčım   mi,
   Then a   master of   company he 3rd person-make cook-object marker me,
   Then a white man from the company took me as a cook again.
3. mi kuk ləŋ ɛm gɛn. master kıŋ. mi stap.   naw ɔl mastər
   I cook for him again. Master King. I stayed.   Now all masters
                         Mr. King.   I stayed there. Now all the white men
4. i-kık,   naw ɔl i-kıkım   ɛm, naw leg bıləŋ ɛm
   3rd person-kick,   then all 3rd person-kick-object marker him, then leg of   him
   were playing football, and they kicked him,   so that his leg
5. i-sweləp.   ɔl mastər tæsɔl i-kık,   naw ɔl i-kıkım   ɛm.
   3rd person-swell up. All masters just 3rd person-kick, then all 3rd person-kick-object
   swelled up.   The white men were just kicking, and kicked him.   marker him.
6. naw   ɛm i-go   ləŋ sıdni ləŋ haws sık.   mi wənfelə mi stap lukawtım
   And then he 3rd person-go to Sidney to hospital.   I alone   I stay look after-object
   So he went to Sydney,   to the hospital. I stayed alone to look after marker.
7. haws bıləŋ ɛm. əltəgedər səmtıŋ mi lukawtım,   mi stap.   ɔrajt,
   house of   him. Altogether things I look after-object marker, I stay.   Alright,
   his house.   I looked after everything,   and stayed there. Very well,
8. naw pæs i-kəm.   naw kiap i-lukım,   i-tɔk:
   then letter 3rd person-come. Then official 3rd person-look at-object marker, 3rd person-talk:
   then a letter arrived.   Then the government official looked at it,   and said:
9. "o,   mastər bıləŋ ju i-no   kæn kəm bæk." naw mastər—
   "Oh, master of   you 3rd person-not (verb) can come back." Then master—
   "Oh, your master cannot come back."   Then the master—
10. dısfelə ɛm i-kəməp—   bıləŋ kəmpəni tu,   ɛm i-save   bajım
    this-one he 3rd person-come there-of company too,   he 3rd person-Habitual
    this one who had come—   he too was of the company, he recruited buy-object marker
11. nufelə boj   ləŋ ɔlgedər   ples—   ɛm i-tɔk   ləŋ mi: "ju   no kæn
    new laborers from all   villages—he 3rd person-talk to me: "You not can
    new native laborers from all the villages—he said to me: "You cannot
12. go ləŋ bıglajn,   maski, ju kuk ləŋ mi gɛn."   mi stap ləŋ ɛm.
    go to work-group, instead, you cook for me again."   I stayed with him.
    go to the work-group, rather you shall cook for me again." I stayed with him,
13. stap stap stap stap.
    stay stay stay stay.
    and kept on staying.

COMMENTS

Syntactic Structure

Notice in particular (sections are numbered in such a way as to facilitate cross-reference with the general discussion on pp. 64–69):

1. Sequencing by *naw* 'now, then' is the rule, not subordination. The
reliance on apposition rather than subordination by relative clauses is
well illustrated by *dısfelə ɛm i-kəməp* 'this one he came there' (line 10),
where the third person pronoun *ɛm* ıs coreferential with *mastər*, and does
not have the form of a separate relative pronoun.

3. The subject is often iterated, as a pronoun, as in *wənfɛlə mastər bilɔŋ kəmpəni ɛm i-kɪčɪm mi* (line 2). This iteration may be one of the sources of the third person prefix on the verb (Section 5b below).

4a. Plural inflections on nouns do not exist in Tok Pisin. However, numerators are often used where singular and plural would be used in English, as in *wənfɛlə mastər* 'a/one white man' (line 2), *ɔl mastər* '(the) white men' (line 5).

4c. *lɔŋ* is a general localizer, roughly equivalent in function to WAPE *fo*, possibly derived in form, but not meaning, from 'along'. *bilɔŋ* is the regular possessive marker, equivalent to 'of', and derived from 'belong'.

5b. Verbs are not marked for tense. Aspect is illustrated by *i-save* (line 10) (noncompletive) from Portuguese, and by *stap stap stap stap* (line 13) (intensified duration). The latter type of aspectual expression is similar to English 'I stayed and stayed and stayed'.

Of particular importance is the system of verbal affixes. A third person marker *i-* precedes the verb stem when the subject is neither first nor second person, and an object marker *-ɪm* follows the verb stem whenever the verb is followed by an object; this object is expressed solely by this *-ɪm* if it is a pronoun, cf. *i-kɪk* 'they kick' (line 3), *i-kɪkɪm* 'they kick him' (line 4), *mi kɔtɪm kopra* 'I cut copra' (line 1). This affix structure closely resembles that of Austronesian languages in the area. The particular forms may be related to the English subject form *he* and the object form *him;* if so, it is important to remember that the only form of the third person pronoun is *ɛm*. The affix structure as well as the distinctions in the pronouns, not illustrated by this passage, demonstrate clearly that pidgin syntactic structure is not 'simpler' than English structure in any very obvious way, at the level of the simple clause.

JAMAICAN CREOLE

Jamaican Creole (JC) is one of a variety of creoles that developed in the Caribbean, the trade center from which African slaves were transported to various parts of the Western Hemisphere, especially North America. The political situation in the Caribbean was highly complex in the seventeenth, eighteenth, and nineteenth centuries. At various times and places there were important groups of traders and colonists of Spanish, Portuguese, French, English, Danish, Dutch, and German origin; Dutch was especially influential through the Moravian Church. The slaves came from various parts of West Africa; those who had been in the factories of West Africa apparently already spoke pidgin; others presumably learned it as they were transported to the Caribbean. As we will see, it is important for the history of Black English that two different kinds of creole arose in the Caribbean, one spoken by the field slaves who had little contact with the plantation owners and indeed relatively little contact with White speakers at all, and one spoken by household slaves who were in close proximity with the colonists.

In modern times relatively decreolized forms of JC are being used more and more in Jamaica. With independence, the issue of whether British English or a direct descendant of the creole should be the standard language has not been resolved, but we may expect a gradual shift away from the British model to a Jamaican Standard which is an outgrowth of the contact of both.

The following passage is from a folktale collected by David DeCamp, illustrating many features we have encountered in the pidgins and also a high degree of variability suggesting extensive modeling on English and English inflections. The story is about Andrew, a "witch-boy" who could foretell the future, and his three sisters, Queen Anne, Jane Anne, and Sally. [j] symbolizes the voiced affricates in *judge* (instead of the more usual [ǰ]), double vowels indicate long vowels, and ['] indicates stress on the following syllable.

ANDREW AND THE OLD WITCH[5]

1. ... 'wel, 'dis 'trii 'gyal, 'jienan,   'kwiinan,   an 'sali, 'diiz 'trii 'gyal,
   ... Well, this three girls, Jane Ann, Queen Anne, and Sally, these three girls,
2. 'went 'out far a 'waak wan 'die, bot 'andro, di 'likl 'yaazikin
   went out for a walk one day, but Andrew, the little yaws-skin [skin pitted
3.   'breda, 'nuo 'wa de go   'hapm   tu dem. an di 'trii a 'dem
   from yaws] brother, knows what is going to happen to them. And the three of them
4. get 'op di 'maaniŋ,   'wan 'maaniŋ 'den, 'tel dem 'mada se dem 'gwaiŋ
   get up (in) the morning, one morning then, tell their mother say they going
5. 'out far a 'waak. dem wil bi 'bak in di 'iivliŋ.   'andro de   'wan 'said de.
   out for a walk. They will be back in the evening. Andrew is at one side there.
6. 'andro him 'hier we   dem 'de sie   an 'hin 'nou 'wa de go   'don,
   Andrew he hear what they are saying and he know what is going (to be) done,
7. far 'him a   uol 'wich. bot 'diiz 'trii 'sista, 'tuu a dem 'duon 'lov
   for he is (a) old witch. But these three sisters, two of them don't love
8. 'andro a'tal bot 'wan, 'kwiin'an   di 'laas   'daata   'lov 'andro.
   Andrew at all, but one, Queen Anne, the last [youngest] daughter, love Andrew.
9. 'enitiŋ   in 'ha de 'iit   in 'giv   'andro.
   Anything she have is eating [anything she has to eat] she give (to) Andrew.
10. so fi fi-'har 'siek, den 'andro 'gwain   'sieb di 'trii a der 'laif.
    So for her   sake, then Andrew going (to) save the three of their lives.
11. 'an di 'mada se, 'wel! 'unu kyan 'guo 'an, guo 'sprii unu'self
    And the mother say, "Well! You can   go on, go spree yourself [have a good
12.   an kom 'bak. hin sie, 'yes 'ma. at 'dis taim a   den 'det dem
    time] and come back." They say, "Yes, Ma." At this time (it) is their death they

[5] From Robert B. Le Page and David DeCamp, *Jamaican Creole. Creole language studies I*. New York: St. Martin's Press, 1960. Pp. 156–157; by permission of St. Martin's Press Inc., Macmillan & Co., Ltd., and the authors.

13. 'de go   'fies. den 'staatid. 'andro, dem 'yaazikin 'breda, 'we   den
    are going (to) face. They started. Andrew, their yaws-skin brother, whom they
14. 'no re'spek, 'hin 'nuo 'wa de go   'hapm tu 'dem . . .
    no respect, he know what is going (to) happen to them . . . (Andrew decides to
15.   di 'trii 'gyal 'staat, an dem 'trabl 'out,
    follow for Queen Anne's sake) . . . The three girls start, and they travel out,
16. biek op dem 'rashin an 'kyari wi   dem, fi 'sov dem, fo 'we   dem de
    bake up their ration and carry with them to serve them, for where they are
17. guo dem 'duon 'nuo, bot dem 'gwaiŋ 'out pan 'sprii. 'aa 'rait. dem
    going they don't know, but they going out upon spree. All right. They
18. 'staat. an wen dem 'staat 'andro . . . 'nuo wat 'de go   'hapm. 'andro
    start. And when they start Andrew . . . know what is going (to) happen. Andrew
19. 'staat 'afta 'dem. 'an dem 'staatid, an dem 'waak fi di 'huol 'die. dem
    start after them. And they started and they walk for the whole day. They
20. 'waak 'waak tel   dem get 'taiad,   den sit 'duon. 'wen den sit 'doun,
    walk, walk until they get tired   (and) they sit down. When they sit down,
21. 'laik 'rait 'hier,   'andro 'stap 'kwait a 'wie bak.
    like right here [i.e., *as we are now doing*] Andrew stop quite a way back.
22. 'kwiinan   sii 'andro an 'nuo sie 'andro de 'kom. bot in 'kyaan 'tel in
    Queen Anne see Andrew and know that Andrew is coming. But she can't tell her
23. 'ada 'tuu 'sista sie den   de 'kom fi 'dem 'nuo 'waant 'andro fi 'kom
    other two sister that then (he) is coming, for they no want Andrew to come
24. wi 'dem a'tal, fo den no 'laik 'andro, for 'andro ha 'suor, an 'andro
    with them at all, for they no like Andrew, for Andrew have sores, and Andrew
25. 'yaazikin. hin 'doti . . .   an 'wen dem 'tiek
    yaws-skin. He dirty . . . (The sisters have breakfast) . . . and when they take
26. 'brekfas 'don, 'kwiinan   'lef a 'likl a fi-'him 'brekfas, 'siem 'plies, fo
    breakfast done, Queen Anne left a little of her   breakfast, same place, for
27. in 'nuo 'andro 'de 'kom. 'andro 'waan 'brekfas, so 'wen 'andro 'kom 'de,
    she know Andrew is coming. Andrew want breakfast, so when Andrew come there,
28. 'andro wi 'tiek i. an den 'staat a'gen, an dem ga'laŋ an ga'laŋ 'tel
    Andrew will take it. And they start again. And they go along and go along until
29. an 'wen dem 'kech a 'faar 'wie 'aaf, 'andro 'riich 'wer dem wor 'iitiŋ 'brekfas.
    and when they catch a long way off, Andrew reach where they were eating breakfast.
30. 'andro 'sii im 'brekfas 'lef de, 'andro 'tiek i, hin 'iit i, an 'dem
    Andrew see his breakfast left there. Andrew take it, he eat it. And they
31. 'gaan. hin 'trabl 'ata dem. an den 'travl fi di 'huol 'die 'tel i 'komiŋ
    gone. He travel after them. And they travel for the whole day until it coming
32. 'nait. 'nou den 'drap 'rait 'in a 'wan uol 'liedi 'yaad.
    night. Now they drop right in at one old lady's yard.

COMMENTS

Syntactic structure

1. The sentences are considerably longer in this passage than in the pidgin passages. Particularly noticeable is the presence of clear relativizers, as in *dem 'yaazikin 'breda, 'we den 'no re'spek* 'their yaws-skin brother whom they don't respect' (lines 13–14). As in WAPE, we find *tel . . . se* introducing quotations (in this case indirect speech): *'tel dem 'mada se dem 'gwaiŋ 'out for a 'waak* 'tell their mother say they are going out for a walk' (lines 4–5). The development of *se/sie* from a verb into a complementizer like *that* can be seen in *bot in 'kyaan 'tel in 'ada*

'tuu 'sista sie den de 'kom 'But she can't tell her other two sisters that he is coming' (lines 22–23), where *'tel* and *sie* are separated, and especially in *an 'nuo sie 'andro de 'kom* 'and knows that Andrew is coming' (line 22), where *sie* cannot mean 'say'.

2. Although *'wa de go don* (line 6) is translated as 'what is going to be done', there is no passive in the true creole variety of JC (as opposed to decreolized varieties); *'wa de go don* literally means 'what is going to be in-the-state-of-doneness'. It is interesting to note that passive constructions with a *be* auxiliary frequently develop in languages from resultative structures of this type. Passives developed this way in Old English; they also develop this way in child language acquisition.

3. As in WAPE, the subject is often repeated by a coreferential pronoun: *'andro him 'hier we dem 'de sie* 'Andrew, he hears what they are saying' (line 6).

4a. Plurality of the noun is assumed from the context, as in *for 'andro ha 'suor* 'for Andrew has sores' (line 24), or is expressed by numerators: *'diiz 'trii 'gyal* 'these three girls' (line 1).

4b. As in WAPE, no gender distinction is made for masculine and feminine third person pronouns; a neutral *i* 'it' is sometimes found, as in line 31. There is considerable variation in the form of the third person singular *him/hin/im/in* and the plural *dem/den;* choice of form depends partly on position in the sentence: *h*-less forms of the singular may occur only within the sentence or clause, not at the beginning, and partly on phonological environment: *n* is preferred over *m* in the environment of a following *t, d,* or *s.* The decreolized forms *har* and *der* are occasionally evidenced in this text; the hesitation form *fi fi-'har 'siek* 'for her sake' (line 10), followed by *di 'trii a der 'laif* 'the lives of the three of them' (line 10), suggests a certain degree of self-consciousness on the speaker's part at this point. As in WAPE there is a distinct second person plural, *unu* (line 11) (compare WAPE *una*).

4c. The preposition *fi* occurs in many Caribbean creoles and may be related to WAPE *fo;* it is used both in the sense of the complementizer *to,* as in *'kyari wi dem, fi 'sov dem* 'carry with them to serve them' (line 16), and in the sense of *for* as in *fi di 'huol 'die* 'for the whole day' (line 19). As *'wan uol 'liedi 'yaad* 'one old lady's yard' indicates (line 32), possessive relations are expressed by a noun-head noun construction, and evidence neither inflection nor a preposition.

5a. The presence of copula verbs is variable in this passage. No copula occurs in *hin 'doti* 'he is dirty' (line 25), but it does occur in an emphasizing construction as *a: at 'dis taim a den 'det dem de go 'fies* 'at this time it is their death that they are going to face' (lines 12–13). Various forms of a *be* verb are also found in aspectual constructions, as discussed in the next section (5b).

5b. Past tense is for the most part not expressed in this passage. However, the form *staatid* 'started' occurs (line 13). It seems characteristic of creoles to introduce inflections in positions where they will be particularly distinct; *staat*, ending in a -*t*, requires a syllabic past tense in English, and therefore provides just the kind of environment that favors the introduction of past tense markers. Three aspects are represented in this passage: intensified iterated activity, completive and noncompletive. For intensified iterated activity we find *dem 'waak 'waak tel dem get 'taiad* 'they walk and walk till they get tired' (lines 19–20), which is reminiscent of a similar intensified duration in Tok Pisin, and by the rather more decreolized form *an dem ga'laŋ an ga'laŋ 'tel . . .* 'and they go along and go along until . .' (line 28), with the coordinator *and*. Completive is expressed by *don* as in *'wen dem 'tiek 'brekfas 'don* 'when they had finished breakfast' (line 25–26). The noncompletive is particularly interesting in this passage, since it is variably expressed by a distinctly creole form *de*, presumably related to the WAPE *di*, by a somewhat decreolized form *Verb + ing*, and by a fully decreolized form, with the *be + ing* auxiliary. Compare *him 'hier we dem 'de sie* 'he hears what they are saying' (line 6) and *'nuo 'wa de go 'hapm tu dem* 'knows what is going to happen to them' (line 3), with *bot dem 'gwaiŋ 'out pan 'sprii* 'but they (are) going out on a spree' (line 17), and with *'wer dem wor 'iitiŋ 'brekfas* 'where they were eating breakfast' (line 29).

6. Of special interest is the use of vowel length to indicate negation with the verb *kyan* 'can', as in *bot in 'kyaan 'tel* 'but she cannot tell' (line 22).

Phonology

Characteristic of Caribbean creoles are forms like *gyal* 'girl', *kyat* 'cat', and *kyan* 'can', with palatalization of the velar consonant [k] or [g] before a low vowel. As in other pidgins and creoles, there are no fricatives [θ] and [ð]; there is also variation in the use of *v*, for we find both *trabl* and *travl* for 'travel' in the same sentence (line 31). Jamaican Creole illustrates the situation with respect to consonant clusters mentioned in the general introduction. Final consonant clusters occur chiefly if the consonants differ ɪn voicing; hence we find *hapm* (line 3). In words corresponding to English words with final consonant clusters in which both consonants have the same voicing, the first consonant of the English word is found, as in *uol* 'old' (line 7), *respek* 'respect' (line 14), and *brekfas* 'breakfast' (line 26). Exceptions are words ending in *l*, which tends to have a vocalic, syllabic quality, as in *travl* (line 31), and in *s* like *neks* 'next' (note this *s* is never an inflection since there is no plural or possessive inflection on nouns, nor a third person singular inflection on verbs).

GULLAH

Of the distinctly creole languages in North America, two are reasonably well known and fairly widely attested nowadays: Louisiana French Creole, and Gullah. Gullah (also called Geechee or Sea Island Creole) is spoken mainly in the coastal regions of South Carolina and Georgia. Gullah has its origins primarily in the field slave creole and has developed somewhat independently of the mainstream of Black English because of the relative geographic isolation of its speakers. The collection of Gullah materials by Lorenzo Dow Turner in *Africanisms in the Gullah Dialect* (1949) represents a major milestone in the study of the history of Black English in America. It includes a detailed list of lexical correspondences between Gullah and various West African languages, a description of the major grammatical and phonological correspondences, and also several texts; these are recordings of Gullah speakers, many of whom remembered slavery. Turner cites 21 African languages to which he found clear correspondences to Gullah in syntax and phonology as well as in vocabulary, of which Ewe, Fante, Twi, and Yoruba figure most prominently, especially in the discussion of syntax. The similarities to Jamaican Creole are striking in many respects. Another important collection of texts, incorporated by Ambrose E. Gonzales, within a fictionalized framework, gives us a broader view of the life of the area and especially of its folklore; this collection is published in various volumes of stories, among them *The Black Border* (1922).

The first Gullah passage cited here is from a narrative about Edisto Island, collected and transcribed by Turner. Turner used fairly detailed phonetic transcription; therefore he makes use of several symbols not used in the other passages. Symbols additional to those found in the other texts are:

Vowels

ʌ   stressed central vowel
ə   unstressed central vowel
ɐ   central vowel, slightly lower than ə or ʌ
ɑ   low vowel, unrounded, as in *father*
ɒ   low back vowel, rounded, as in British *not*
~   nasalization of vowel

Consonants

ʃ   initial consonant in *sheep*
c   voiceless palatal stop (somewhat like [č], but not affricated)
ɟ   voiced palatal stop (somewhat like [ĵ], but not affricated)
ɾ   retroflex flap
ɲ   palatal nasal, close to [ny], except that the palatal is coarticulated with the nasal, not articulated after the nasal

HARD TIMES ON EDISTO[6]

1. unɔ pɪk ə bascɪt ə bin fə fɔɪw n   wʌn sɛnt. tu   bascɪt—wɒt ɪt kʌm tu?
   You pick a basket of bean for five and one cent. Two basket—what it come to?

2. ɒɪ wʊdn   go de   tɪde; nɒt mi! ɒɪl it dɪ bin, bʌt ɒɪ ē   gɒɪn go
   I wouldn't go there today; not me! I'll eat the bean, but I ain't going go

3. pɪk nʌn dɛ . . .   bʌkrə   ʄi dɪ pipl kɒn—kʌləd pipl kɒn fə
   pick none there . . . White-man give the people corn—colored people corn to
                      The white man give the people corn—colored people corn to

4. mɛk krɒp. ɛnti   bʌkrə   wɒt brag, sɛ dɪ nɪgə mɛk im krɒp ɒf
   make crop. Ain't-it white-man what brag, that the nigger make him crop off
   make crop. Ain't it the white man what brag that the nigger make crop for him off

5. grʊɪn kɒn? ʄi   yu dɪ barɪl ə kɒn n dɪ sak. yu go   də
   ground corn? Give you the barrel of corn and the sack. You go (and) are
   ground corn? (He) give you the barrel of corn and the sack. You go to

6. grʊɪn əm. dats ɒl. de ē   pe no mʌnɪ. dat ē   nə du nɒu.
   grinding them. That's all. They ain't pay no money. That ain't not do now.
   grind it.

7. bət mi nɛwə gɒt dɪ   wʌn. no, ɒɪ satɪsfɒɪ; an aɪ kʊk əm n it əm.
   But me never got the (first) one. No, I satisfied; and I cook it and eat it.

8.   nɒt ə bag in dɪ stebəl; an de ʄɪt tuʄɛɾə tʊ dat hɒl.
   (There's) not a bag in dɪ stable; and they get together to that hall. (They)

9. sɛ de mɛk dɪ krɒp ɒf dɪ nɪgə—dɪ kɒn. nɒu de sɛ de had ə
   say they make the crop off the nigger—the corn. Now they say they had an
                                              Now they say they had culled

10. ʊɪ ʃ pətetə kʌl an dɪ pipl ha fə pɪk əm in. dɛn de ʄɪt ɪt
    Irish potato culled and the people have to pick them in. Then they get it
    Irish potato and the people have to pick it (cotton) in. Then they get it

11.   fərəm. pɪk dat kɒtn in fə dɪ ʊɪ ʃ tetə.
                for them. Pick that cotton in for the Irish potato.
    (culled potatoes) for them. They pick that cotton in for the Irish potato.

12. ɛnti?—   ɛnti rɛbəl tɒɪm kʌmɪn bak? ɒl hu nɛwə ʃʌm—   ɛnti
    Ain't it?—ain't it rebel time coming back? All who never saw them—ain't it
    Ain't it?—ain't slavery coming back?   All who never saw it—ain't it

13. də kʌmɪn bak? ɒɪ sɛ, "taŋk gɒd de ē gɒt mi han, ce   ɒɪ cɪn
    be coming back? I say, "Thank God they ain't got me hand, because I can
    coming back?

14. sɪt dɒuŋ n krɒs mɒɪ fit." nobɒrɪ ē wʌrɪ we   dɒɪanə bin, ce
    sit down and cross my feet." Nobody ain't worry where Diana is, because

15. mɒɪ tɒɪm dʌn kʌm tru.   ɒɪ dʌn bin tru   dat. nɒu dɪ cɪlən
    my time done come through. I done been through that. Now the children

16. də frɛt. ɒɪ sɛ dem bʌkrə   gɒt dem ɲɒŋ cɪlən fə wʌk fə
    are fretting. I say them white people got them young children to work for

17. dɛm—dɛm on. yu si? hē! yu ɛn nɛwə gɒɪn   ʄɪt no ol
    them—themselves. You see? Huh! You ain't never going (to) get no old

18. pipl. ɒl dɪ ol pipl dʌn gɒn.
    people. All the old people done gone.

[6] From Lorenzo Dow Turner, *Africanisms in the Gullah dialect*. Chicago: University of Chicago Press, 1949. Pp. 260–263. Where only one line of gloss occurs, the gloss is by Turner; where two occur, the first is by the present author, the second by Turner.

COMMENTS

Syntactic structure

1. As in JC, there is clear evidence of relativization, for example, *ɛnti bʌkrə wɒt brag* 'Ain't it the white man what brag' (line 4). No clear example of the serial construction involving 'tell' and 'say' occurs in this text; however, *sɛ* appears in its function as a complementizer in *ɛnti bʌkrə wɒt brag, sɛ dɪ nɪgə mɛk ɪm krɒp ɒf grɐɪn kɒn?* 'Ain't it the white man what brag that the nigger make corn for him off ground corn?' (line 4–5).

4a. As in the other passages, there is no evidence of pluralization through the *-s* inflection: *tu bɑscɪt* 'Two baskets' (line 1). However, plurality as such is clearly evidenced in Gullah by the plural form *fɪt* (as opposed to *foot*) in line 14. The *-s* plural is presumably not available, in part because of the pidgin origin of Gullah and the typological absence of noun plural markings in pidgins, and in part because the *-s* plural marker, if acquired through decreolization, would necessarily be in many instances in violation of the phonological constraints on final consonant clusters with shared voicing already noticed elsewhere.

4b. Note the use, as in JC, of both *əm* and *ɪt* to express the third person singular neutral (compare *əm* in lines 6 and 10 with *ɪt* in line 10). As in JC, this alternation suggests a time when third person pronouns were indistinguishable for gender. *unə* (line 1) is the second person plural pronoun (compare also WAPE and JC).

4c. As in WAPE and JC we find the preposition *fə*, as in *pɪk . . . fə fɒɪw n wʌn sɛnt* 'pick . . . for five and one cent' (line 1), *kɒn fə mɛk krɒp* 'corn to make crop' (line 3–4). Additional prepositions derived from English are also used extensively in Gullah. *In* is used for both *in* and *into*, *on* for both *on* and *onto* (a situation characteristic of spoken English in general), and *to* for both *at* and *to;* in other words, no overt distinction is made between static and dynamic locational prepositions in these cases. In this respect, as in many others, Gullah represents a stage in the transition from an essentially one-preposition language such as WAPE to a completely decreolized form of English with the whole complex set of prepositions available in Standard English.

5a. The main verb copula is present when it expresses existence in location, as in *nobɒɽɪ ẽ wʌrɪ wɛ dɒɪanə bɪn* 'Nobody ain't worry where Diana is' (line 14), but not when it expresses description, as in *ɒɪ sɑtɪsfɒɪ* 'I satisfied' (line 7). In the negative, the copula has its own special form, as is frequent in the languages of the world; in this case it is *ẽ*. There is also a special negative copula used in questions *ɛnti*, equivalent to *isn't it* in such constructions as *Isn't it time we finished?*

5b. Aspects are represented by completive *dʌn*, as in *mɒɪ tʊɪm dʌn kʌm tru* 'my time done come through' (line 15), and a noncompletive which is strictly speaking a continuative, that is, it implies duration of events and states, not simply the fact that they are not over. Continuative is expressed, as in WAPE and JC, by a *də* form: *dɪ cɪlən də frɛt* 'The children are fretting' (line 15–16), but also, as in JC, by a variety of partially decreolized forms (however, there is no fully decreolized form in the text such as we found in JC). So we find *ɛnti də kʌmɪn bak?* 'ain't it coming back?' (line 12–13) with both *də* and *ɪn* (*-ing*), as well as the negative question copula *ɛnti;* notice this construction with what essentially functions as two copulas immediately follows a hesitation form in which *də* is not present: *ɛnti?—ɛnti rɛbəl tʊɪm kʌmɪn bak?* 'Ain't it—ain't it slavery coming back?' (line 12); this suggests some uncertainty about the use of the relatively decreolized form with *-ing*.

6. This passage illustrates extensive use of the so-called double negative, the construction in which a negative is used with every element that permits a negative within the sentence. This type of "negative agreement" occurs in many varieties of Nonstandard English and was characteristic of emphatic negative constructions in English up to the seventeenth century.

Vocabulary

The common creole term *bʌkrə* is not confined to Gullah. Turner suggests that it is derived form Ibibio and Efik *mbakara* 'white man', literally 'he who surrounds or governs'.

Phonology

Apart from the palatal stops [c] and [ɟ] which have already been mentioned, we may note the velar nasal in *dɒʊŋ* 'down' (line 14) and the palatal nasal in *ɲɒŋ* 'young' (line 16), both general creole forms. As in JC consonant clusters normally occur in final position only if the two consonants have different voicing, as in *pipl* 'people' (line 3); however, this passage shows that they may also occur despite sameness of voicing if the clusters are formed by the elision of two different words, such as *wʊdn* 'wouldn't' (line 2) and *dats* 'that's' (line 6). The latter, involving a form of the copula, shows clearly how the development of final consonant clusters with voicing sameness is a function of decreolization.

A SECOND GULLAH PASSAGE

It is interesting to compare a passage from Gonzales. While largely unaware of the African heritage of Gullah, and indeed expressing surprise at how little remained of the 'jungle words', Gonzales had a good ear and recorded the language well and with great sympathy. As is characteristic of literary use of a dialect, the Gullah in Gonzales' work is presented as if it were a relatively homogeneous, invariant system, and is characterized by certain 'markers' or stereotypes. In this passage we may note especially the use of the pronoun *him* to refer to both Jane and Uncle Bill Rose, expressions like *alltwo* for quantifiers, the preposition *fuh* ([fə] in Turner's text), the completive *done* (line 44), and an iterative, distributive form *does* (e.g., lines 24–26) which took over one of the functions of the distinctly more creole *də* of more archaic Gullah. Both *buckruh* 'white man' and the form *nyung* 'young' are familiar Gullah forms from Turner's text. Gonzales has taken particular care to capture the nonexistence of final consonant clusters with shared voicing, often using an apostrophe where a consonant would be present in Standard English; compare *twis'* and *ole* with *jump* where there is a voicing contrast. One of the noticeable stylistic features of this passage is the long sentence interspersed with explanatory parenthesis (*dat is de . . .*). While imparting breathlessness and an additionally ironic view of the purist's diction, it presumably does not catch the actual speech situation considering the infrequency of relative clauses in creoles and in spoken language in general, and especially considering the obvious decreolization evidenced by the presence of the full, unelided verb *is* in structures that are neither locative nor existential.

THE CAT WAS CRAZY[7]

Suddenly, on the edge of the gathering, an old negro, bent with age and with a face furrowed by grief, appeared. He led by the hand a little black girl about ten years old. Her eyes were round with fright, and about her thin legs a ragged red calico skirt flapped like a weather-
5   stained flag at half-mast.

The old man skirted the group, eagerly scanning each face as though looking for a sympathetic ear into which to pour his sorrows. . . .

"Maussuh, please, suh, tell me ef cat kin git crazy?"

"Do you mean is it possible for a cat to have rabies?"

10   "No, suh, 'taint rabbit, 'tis cat."

"I apprehend," said the English purist, "that you desire to ascertain whether it is possible for a cat to have the rabies. I may say, for your information, that there are, literally and mathematically speaking, 18 phases of insanity to which humanity is subject, ranging from the emotional

15   insanity of commerce, to the popular *mania a potu*, vulgarly called *delirium inebriosa*. I do not care to give an off-hand opinion as to whether or not a cat may have one or more of these kinds of insanity, unless you will accurately describe the symptoms and put your questions categorically. It is manifestly a work of supererogation—"

[7] From Ambrose E. Gonzales, *The black border; Gullah stories of the Carolina coast*. Columbia, S.C.: The States Printing Co., 1922. Pp. 227–229.

20   "Great Gawd, maussuh!" said the old man, turning appealingly to the
tall gentleman. "Please, suh, tell dis juntlemun dat my cat nebbuh had
no rabbit, 'e only had kitten'. Yaas, suh. My cat name Jane, en' 'e
b'long to dis leetle gal chile w'ich is my gran', en' him (dat is de gal)
   name Jane, en' Jane (dat is de cat) b'long to Jane (w'ich is de gal)
   en' Jane does use to folluh Jane eb'ryweh
25   'e go, en' Jane does berry lub Jane, en' w'enebbuh Jane does ketch rat,
   'e fetch'um een de house, en' w'enebbuh Jane does git 'e bittle fuh cat,
   'e always keep some uh de bittle fuh Jane, en' w'en Jane (dat is de cat)
   had nine kitten' een Mistuh Claa'k' smokehouse on de t'ree Chuesday een
   dis same berry munt', den Jane (dat is de gal) set up all night fuh nuss
30   Jane (dat is de cat) en', please Gawd, maussuh, jis' as soon as de nyung
   kitten' eye' biggin fuh op'n, one shaa'pmout' black dog, wid 'e tail stan'
   like dese bu'd fedduh buckruh 'ooman does lub fuh pit on 'e hat w'en
   Sunday come, dis dog jump obuh de fench en' bite'um, en' Jane (dat is de
   cat en' de gal alltwo) git berry agguhnize en' twis' up een alltwo dem
35   min', en' Jane (dat is de cat) him jump obuh de fench en' run'way, en'
   de dog en' Jane (dat is de gal) run attuh Jane (dat is de cat) 'tell w'en
   Jane (dat is de cat) staa't fuh run down de lane, Jane (dat is de gal)
   see ole Unk' Bill Rose—w'ich'n him is de Gub'nuh' Claa'k, walkin' good
   fashi'n down de lane. Now, de gal holluh att'um fuh ketch de cat, but
40   eb'rybody know dat Unk' Bill Rose is leetle kinduh bowleggit, en', alldo'
   him hol' alltwo 'e foot togedduh, 'e foot couldn' specify, en' Jane (dat
   is de cat) jump clean t'ru Unk Bill Rose' britchiz, en' 'e git'way en'
   gone, please Gawd, en' lef' Jane (dat is de gal) en' lef' 'e nine kitten',
   w'ich all dem eye' ent done open, een Mistuh Claa'k' smokehouse, en' gone
45   en' jump obuh de fench w'ich run roun' de 'Sylum yaa'd—en' dat de reaz'n
   w'ymekso I know berry well Jane (dat is de cat) mus' be gone crazy, 'cause
   he gone *spang* een de 'Sylum!"

VERNACULAR BLACK ENGLISH

There is no more reason to speak of one Black English than there is
to speak of one British English. There are many different forms, varying
in part according to geographic provenience, but even more according
to social, especially socioeconomic factors. The variety of Black English
most frequently discussed in the context of language teaching and reading
problems is urban Black English, as spoken in New York, Washington,
and Detroit. However, many other varieties have also been studied, and
an example will be given below of a variety spoken in Memphis,
Tennessee.

Black English is clearly in many respects different from Gullah, partly
because it originated primarily in the language of the household rather
than the field slaves, partly because it experienced somewhat less isolation, partly because it has been heavily influenced by urbanization. Most
importantly, it is a vernacular with a far wider range of functions than

most creoles. Urbanization tends to dilute and even obscure geographic distinctions (the so-called "melting pot" syndrome), but it likewise tends to increase social distinctions and has led to the development of sharply different social dialects within the same geographic area.

The variety of Vernacular Black English (VBE) spoken in the urban ghettos, and least affected by the language of mainstream English, is characterized by many linguistic features that are strikingly similar to the ones I have been discussing. As a spoken variety, VBE naturally does not evidence such elaborate subordination structures as Standard English in some of its written forms; comparative infrequency of complex subordination by no means proves, though it does not rule out, the creole origins of VBE. Many of the other characteristics, however, point directly to such origins or are at least suggestive of them. In particular, we find the following characteristics.

Syntactic Structure

2. Active sentences predominate. Passives with *be* and especially *get* are, however, found. The *get* passive, when used in Standard English, is used largely for passive relationships in which the patient of the action is also in some degree involved as an actor. For example, *He got himself killed, He got killed,* as opposed to *He was killed.* This action-oriented passive is a natural precurser of the *be* passive in the decreolization process. It is becoming increasingly common in vernacular Anglo-English, where it seems to be a function of a reaction to the obscurantism of officialese as well as of the influence of VBE itself.

3. Iteration of the subject, as indicated in the introductory section on syntax, is frequently found in spoken language. However, it may be considered a special feature of VBE insofar as it is used with greater frequency than in most other varieties of English. This may point to ultimate origins in a language like WAPE where iteration of the subject by an anaphoric pronoun is so frequent as to be almost obligatory.

4a. Occasionally nouns are not marked for plural; however, absence of plural inflections is largely limited to constructions like *three mile,* where the noun indicates some unit of measurement. The occurrence of *foots* and "double plurals" like *childrens* and *mens* suggests that in the development of the vernacular from creole, the common English plural -*s* was generalized to all nouns and added to words already pluralized in irregular ways (*children* is itself a "double plural" derived in the Middle English period from an irregular plural *cildru* and a regular but now obsolete plural -*en*). The possessive relationship is often signaled by the -*s* inflection, but it is by no means obligatory. It is absent more frequently than the -s plural which suggests that the inflections were acquired in the decreolizing process according to their meaning more than their sound. Word order and stress patterns often signal possession quite unambiguously; furthermore the *of* possessive provides an alternative mode of expression which conforms to the structure of Modern English and which favors prepositional over inflectional expression of underlying relationships such as possession, direction, and so forth.

4. Uninflected pronouns are occasionally found in the South; in most varieties of VBE, however, a distinction is made between *I, me*, and *my*. As in other varieties of spoken English, the *I* form is largely limited to constructions with a single subject; if the subject is coordinated, the *me* form is preferred, as in *Him and me left*.

5. One of the best-known features of VBE is the structure of the copula and of verbal aspects. Another important feature is expression of tense.

5a. Copula constructions with the main verb *be* functioning descriptively, as in *She is happy*, or to indicate set membership as in *She is a teacher* are expressed in a variety of ways. There is a range for nearly all speakers of VBE from expressions where no form of the copula is present, as in *She a teacher*, to contracted expressions of the copula, as in *She's a teacher*, to occasional use of the full verb, as in *She is a teacher*. Some speakers show no number agreement between the subject and the verb, as in *The boys was there;* in other words, the highly irregular pattern of the copula has been generalized. Copulas are, however, always present in infinitives like *You got to be good* and imperatives like *Be cool*, and where the structure of the sentence is such that the copula occurs at the end, as in *I don't care what you are*. It has been shown that the copula can be absent just where it can be contracted in spoken Standard English, as in *She's a teacher*, but not *I don't care what you're*. If this is so, we are dealing with deletion of the copula, and then VBE may be said to have been assimilated to this extent into the mainstream of English structure; the reason that there is absence of copula, however, is the creole origin of VBE, and historically we may see the variability in the use of the copula as a result of decreolization during which the copula was added rather than phonologically deleted through contraction.

5b. In VBE past tense is marked where the phonological rules admit, that is, where the -*ed* (phonetically [t], [d]) past tense would not create a consonant cluster of which both members are voiced or unvoiced; hence we find *came, went, bought*, but *walk* for past tense. This indicates that the meaningful marker "past tense" is present in VBE, but may not always be expressed because of the phonological constraint against clusters which share voicing. Some common verbs like *say* are not inflected for past tense, rather as *put* and *hit* are not in Standard English. Present tense is typically unmarked except in the copula, although instances of -*s* do occur. The imbalance between the marking of past and present reminds us of the fact that tense inflections appear first in creoles in the past, not the present (cf. JC *staatid*); this is itself probably ultimately relatable to the fact that the speech act automatically presupposes the present, and therefore the present tense marker in many instances adds no information, while past tense does.

Among aspect markers particularly characteristic of VBE are *done, been,* and invariant *be,* of which *done* is the only one that commonly occurs in other varieties of English, though often not with exactly the same range of structures and meanings. *Done* indicates completion, *been* remote past, as in *I been had it there* "I had it there a long time ago"; both are mainly used in the South, and both are found in creoles. The invariant *be,* most typical of speakers under 20 years old, but understood by all speakers of VBE, is used to express the distribution of events over time. It is favored in constructions expressing intermittent distribution and therefore is most often found with adverbs like *everytime,* and *whenever. She gone* means "She has left," *She be gone,* on the other hand, means "She has gone and she's often gone"; to say *She happy* is to characterize her as a happy person, but to say *She be happy* is to say that she is happy from time to time. This means that permanent identifications such as *She my mother* cannot be expressed with invariant *be.* (Other sources for invariant *be* exist, such as *She be here soon,* where *be* is the main verb with *will* deleted; this *be* is not aspectual.) The distributive *be* bears some resemblance to the *de* of Jamaican Creole and Gullah and is often considered the one indisputable creole feature in VBE. While there can be no question that it is derived from an earlier creole, it is interesting to speculate why this very distinctive creole feature was retained in the face of strong decreolizing forces. One possibility that is worth considering is that some creole features were retained because they were reinforced by the speech of Whites, and it is marginally possible that some relics of earlier English reinforced invariant *be;* this is true not only of the subjunctive of *if you be there,* but also of a now obsolete distinction between Old English *beon* and *wesan,* a distinction that survived at least in Scotland till the nineteenth century, and which has some resemblances to VBE *be* versus copula (*beon* was used for future, habitual, and distributive aspect, *wesan* for identification and also for all the uses of *beon*). In any event, an aspectual distinction such as is currently made in VBE is in no way uncharacteristic of English as it has been known in the last 1500 years.

Phonology

Much has been written about the phonology of VBE, in particular, the so-called consonant cluster deletion rule (see Chapter 8 by William Moulton). It should be clear by now that historically it makes little sense to talk of consonant cluster deletion; rather, the historical process was of adding consonant clusters during gradual adaptation to English. The claim that consonant clusters are present only where the consonants are different in voicing and that they can be derived by exactly the same rules as can consonant cluster deletions in rapid speech by speakers of Standard English provides one more argument that VBE is no longer a system separate from English, but rather has been directly absorbed into the system of English. It is important to realize, however, that the absorption is not complete and that elsewhere, for example in the aspectual system, there are clear indications of a partially independent pidgin and creole heritage.

AN EXAMPLE OF VBE

The following is an excerpt from a narrative told by a 14-year-old girl from Memphis, Tennessee recorded and transcribed by Emily Pettigrew Morris. In this transcription consonant omission is shown by italicized consonants.

VELMA'S STORY[8]

    Elaine, Ardina and Elaine West, dey in the club. Dey had, —.
Dey done got to fightin. Dey got to fightin on the night of my birthday party. And uh Elaine West and Elaine Moore got to fightin. See Elaine West —. We went to see "The Bible." Elaine West slip her dress, —
5 her sister dress. You know Sharon got some real pretty clothes. And Elaine slipped Sharon's dress out o the house and took it over Mary Alice en house that night and Mary Alice kept it for 'er. N next mornin Elaine put on all her clothes 'cept her dress, and put 'er coat on, and went over Mary Alice en house and put the dress on and went to school. And Elaine
10 Moore told Sharon and Sharon got mad. . . .
    Didn't you see 'at big black scar up there? Shar' — Sharon be neat eriday. See Elaine don't take care of her clothes. Elaine git bout ten dresses and Sharon cin git ten and they can git'em on the same day. And Sharon, eritime she wear her dress, she wash it out and iron it and have
15 it ready for n next day. Elaine wear her dress. She wear 'em and, se-, and — and Sharon change clothes when she com'um school. Elaine play in ne clothes, git to fightin in 'em and tear 'um up. Her and Mary Alice got

---

[8] From Dagna Simpson, Emily Pettigrew Morris, & N. Louanna Furbee, Transcriptions. In A. L. Davis (Ed.), *Culture, class, and language variety*. Urbana, Ill.: NCTE, 1972; pp. 204–205. By permission of NCTE. The transcription is by Emily Pettigrew Morris.

to fightin one time n Mary Alice ripped the clothes off 'er. And Elaine,
see Elaine had been talkin bou*t* my mama. Talkin bou*t*, talking bou*t* my mama
20   and talkin bou*t* Mary Alice an*d* Mary Alice jumped on 'er. rippin 'er —.
Ripped her clothes off. Dat was before my party.

Comments

This passage illustrates the fluctuation in use of inflections and of final
consonants and consonant clusters typical of rapid speech. Of particular
interest are:

(4a) *her sister dress* (line 5) beside *Sharon's dress* (line 6) contrasted
to regular use of the -*s* plural.

(4b) *She wear'em* (line 15) beside *Her and Mary Alice got to fightin*
(lines 17–18)

(5a) *dey in the club* (line 1) without copula, but *Dat was before my
party* (line 21) with copula.

(5b) clear marking of past tense in *got to fightin* (lines 17–18), as
opposed to present tense *git to fightin* (line 17); also present tense *she
wear her dress, she wash it out and iron it* (line 14) all without overt
tense markers. Notice also completive *done* in *Dey done got to fightin*
(line 2) emphasizing the immediacy of the action, and distributive *be*
in *Sharon be neat eriday* (lines 11–12); apparently in this narrative
Sharon's neatness is first considered as something that recurs or iterates,
while the washing and ironing that effect it are considered as an ongoing
uninterrupted activity, since the latter are expressed in the present tense
without *be*.

ANOTHER PASSAGE IN VBE

The following passage was not recorded, but was deliberately translated
from the Gospel according to St. John to be used as reading material
for urban schools by Walt Wolfram and Ralph Fasold. Insofar as it was
devised to illustrate many features of VBE it contains a large variety
of grammatical structures already discussed here; however, the spelling
largely approximates Standard English, since it was considered advisable
to use a spelling that would facilitate transition from reading Black English to reading Standard English. Insofar as this is a written text it is
homogeneous and does not represent the high degree of fluctuation we
saw in the previous passage. Its usefulness here is that it provides stereo-
typic illustrations of many of the structures discussed in the preceding
pages.

JOHN 3:1–15 (BLACK ENGLISH VERSION)[9]

It was a man named Nicodemus. He was a leader of the Jews. This man,
he come to Jesus in the night and say, "Rabbi, we know you a teacher
that come from God, cause can't nobody do the things you be doing 'cept
he got God with him."
5   Jesus, he tell him say, "This ain't no jive, if a man ain't born
over again, ain't no way he gonna get to know God."
Then Nicodemus, he ask him, "How a man gonna be born when he already old? Can't nobody go back inside his mother and get born."
So Jesus tell him, say, "This ain't no jive, this the truth. The
10   onliest way a man gonna get to know God, he got to get born regular and
he got to get born from the Holy Spirit. The body can only make a body
get born, but the Spirit, he make a man so he can know God. Don't be
surprised just cause I tell you that you got to get born over again. The
wind blow where it want to blow and you can't hardly tell where it's
15   coming from and where it's going to. That's how it go when somebody
get born over again by the Spirit."
So Nicodemus say, "How you know that?"
Jesus say, "You call yourself a teacher that teach Israel and you
don't know these kind of things? I'm gonna tell you, we talking about
20   something we know about cause we already seen it. We telling it like it
is and you-all think we jiving. If I tell you about things you can see
and you-all think we jiving and don't believe me, what's gonna happen
when I tell about things you can't see? Ain't nobody gone up to Heaven
'cept Jesus, who come down from Heaven. Just like Moses done hung up
25   the snake in the wilderness, Jesus got to be hung up. So that the
peoples that believe in him, he can give them real life that ain't
never gonna end.

Comments

The number of features common to those already discussed are so great
that it would be otiose to repeat them. However, particular attention
should be drawn to the *It was a* ... construction (line 1), the *tell* ... *say*
construction (line 5), and the *get-passive* (line 12), since these were not
illustrated in Velma's story.

[9] From Walt A. Wolfram & Ralph W. Fasold, Toward reading materials for speakers
of Black English; Three linguistically appropriate passages. In Joan C. Baratz &
Roger W. Shuy (Eds.), *Teaching black children to read.* Washington, D.C.: Center
for Applied Linguistics, 1969. Pp. 150–151. By permission of the Center for Applied
Linguistics and Walt A. Wolfram. Wolfram and Fasold's article provides extensive
grammatical annotations which should be consulted for further reference.

CONCLUSION

Viewed from the perspective of English-related pidgins and creoles, there seems to be no question that aspects of VBE can best be explained in the light of centuries of linguistic change, and development from a pidgin to a creole, through various stages of decreolization, to a point where VBE, though largely assimilated into the various English vernaculars, still has features which clearly distinguishes it from them. To claim that VBE derives from a creole, therefore, is to focus on its social and linguistic history, and on the relative autonomy of the Black community in America. This claim also counters head on the argument that VBE is "deficient" or "sloppy" because it differs from other varieties of English.

ACKNOWLEDGMENTS

Thanks are due to Charles Ferguson, Mary Key, William Labov, and Patricia Nichols for comments on a preliminary version of this presentation. Needless to say, they are in no way responsible for possible misrepresentations of the very complex issues at stake.

SUGGESTED ADDITIONAL READINGS

DeStefano, J. S. (Ed.) *Language, society, and education: A profile of Black English.* Worthington, Ohio: Charles A. Jones Publishing Co., 1973.

Dillard, J. L. *Black English: Its history and use in the United States.* New York: Random House, 1972.

Florida Foreign Language Reporter, 1972, **10** (Black Dialect issue).

Hymes, D. (Ed.) *Pidginization and creolization of languages.* New York: Cambridge University Press, 1971.

Labov, W. *Language in the inner city: Studies in the Black English vernacular.* Philadelphia: University of Pennsylvania Press, 1972.

Wolfram, W., & Clarke, N. H. (Eds.) *Black–white speech relationships.* Washington, D.C.: Center for Applied Linguistics, 1971.

Wolfram, W., & Fasold, R. W. *The study of social dialects in American English.* Englewood Cliffs, New Jersey: Prentice-Hall, 1974.

5

Sociolinguistic Configurations of African Language in the Americas: Some Educational Directives

Angela Gilliam

*State University of New York,
College at Old Westbury*

When approaching the subject of language from a noncolonial perspective, one of the sounder methodologies is to analyze the political role of language in the development of the Western Hemisphere, especially as it pertains to the subject peoples—the Native American and the African ex-slave. Two interesting facts immediately present themselves—one, that the vehicle of communication established within the incipient slave economy of Europe and in the subsequent colonization of the hemisphere was to be the European language. This pattern of communication—what David Dalby (1970) refers to as "Black through White"—has remained constant to this day, even though the forms of linguistic imposition and modification have become at once more subtle and complex. For example, there is still no vehicle through which the oppressed can learn about other oppressed, or even define themselves, that is not somehow governed by the traditionally dominant forces, either through the use of the language itself or the instruments through which we perceive that communication. In other words, the hardware and the software of radio, television, publishing houses, magazines, films, cameras, sociological studies, education, advertising—whether in the United States itself or in its political/military sphere of influence—are controlled by those who control the means and distribution of production.

In line with the above, it is also interesting to note that in all colonial societies there is the tendency to value Gongorism[1] as a way of defining the extent of the "civilizability" of the so-called primitive and to place within a confining sociological frame his presumed nonverbality and inarticulateness. The mystification of language is not only a way of obfuscating reality but forcing the castes to accept the obfuscation instead of the reality. As Lloyd Brown (1971) states, "The language of communication is symbolic of the colonial experience itself [p. 5]."

This colonial reality perforce also influences any study about language and about the language of Blacks. When one attempts to piece together a hemispheric unity or historical logic in terms of the Black experience with slavery, or the African linguistic sphere of influence, the material in all of the pertinent languages leaves much to be desired. For example, when Dalby (1969) noted that the word "okay" probably stemmed from the Malenké word "okeh" (meaning "that's it"), his idea caused a great furor—not just because other linguists had traced the word back to the French "au quais" (meaning "at the docks") but also because of their inability to face the larger issues: (1) that Blacks would have been using lexicon and syntax other than that which Whites had taught them, and (2) that Blacks *had* influenced European languages.

As Lorenzo D. Turner discusses at length in his pioneering work, *Africanisms in The Gullah Dialect* (1949, pp. 5–11), many linguists feel Gullah is really the remains of British "baby-talking" to their slaves, a concept Turner shows to be fallacious thinking. Nonetheless, this author has noticed monolingual Americans in other countries speaking louder, more slowly, and in "Tarzan" English to the non-English-speaking persons they are trying to get to understand them. This is only in 1- or 2-word sentences however. No one could sustain language acquisition this way. Further, the habit is quite possibly postcinema imitation of "dealing with the natives."

When we turn outside of the United States and look at the African experience in the Americas, we get little more clarity on the same issues, primarily because certain factors and histories are repeated in the other environments. If we take a look at the African cultural sphere of influence, we find that very large numbers of Africans settled in the circum-Caribbean area, which we can define as the Greater and Lesser Antilles, the coastal parts of northern and eastern South America, coastal Mexico and Central America, and the southern United States. In all of those speech communities, Africans have influenced the phonology, lexicon, and syntax of those regions and, furthermore, these speech patterns have been

---

[1] Gongorism originally referred to the poetic style of the Spaniard Luis Gongora y Argote (1627)—a literary style characterized by studied obscurity (Webster). This pedantry appeared during the decline of the Golden Age of Spain when to be understood by the masses was degrading to the poet.

used by the oligarchy to define aspects of lower-class culture, of which language is a primary indicator. In the plantation economies any activity connected with manual labor was "open" to the African, as were certain of his musical expressions, especially that music which seemed to be connected to Christianity. It is no wonder then that cuisine is African in the circum-Caribbean and that "kalalloo" which is found in St. Thomas or Jamaica is also found as "carurú" in Salvador, Bahia.

However, if we are careful enough in our linguistic research to not fall into conventional academic traps of looking at cultures vertically instead of horizontally, the scientist should be able to not only trace carefully the trade routes of certain words and linguistic styles, but also to adequately analyze the social relationships that determined this influence and modification. Where did "savvy" come from—the Portuguese or the Spanish? I believe it is exclusively Spanish, since it is in wider use in the southwest; and were it to have come from Portuguese, southern Blacks would have used it, as was the case with *most* Portuguese pidgin lexicon found in American English. However, there are exceptions to this, and "pickaninny" presents several questions. Dillard (1972, p. 122) maintains that "pickaninny" was transmitted to Whites by Blacks. The word was, undoubtedly, but the meaning most likely wasn't. The word comes from the Portuguese word "pequeno" which means "little," or "little one." In Portuguese and Spanish also, one can reduce the value or add affection *or* even be paternalistic by adding the diminutive to an adjective or a noun. The paternalism would only be present in such words as relate to the description of a person, that is, "indio" (Indian) becomes "indito," which is extremely paternalistic. It is like saying "little Indian." "Pequenino" which is the diminutive form of "pequeno" really only means "teeny, weeny little one." It has no special pejorative social or racial significance as "pickaninny" does in the United States. Furthermore, in Guyana and the West Indies "pickaninny" is also a term of affection used by Blacks to their children.

The questions become these: At what point did the word come to mean "Negro child" in English? Was that meaning generated from the White or the Black? When and in what context did Blacks start to perceive it as a self-devaluative word? Furthermore, since *words do not become functional in a society that has no operational use for them* (Gilliam, 1972), why did the meaning change in the United States and *not* in the original Portuguese, especially since there are many other paternalistic ways of saying "Negro child" in Portuguese? Perhaps it was transmitted by Black "ladinos."[2] When a word is borrowed from another language,

[2] Black "ladinos" were Africans who had been enslaved in the Iberian Peninsula and had acquired some Spanish and Portuguese language and customs. In the Western Hemisphere, the term became a sign of status to have been a "ladino" rather than a "bozal," which meant "direct from Africa."

the degree to which it retains most of the original phonology and lexical meaning is usually in direct proportion to the degree the related concept was absent in the borrowing language, that is, if "algebra" has existed in an English conceptual framework, the word would not likely have been borrowed from Arabic (al-jabr) almost *in toto*. Rather, it would have been translated. Translation only truly occurs where circumstances and cultural environments have been similar. Therefore, "good hair" and "bad hair" (which exist in Spanish, Portuguese, and English with the same sociological meaning in all three languages) definitely relate to the ethno-class ascriptions in the areas where these terms are used.

One of the other questions that arises is why Africans in some parts of the circum-Caribbean also retained more of the collective habits of physical articulation (oral reproduction) than those in English-speaking areas. We understand that relexification (thinking in one language and using a word of another to express the original thought) has occurred in all the colonial circumstances, especially where those circumstances were so conflictive vis-à-vis language, as in the southern part of the United States. However, the collective retention of articulative habits constantly produced American-created words like "candungué" (Alvarez-Nazario, 1961, p. 301), whereas the same did not happen as often here.[3]

The traditional work of Brazilian linguists attempts to place *original* African meaning, implying that linguistic development and creativity was absent in the Western Hemisphere. Further, every work on the subject down-plays this influence in mainstream Brazilian life, that is, in a colonially based culture where excolonies still feel *culturally* inferior to the European axis, those cultures or geopolitical entities that feel the most threatened in terms of racial or linguistic purity are the ones with most African influence, because that influence is still associated with the slave—the least common denominator of inferiority. (In some places this varies depending on whether the Native American is the societal scapegoat, such as Peru, Bolivia, Mexico, etc. In those regions, the Indian culture represents the lower class. One notable exception is Paraguay where Guaraní has enjoyed *almost* the same prestige as Spanish and virtually all classes are bilingual.) In succinct terms, the Southern United States *accent*—which is African influenced—is "inferior" to that of Boston where the phonology and syntax most approximates British English. Furthermore, many Blacks in the United States—like their counterparts in other parts of the circum-Caribbean—feel that an acknowledgment of their linguistic heritage attests to "sloppy tongues" (alias African habits of physical articulation) and that "we can speak just as well as any European." Therefore, we conceptualize Black English and Black

[3] Alvarez-Nazario conjectures that "candungué" is a *free phonetic transformation* of the Bantu word "candombe."

Portuguese as a function of *class*, since those who reinforce their collective articulatory habits are poor, unintegrated, or unassimilated Blacks. It therefore threatens our upwardly mobile pretensions to use Black English, Black Spanish, or Black Portuguese *unless* that lexicon or syntax has passed into the mainstream. For example, in this country Black English may be Standard English of the next century. Within a span of five years certain Black syntax and lexicon has become known as language of youth. The theory is this: the forces that are changing the colonial European languages are the non-Europeans upon whom these languages were imposed. This is especially cogent when we realize that most of the speakers of English, Spanish, Portuguese, or French are non-Europeans.

In the Brazilian context, the fact that the African woman was the vehicle through which many a child—whether her own or that of the master—learned language and culture contributed more than phonology and lexicon to the language, it also contributed to what Chomsky (1965) refers to as the deep structure. This is the point that most Brazilian social scientists, who traditionally minimize the Africanity of the *shared* culture, refuse to accept. Indeed, the same thesis could be modified and posited in the context of the United States.

What concerns us at this point is the analysis of cultural conflict in the upwardly mobile Black in Brazil who is forced by his circumstances to control his speech and/or to be equivocal about the retention of any of its features that could be construed as "slave behavior." There are two linguistic streams then that are the theme of this study: (1) the role of "gíria" in modifying Brazilian language, and (2) more specifically the attitudes of the masses of people about gíria which determine the relationships governing its usage. Gíria is a highly stylized language system occurring within the Portuguese morphological structure, spoken first by lower-class Blacks and other poor people in the slums of Rio and/or in jail. (The mutual contact between the two locations has the same sociological relationshp that it does in the United States.) It then eventually became known as the language of the youth after it spread to other urban Black communities. An interesting observation is the fact that "terrível" (terrible) has the identical meaning in some Brazilian urban centers that "terrible" (pronounced "turble," as in Amiri Baraka's *In Our Terribleness*, 1970) has in the United States when it means "superbad." This then clearly reflects not just an unusual coincidence but it also tempts one to question the reasons for such similarities in this kind of linguistic construct, especially given the fact that the avenues of Black American culture directly to the "favela" are rather circuitous.

The other stream of influence in Brazil occurs in the northern state of Bahia where countless Africans have always outnumbered Whites and have so influenced the language that in spite of the evidence of a rigid class society, many people feel it is impossible to distinguish between the phonology of Blacks and Whites. Rather, the increased amount of Yoruba words is primarily the distinguishing factor.

Language is an organic, adaptive, and horizontal aspect of culture. Just as there are radical Mexicans who accept rather than disparage their "Indianness," there are English-speaking Africans—in Africa, Australia, the United States, and the Caribbean—who are "taking the white man's language, dislocating his syntax, recharging his words with new strength and sometimes with new meaning before hurling them back in his teeth, while upsetting his self-righteous complacency and clichés ... [Cook, 1969, p. 52]." Those are the words of Mercer Cook, yet they also remind one of Okot p'Bitek, who in *Song of Lawino* (1969) did his own translation from Acholi, and English is better served because of it. Or, take the onomatopoeic poetry of Nicolás Guillén (1952) or Solano Trindade (1970), who not only manipulate their Spanish and Portuguese, respectively, with an iron hand, but who also retain the African onomatopoeic phonology while making political statements.

If we agree that language and culture are not only organic but that there is no primitive language any more than a rat is a primitive form of the giraffe, then one can accept aspects of substratum theory, that is, that in colonial situations, the language of the dominant powers is modified—defensively at first—by those upon whom it is thrust as a foreign tongue. If that is a given, then one would have to accept the concept that the social relationships and attitudes surrounding that language modification determine the style, the degree, and the configurations of the change.

At issue at this point is how people *view* their linguistic heritage, which is part of our unconscious culture. Unconscious culture is that life-style which people inherit and utilize without being aware of its adoption; conscious culture is of course those accoutrements and customs that one consciously attempts to assume or acquire (Gilliam, 1972). One might say that for most American Blacks, Black English is unconscious and Standard English is conscious. The major conflict about Black English stems from the source of its supporters, that is, since much of the academic push to use Black English in schools often comes from misinformed White sholars (who often are either unclear in their objectives, or else concentrate on esoteric topics such as "copula"), Blacks have a tendency to dismiss any African linguistic nexus altogether.

It is in this context, then, that we discuss the Black's consistent effort to cleanse his speech of its historical reality or, to use the term of Mexican anthropologist Arturo Warman (1970, p. 13), to "desnativarse" (to denativize oneself). Indeed, it is unfortunate to note that sometimes the Black community's interest in African names, Swahili or Africanity *sui generis,* is not to open and expand its consciousness to the roots of its existence and to become receptive to other cultures, but rather to extend the European concept of exoticism where African is romanticized right out of reality and where we wax lyrically about the existence of African "kings and queens." This merely becomes an updated version of "we are really just like Europeans, too." The only difference is that the Black community has taken a colonially imposed fictitious definition of Africa and turned it into a source of pride—but it is still fictitious.

What are the implications of this discussion for the Black child? I see them as being many. On the one hand, we must start to look at our language as our given culture that is *horizontal*—no better, no worse. What comes from that view is the right to be creative and original and to use new forms to elasticize the English conceptual framework. What also follows is the need to look at other languages and cultures horizontally, in accordance with immediate need and survival. This means not only learning Standard American English (within a methodological framework of English as a second language, perhaps), but learning Spanish if one lives in New York or California, and also learning a linguistic history of English within a certain political context. It is interesting to know how the Swahili word "mbenzi" or "wabenzi" came into being, and what the political implications are of the word being created.[4]

Children should learn how language influences their behavior. They should learn that if they use a sentence like "Columbus discovered America," they are not going to see anything wrong in a television program of 1971, entitled "China—Lost and Found." The praxis of bilingualism, for example, is to consciously make one aware of multiple definitions of existence. When a child learns a language, he unconsciously accepts a view of the world that is inherent in the particular structure of that language. Prior to 1945, there was no concept in Japanese for "privacy." Imagine the recent linguistic and cultural implications now that "puraibashi"—the word and concept—have been added to Japan's society. In the words of Eskimo activist, Charles Etok Edwardsen, "Ownership has few dialects." Swahili or Eskimo are important because there is little room for *direct* translation. The optimal bilingual situation is where translatability is sufficient for one to comprehend but dissimilar enough to expand awareness. Portuguese is also important; how else can one read Amilcar Cabral without going through a translator *whose politics may condition* the translation?

What happens now is that the Black child learns about life's alternatives from what Nietzsche called "frog perspectives"—looking at the

---

[4] "Mbenzi" is a Swahili adjective or noun singular to mean "bourgeois," he who seeks to own and/or drive a Mercedes Benz (hence the infix "benz"). "Wabenzi" is the adjective or noun plural.

world from down below. Education itself, for the Black child at least, rarely deals with the child's unconscious culture but rather amounts to what Paulo Freire (1971) calls cultural invasion. I think here of the Black Brazilian novelist, Romeu Crusoé, who wrote in his book, *The Curse of Caan*, "Why in the Hell did I gush out my bitterness in white man's language? I knew that to the degree that I was educating myself, as a consequence—by climbing upwards—my suffering was growing [1955, p. 134]."[5] This happens when we do not make sure our children use *their* unconscious culture to bridge horizontally other cultures. In United States schools, education does not begin from a position of one's origins—and that which children know—to the unknown.

Because of this process, Blacks as a group do not have control of the tactical and strategic propaganda (which R. Cirino, 1972, calls the short-range and long-range modes of propaganda) needed for the perpetuation of their culture and values. The education of Black children must some-how enable them to define themselves in other than "abstract terms, the Negro condition to the outsider in terms of the outsider's interests [Lewis, 1973, p. 587]." All oppressed children, regardless of the languages they speak, should know what "inarticulate, nonverbal, and culturally de-prived" *really* mean—not only how those terms relate to language but how that type of definition of themselves relates to their oppression.

In his work of creating education-for-liberation models, Paulo Freire (1971) says, "Men emerge from their submersion and acquire the ability to intervene in reality as it is unveiled [p. 100]." The role of the progres-sive linguist/teacher/interpreter is to provide the child with the intellec-tual circumstances and tools to intervene in his own reality.

REFERENCES

Alvarez-Nazario, M. *El elemento Afro-Negroide en el Español de Puerto Rico*. San Juan: Instituto de Cultura Puertorriqueña, 1961.

Baraka, A. *In our terribleness*. Indianapolis, Indiana: Bobbs-Merrill, 1970.

p'Bitek, Okot, *Song of Lawino*. New York: Meridian, 1969.

Brown, L. The moral significance of European languages in African literature. *Today's Speech*, 1971, Spring, 3–11.

Chomsky, N. *Aspects of the theory of syntax*. Cambridge, Massachusetts: MIT Press, 1965.

Cirino, R. *Don't blame the people*. New York: Random House, 1972.

Cook, M. African voices of protest. In M. Cook & S. E. Henderson, (Eds.), *Militant Black writers in Africa and the United States*. Madison: The University of Wisconsin Press, 1969.

[5] Portuguese original: "...mas porque diabo, vertia meus amargores em língua de branco? ... Sabia que, à proporcão que me instruisse, por consequencia, elevan-do-me, cresceram as minhas dores."

Crusoé, R. *A Maldicão de Canaan*. Brazil: Irmãos Di Giorgio & Cia, 1955.

Dalby, D. Americanisms that may once have been Africanisms, *London Times,* July 19, 1969.

Dalby, D. *Black through White: Patterns of communication*. Bloomington, Indiana: Indiana University Press, 1970.

Dillard, J. L. *Black English*. New York: Random House, 1972.

Freire, P. *Pedagogy of the oppressed*. New York: Seabury Press, 1971.

Gilliam, A. Black and white in Latin America, *Pan-African Journal,* 1972, **5,** 324.

Guillén, N. Negro Bembón. In *Sóngoro Cosongo*. Buenos Aires: Editorial Losada, S.A., 1952.

Lewis, D. Anthropology and colonialism. *Current Anthropology,* 1973, **14,** 581–602.

Trindade, S. Trem sujo de Leopoldina. In M. de Andrade (Ed.), *Antologia da literatura Africana de expressão Portuguesa*. Kraus Reprints, Kraus-Thompson, Germany, 1970.

Turner, L. D. *Africanisms in the Gullah dialect*. New York: Arno Press, 1949.

Warman, A. Todos santos y todos difuntos. In A. Warman, M. N. Nolasco, G. B. Bonfil, M. Oliveira de Vazquez, & E. Valencia, (Eds.), *De eso que llaman la antropologia Mexicana*. Mexico: Editorial Nuestro Tiempo, 1970.

6

The Black–Southern White Dialect Controversy: Who Did What to Whom?

Ernest F. Dunn

Livingston College, Rutgers University

INTRODUCTION

Slovenly and careless of speech, they seized upon the peasant English used by some of the early settlers...wrapped their clumsy tongues about it as well as they could and it issued through their flat noses and their thick lips as so workable a form of speech that it was gradually adopted by other slaves...with characteristic laziness these Gullah negroes took short cuts to the ears of their auditors, using as few words as possible, sometimes making one gender serve for three, one tense for several and totally disregarding singular and plural numbers...[Gonzales, 1922, p. 10].

The linguistic legacy attributed to the Black man in the Western Hemisphere was that of a slave transplanted here from Africa who was capable of speaking only an unintelligible, savage gibberish. In order to adapt to these new surroundings, he slowly began to acquire a semicivilized mode of communication. However, his childlike nature, intellectual inferiority, and certain physiological features supposedly imposd insurmountable barriers to proper acquisition of English. Within this particular stance, persons such as Gonzales concluded that the murderous attempt to articulate the refinements of the English phonological system through thick lips and oversized tongues, coupled with the inability to deal with the sophistication of the grammatical system, engendered a strangely strangled brand of English.

These and numerous other misconceptions have persisted, sustained by "research" on Black speakers of English in this hemisphere. Undoubtedly, some misconceptions accompanied the African slave on his treacherous middle passage. Some may have preceded his arrival. One can well imagine that many of the Europeans who first ventured into Africa thought themselves somehow mysteriously suspended in time and space, transported to the Tower of Babel. They found themselves in a diverse linguistic environment, encountering innumerable tribes and countless unrelated spoken languages, languages so unique to European experience that they had to be regarded as void of intellectual rhyme or reason.

Such was the perception, but not the reality. Although the languages were many and various, there were typological and lexical features which allowed for linkages into families. Africa was not a wild Babel of mutually exclusive languages. Using rigorous, linguistic methodology, African languages can be classified and grouped into four major families: Congo–Kordofanian, Nilo–Saharan, Afroasiatic, and Khoisan. Of particular significance is the fact that the Blacks who were brought to the Americas during the slave trade era spoke almost exclusively the languages of only a subfamily within one of the families, that is, the Niger Congo of the Congo–Kordofanian. The linguistic diversity so apparently lacking in pattern or structural framework was, in reality, a subfamily of languages woven together in a fabric of structural similarities. It was this commonality which eventually provided for the broad grammatical base on which to build the bridge of communication between African and European, and which previously provided for communication between African and African of differing language backgrounds.

Another misconception which, fortunately, has been called into question by a number of researchers asserts that the varieties of English spoken by Blacks, particularly in America, were void of any African trappings or influence. In fact, Black versions of English were considered no different from that of Whites, each varying in accordance with the parameters of geographic area and educational background. This misconception was initially promulgated for one obvious reason, but strangely enough its survival has resulted from a variety of reasons, some of which are almost diametrically opposed to each other. During the late 1920s of this century, this idea was utilized by writers such as Kurath and Krapp to allay any claims that Blacks had made any significant contribution to the development of English in America. According to these scholars, the native African dialects were completely lost. These loses were attributed to "Krapp's Law" which stated that whenever two languages come into contact where one was representative of a high level of culture and sophistication and the other of a low level, the latter yielded and adapted to the speech patterns of the former. Little or nothing happened in the reverse direction (Krapp, 1924).

The propagation of this myth, not allowing the possibility of Black influence, delegated the functioning of Blacks solely to that of imitator in acquiring language. Beyond this, the minimizing of Africanisms in Black speech patterns allowed them to account for any diversions as being inappropriate and incorrect. Such diversions or differences they then accounted for by ascribing a number of characteristics of Black English to vestiges of older forms of English (the conservation-in-isolation type rule phenomenon). This type of rule stipulates that the more isolated the speech community, the less likely is its language to change. In time, the synchronic linguistic system of such an isolated community is considered archaic in another dialect, which has undergone changes due to linguistic contacts beyond its boundaries. Of course these men did not stop there but went on to conclude that Black English speakers hung on to these archaisms due to social backwardness. This orientation was definitely racist in character and was a chief contributor to the stigma which still accrues to Black English.

As illuminated by Dillard (1972, p. 187) such explanations were patently bogus, and were engendered out of an attempt to support a shaky and untenable concept known as the East Anglian origins theory. This proposition suggested that Blacks originally learned archaic dialects spoken in some of the remote localities of Northern England. Even more absurd was the idea that the Blacks remained in a perpetual state of archaism, unable to bridge the linguistic gap separating them from Whites. Dillard suggests that the concept was one of the harshest if not the most racist theory promulgated upon the Black man. One could only conclude that such inability was the result of mental deficiency.

Some liberal thinkers have given support to this doctrine, thereby feeling that they were doing Blacks a favor. The minimizing of differences certainly would hasten the processes of integration and would establish equality among races. The playing down of differences of culture, language, and other modes of behavior was an endeavor embarked upon by both Blacks and Whites. Apparently both sides failed to appreciate the dearness of the price the Black man was being asked to pay, namely, the denial of his own cultural heritage. If awareness of this did indeed exist, then perhaps all concerned believed the prize worth the price, the prize being the flow into the mainstream of American culture.

The price that was paid proved to be even more costly than many might have expected. Support for the doctrine did not bring the Black man into the mainstream. On the contrary, the argument came full circle, and turned upon Blacks in a manner reminiscent of the original authors. Having buried the notion of an African substratum surviving in the dominant American culture, the Kurath–Krapp hypothesis was used, for example, to perpetuate the myth that the use of Black English beyond a certain point of maturation indicated a low barometric level of achievement capability. One was able to postulate such culprits as cultural deprivation and social deficiencies for the failure of Black children to master the sophisticated, grammatical structures of standard English. Further "research" allowed one to identify some of those social deficiencies as a lack of strong family structure, the resultant poor motivation, underdeveloped linguistic and cognitive capacities, as well as an illiterate, nonverbal environmental background.

As a consequence, we found ourselves at a point where sociopsycholinguisticians were prepared to formulate theories to the extent that the "deficiencies" in Black English should be viewed as a pathological phenomenon. The linguistic skills of Black children were to be viewed as an illness to be cured, or even better, to be rooted out like a cancerous growth. And why not? Seemingly we had destroyed the rationale for viewing these deviances as a ground of systematic differences to be examined from diachronic and synchronic linguistic perspectives.

PRESENT STATE OF THE CONTROVERSY

Until very recently, perhaps to this day, there remains a number of scholars who provide life-giving energy to the theory that Black English is merely the end product of the process whereby the Southern Black took his cue imitatively from the linguistic environment that engulfed him. This particular stance was blatantly asserted in an editorial in *Crisis* magazine:

> This language (Black English) is merely the English of the undereducated with principal variances in accent and structure from locale to locale throughout the English speaking world.
> ... The so-called Black English is basically the same slovenly English spoken by the South's undereducated poor white population [*Crisis,* April–May, 1971, p. 78].

This position fortunately has not gone unchallenged. Within the past decade a few scholars have emerged to lend support to a diametrically opposing view. Their thesis has been that there are radical differences in the underlying grammatical structures in Black English. Marvin Loflin (1969), for example, suggested that when a thorough and proper analysis had been achieved, it would demonstrate that Black English should be treated as a foreign language. This thesis was also supported by Beryl Bailey (1965) who noted, "the Southern Negro 'dialect' differs from other Southern speech because its deep structure is different, having its origin as it undoubtedly does in some Proto-Creole grammatical structure [p. 172]."

Perhaps Imamu Biraka (Le Roi Jones) put it best when he asserted that "It is absurd to assume, as has been the tendency among a great many Western anthropologists, (linguists) and sociologists, that all traces of Africa were erased from the Negro's mind because he learned English. The very nature of the English the Negro spoke and still speaks drops the lie on that idea [1968, p. 9]."

It was truly absurd to assume that the Black African was a linguistic *tabula rasa*, totally unaffected by any prior linguistic experience or expertise, able only to mimic in a semiacceptable fashion the language of the White man. The question to be raised at this juncture is "How came this absurdity?" The answer to this question was alluded to in the Introduction. To answer this question fully, however, requires a brief exposé of the development of Black English and the reactions to it at various stages of its development.

HISTORICAL ORIGINS

While some linguists recognized the fact that the Africans spoke actual languages, some European explorers, bent on "discovering the world," usually concluded that the African spoke a savage gibberish. Even today, White comedians, and, sad to say, even Black comedians, flippantly give forth a meaningless variety of gibberish whenever they give impersonations of African encounters. In similar situations where they are mimicking European languages, usually some care is taken to provide some phonological, morphological, and even some lexical features of the language (à la Artie Johnson). Such "courtesy" is never afforded African languages.

The truth of the matter is that Africa is one of if not *the* most linguistically diverse continents in the world. Linguists estimate that 850 to 1000 languages are spoken there. Initially confronted by this diversity, the European explorer was faced with a dilemma.

There was a need for a system of communications. How best could this be accomplished with a minimum of time and effort? It would have been preposterous and an act of denigration for the European to learn the indigenous language. Furthermore, there were too many to master. On the opposite side of the situation, the African obviously could not be expected to learn the European language. The dissolution of the dilemma was to promulgate a pidgin language(s).

As these pidgins (English, French, and Portuguese based) came into existence, Europeans were bound to interpret the pidgins as "baby talk dialects." This surely reinforced the misconceived inferences by Europeans concerning the African's linguistic or cognitive capacity. Even now, it is still assumed and asserted that the background of such a language was obviously an imperfectly learned form of English or whatever language in question. This assertion, however, implies or presupposes *ipso facto* that perfect English was the linguistic goal of the speakers. It further presupposes that the African moved into a linguistic ambience, the parameters and perimeters of which were defined by the European languages only.

There is no evidence to support these presuppositions. More likely, the situation was that the African and the European sought initially to learn a pidgin and, according to Hall (1966), "For a language to be a true pidgin, two conditions must be met: its grammatical structure and its vocabulary must be sharply reduced, . . . and also the resultant language must be native to none of those who use it [p. 5]."

The pidgin languages that developed in West Africa rightly sought a middle ground, *a mischsprache*. From the European languages, English, French, and Portuguese, some lexical items were extracted. This provided for the European's ease of entry into the pidgin. The predominant grammatical structures of the pidgin, plus some phonological features, were contributed by the African languages. Whether by design or accident, it was most fortunate that African grammatical structures took precedence. It was very easy for the speakers of the various languages to manipulate these underlying grammatical bases of the pidgin as they were representative of broad-based grammatical structures present in their languages. As mentioned in the Introduction, the geographic area of the African continent from which slaves were primarily taken, from Senegal to Angola, represents one primary linguistic area, the area of the Niger–Congo subfamily of languages.

This subfamily of the larger phylum, Congo–Khordofanian, may be subdivided into six genetic subgroups (see Fig. 1). The first group is the West Atlantic. The languages of this group are spoken in Senegal, Gambia, Guinea, and Sierre Leone. Included in this group are such known languages as Wolof, Fulani, Temne, Gala, and Kissi. Of this group Wolof is probably the most important in regard to the slave trade. Dalby (1971) has suggested that Wolof speakers were used as navigators and thus Wolof more than any other African language was spoken more freely in the context of the slave trade. This would in part explain why the majority of African words which have survived in Black English in the United States are Wolof in origin.

The second member in this subfamily is the Mande or Madingo group. These languages, which include Malinke, Bambara, Susu, Mande, Kpelle, and Gio, are spoken in Sierre Leone, Guinea Liberia, Upper Volta, Mali, and the northern part of the Ivory coast.

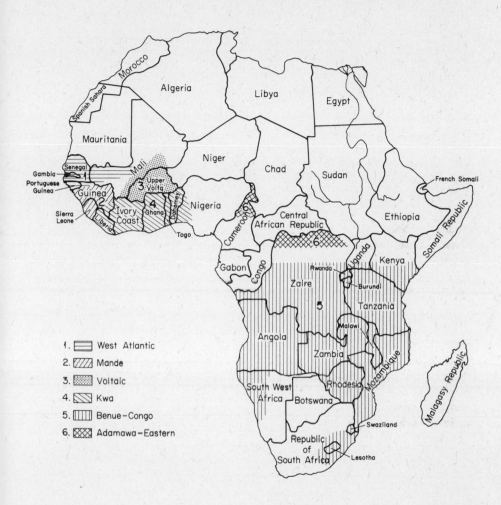

1. ▭ West Atlantic
2. ▨ Mande
3. ▦ Voltaic
4. ▧ Kwa
5. ▥ Benue–Congo
6. ▩ Adamawa–Eastern

The third, the Gur group, is composed of languages spoken in Upper Volta. Mali, Northern Ghana, Togo, Dahomey, and the former Borgu Division in Nigeria. Included in this group are such languages as Gur, Senefo, Loli, and Dogon.

The Kwa subgroup is the fourth member of this group. Kwa languages are spoken from Liberia to Southern Nigeria. Well-known languages in this include Kru, Ewe, Bini, Yoruba, Igbo, Akan, and Twi.

Benue–Congo is the fifth and largest of the subgroups. It includes the 300 or so Bantu languages. Speakers of these languages range from

Nigeria through Central, South, and East Africa. In addition to the Bantu languages, other known languages in this group include Tiv and Jukun.

The sixth group is the Adamawa Eastern languages which are probably not known to most western readers save possibly from Adamawa, Sango, and Ndogo. These languages are spoken principally in the Cameroon and Zaire.

All of these languages comprise a family estimated at 500–600 languages. The languages are principally bound together by a noun classification system of paired affixes, one for the singular and one for the plural form. Generally these affixes are prefixes, e.g., *m*tu, 'man,' *w*atu, 'men'; but in some instances they occur as suffixes, e.g., yul*a*, 'breast,' yu*a*, 'breasts'. There are languages in this subfamily, such as those in the Mande and Kwa groups, which have lost these affixes. Diachronically the drift in the Niger–Congo subfamily has been in the direction of such loss. One still, however, has sound–meaning resemblances in a number of lexical items as a means of positing the genetic linkage among these languages. Based on the African language vestiges found by Turner in Gullah (1949) and the languages Koelle (1963) found spoken in Freetown, Sierre Leone, one would venture to say that slaves were taken from a rather wide representative group of these languages.

Within this context, the pidginization process gave rise to a highly sophisticated system of communication, a system molded by the principles of simplicity and efficiency. Void of the redundant trappings normally present in natural languages, this type of linguistic system relied on maximum utilization of a minimum number of linguistic structures. Further, this system provided for bridges of communication between African and European and between African and African, each of whom spoke different indigenous languages.

The pidginization was further facilitated for Africans by the underlying deep structural similarities in their grammatical systems. According to Van Sertima (1970), "Under the surface of differences—there existed certain basic patterns, patterns which were to assert themselves like engineering blocks and architectural blueprints when it became necessary for the slaves to build a bridge of communication between the European and African tongues [p. 3]."

Pidginized languages continued to develop on both sides of the Atlantic Ocean. On the American side, however, the reasons for such development were more invidious since there was a deliberate attempt to suppress the native languages of the slaves.

The restricting of communication in the African languages provided insurance against and decreased the potential for plotting rebellions and escapes, a political control mechanism. In addition, this factor, together with the physical and emotional separation from land, klan, and family, contributed to the dehumanization process. For the slaveowner, it would have been self-defeating to allow the slave to acquire a suitable surrogate for his original language. If this indeed were the situation, it is somewhat paradoxical. If one accepts the point of view that the slave would function at a minimal level in this new language, what need would there be for further restrictions? In the opinion of this author fear lay at the base of the restrictions. In addition to the fear of internal communication was a growing fear that the hard crust of nonhuman emotions, essential to maintain a man as a captive animal, might crack. Recognition of slaves as human beings and all of its implications were antithetical to slavery. The ability to learn the pidgin, but more importantly, to learn the accepted dialect well, would strongly mandate the recognition of the slave as a person, a person much like the slaveowner. After all, the possibility of something less than human possessing the capacity to manipulate the White man's linguistic structures would threaten his cherished beliefs. Thus an inherent paradox of the slavery system was raised. The slave owner became less than human in order to treat his slaves inhumanely. He closed his mind to the possibility that a Black could speak the slaveowner's language, while simultaneously prohibiting this to happen. Of course there was a safety valve. For each slave who learned to speak, read, and write in the standard vernacular, one could simply wink and say that a slight addition of "White blood" flowed in the slave's veins which accounted for this achievement.

Such advances and speakers, of course, were a very small minority. The majority spoke a pidgin, an unacceptable form of English which eventually became a first language for the subsequent generations. According to Dillard (1972, p. 85), this language was sometimes referred to as Plantation Creole. This was the Proto-Creole to which Bailey (1965) alluded.

In their earlier stages of development, these Creoles exhibited a number of African linguistic traits which are now not as numerous or readily distinguishable in the various manifestations of modern vernacular Black English in the United States. The tonal features, for example, which must have been pesent in the Creole are no longer present in Black English today. In some variations of Black English as evidenced by certain Jamaican Creoles, Guyanese, and Surinam Creoles, and West African Krios and Pidgins, tone continues to play a significant role. Although we have no conclusive synchronic evidence to support the assertion that tone was once a feature of American Black English, it's hard to imagine that such tonal phenomenon developed everywhere except in the U.S. Beyond that, it is inconceivable that a Yoruba, Igbo, Twi, or Mande speaker would not superimpose some tonal system on this new language he was forced to acquire. Advantageously, the subtle distinctions inherently distinguishable to them providing varying nuances of meaning were simultaneously not received by the western ear trained to disregard such pitch distinctions at that level.

The labiovelar stops so prevalent in West African languages and retained in Gullah may also have once been in the phonological inventory of the Creoles in the Southern states. Probably more African lexical items were once in inventory, especially names as Turner (1949) found true for Gullah. A number of Afro-Americans are discovering that many of their parents, grandparents, and great grandparents had African names or nicknames that they ceased to use.

In spite of these losses, there remains a number of linguistic vestiges pointing to an African legacy. The influence of the structural feature of open syllable (having no consonants in the coda position), so prevalent in West and Central African languages, is demonstrably evident in the phenomena of consonant cluster reduction, the devoicing of single voiced consonants, and the loss of voiceless consonants, nasals, and liquids in that position in the varied manifestations of Black English, e.g., desk → des, bed → bet, man → mã and kar → ka(car).

Another phonological feature whose influence can be observed is the absence of the interdental fricatives θ and ð (orthographically th in English) in all African languages save Sherbro and Kiswahili. In a number of dialects of Black English, θ is realized as t word-initially and sometimes finally and as f medially and finally, while d is realized as d in word-initial position and as v in medial and final positions, e.g. [θif] → [tif] 'thief', [bæθ] → [bæf] 'bath', [ðis] → [dis] 'this', [brið] → [briv], 'breathe'.

In the area of morphology, the absence of inflectional affixes for plural, possession, and tense may be traced to African structural influence. The absence of the copula in some constructions and the use of 'be' as the habitual aspect are further linguistic vestiges at the grammatical level. Lexically there are a number of African words preserved. More have survived in Gullah and the Caribbean creoles than in Black English in the United States. Yet such items as "jitterbug," 'juke', as in jukebox, 'dig', 'hip', 'guy', 'okay' and 'gobber', still present in American Black English, strongly suggest African origins.

There are many more such features, phonological, morphological and grammatical, which have been illuminated by Dillard (1972) and much more so by Dalby (1971) and Dunn (1974). Undoubtedly, further studies of Black English will yield more.

SOUTHERN BLACK–WHITE INTERACTION

For my own part, after a somewhat careful study of East Alabama dialect, I am convinced that the speech of the white people, the dialect I have spoken all my life and the one I have tried to record here is more largely colored (no pun intended?) by the language of the Negroes than by any other single influence [Payne, 1903, p. 279].

No one can argue with the notion that Black English was influenced at various stages by Southern White dialects. The language did not develop in a vacuum. It has undergone a number of diachronic changes, due in part to the linguistic bombardment of other systems. In more recent times, we have been able to observe the influences exerted by its collision with Standard English. The result has been hypercorrections in the moprhology such as doubly marked plurals, e.g., mens, certain grammatical adjustments, the copula occurring in environments where it previously did not, the addition of the sounds orthographically symbolized by *th*, to mention just a few.

The acceptance of this premise, however, does not mandate that one proceed further to accept the *non sequitur* that Blacks therefore were *only* imitators and not also contributors to language development. Only up from a racist posture, with no real concern for the actual facts, could men such as H. P. Johnson (1928) have summarized that "... Negroes have made only one contribution to the language of the English speaking world. They have given it the word, buckra, which means white man [p. 381]." The absurdity and venal invidiousness of such a statement has been adequately disproven by Dillard (1972), Dalby (1971), and Dunn (1974).

There were earlier scholars who were able to move beyond the White dominant influence theory to recognize that in the linguistic confrontation between White and Black dialects, the influence was reciprocal. The author of the opening statement of this section suggested that the influence of Black speech patterns upon Whites may have been greater than the converse of the situation, i.e., White influence upon Blacks.

Although such pronouncements flew in the face of the racist ones and called into question the credibility of such theories as East Anglia, they can be found in a host of writings. This represents a meaningful testimony to truth at times prevailing. And why shouldn't such statements have been made? Nichols (1874) was correct in observing that "Southern speech is clipped, softened and broadened by the Negro admixture. The child learns its language from its Negro nurse, servants, and playmates, and this not unpleasant *patois* is never eradicated [Nichols, 1874, quoted in Meredith (1929, p. 291)]. There are two points contained in this statement which are most significant. First of all, there is the assertion that children, Black and White, spoke Black English during their formative years and speech development stages. Patterns were developed that were never totally lost. The Black influence was to some degree permanent. Second, and perhaps more important, is the reference to the language as being a "not unpleasant *patois*." Dillard (1972) includes a number of references alluding to Black English as "broken English," "thick," and "inelegant," an accent worthy of correction. He also includes a reference to the possibility that the languages may have been euphonious to the ears of White children—perhaps an unintended, but nevertheless a rather backhanded compliment. Nichols' (1874) inference, however, proceeded further. Could it be that he was referring to the notion that Whites, even adults, may have actually liked the *patois qua patois*? Were they enthralled to some degree by an element of exoticism, slowly distinguishing sounds not common to their own dialect, by features such as rhythmic tonal patterns and ideophonic onomatopoeia not acceptable in their systems? Might it have been the alluring sweetness of "forbidden fruit?" Did the bilingual owner who spoke one language in business and another to his slaves really enjoy his incursions into the vernacular? Or was this a put down? Whatever it was that lead Nichols to trigger this phrase, it seems obvious that language itself was not the *real* problem.

There is the possibility that the innovative influence of Blacks upon White dialects was readily distinguishable when Southern White dialects were contrasted with White Northern dialects. Researchers were unsuccessful in their attempts to account for all the contrasts on the basis of people migrating here from differing dialectal regions in England. In the search for other factors, the strong influence of the Black presence so prevalent in the South, so absent in the North, simply could not have been ignored.

All of these factors seem to suggest that the problems which subsequently arose in the Black–White confrontation were more sociological than linguistic in nature. One is led to believe that the attempt to deny an innovative linguistic influence by Blacks resulted from the recognition of that very influence. There was concern that few Southern Whites spoke the "yankee twang of the regular down Easter . . . , nice in enunciation and accent . . . [Kemble, 1863, pp. 210–211]." Such an awareness produced a social stigma, a special variety of disgrace that was the "shame of the South." Cognizant of this fact, Harrison (1884) lamented, "It must be confessed, to the shame of the white population of the South, that they perpetuated many of these pronunciations in common with their Negro dependents; and that, in many places, if one happeed to be talking to a native with one's eyes shut, it would be impossible to say whether a Negro or a white person were responding [p. 232]."

If such shame was not the original element which precipitated the theory of White exclusiveness, it certainly provided for the proponents of this theory another vital ingredient for its *raison d'être*. The influence of Black speech patterns was a stigma with which Southern Whites did not wish to be marked. The desire to be rid of this stigma was intensified following the so-called Emancipation. Scholars like Dillard (1972) rightly point out that the movement of the Black into a freer environment placed him in competition with the poor working-class White who was forced to fall back upon his "Whiteness" as his only claim to superiority. To such people the tracing of any of their language or behavior patterns to Negro influence was the bitterest of insults. This attempt to disociate and find no identical features with the Black man led to hostile and violent attacks upon Blacks. The poor White saw his social salvation and the guarantee of his existence in the put down of the Black man. Linguistically this led to stressing those features of language which they considered uniquely Black. These phrases they would utilize to "put Blacks in their place." This kind of activity continued into the 1950's and 1960's, culminating in the "Amos and Andy" syndrome whereby a White felt he could reduce any Black to nothing simply by addressing him with a "Hello dah!" Interesting enough, the Amos and Andy speech patterns which fed this syndrome were the creation of Whites who, of course, would have you believe that Blacks actually spoke that way.

What Dillard and others have not presented was the reaction to the influence of Black speech patterns by the White middle class and well-to-do aristocrats. Prior to the Emancipation, most well-to-do persons tolerated the Black speech patterns in their children only up to a certain age. The formal educational experience was designed, in part, to extricate out of the child the linguistic and behavioral patterns he or she had acquired under the tutelage of her "mammy" and the "plantation play-mates": . . . Those who have black nurses . . . are at such pains and cost for teachers to unlearn them what they need never have learned, had they kept illiterate people from them at first [Anne Royall, quoted in Mathews, 1948, p. 94]."

With the freeing of slaves and the defeat of the Confederacy, the former aristocrats found their position of superiority reduced on the societal totem pole. While on the one hand they could deride Black speech, their patterns in turn were derided by Northern Whites who considered that the majority of Southern Whites spoke inferior dialects. Lest Northerners should conclude that they spoke their "drawls" because of Black influence, fate dictated that they seize the initiative. Men like Krapp (1924) and Kurath (1928) were no "rednecks" speaking out in protection of poor Southern Whites. They were seeking to soothe the wounded egos of the middle and upper classes who were also seeking some manner by which to restore their pride. So intent were such men in their efforts to exorcise any evidence of Black influence that they sought to negate totally the remotest possibility of a genuine Black dialectal experience save for the resultant skewing of White dialects.

Although for different reasons, both rich and poor alike in the South sought disassociation. This reason perhaps as much as any contributed to the resultant segregated schools. The process of White education could not succeed in the presence of Blacks since part of the purpose of that education was to put aside Black influence. Although Blacks subsequently suffered from the separate and far-from-equal schools they were allowed to attend, that system shall remain as a historical monument to the influence that Blacks exerted upon Whites.

FROM A BLACK PERSPECTIVE

For a number of years following the Emancipation, Blacks cherished their cultural heritage. They did not forget they were an African people and some of the best known Black writers of the nineteenth century sought to link themselves with that tradition. James Weldon Johnson (1927) and Paul Lawrence Dunbar (1913), for example, relied heavily upon the imagery and symbolism of the African experience. Langston Hughes (1958) kept the tradition alive through the Harlem Renaissance. Logically this should have led American Blacks into the Negritude movement. Yet the two movements did not join forces. The Negritude movement proclaimed by Cesaire (1956), Senghor (1964), and others was joyously embraced by Caribbean and West African leaders, writers, and poets. African exiles in France and Britain also embraced the movement and sought to aid in the coming of a new day for Black peoples. In America the movement went virtually unnoticed. As alluded to in the Introduction, the movement at this time was not toward Black awareness but toward assimilation into the dominant culture. Assimilation, linguistically, dictated the adoption of the dominant language. Unlike the Irish, Italians, Germans, and other European ethnic groups who approached Standard English from acceptable language background, the Black child approached Standard English from the background of a "bastardized" version of English, or so it seemed. Black children were constantly bombarded with the fact that their language patterns did not conform to proper usages acceptable to institutions of learning.

Having been stripped of his African legacy, the Black child was damned for his linguistic deviations while at the same time deviations by children from other ethnic groups were accepted as natural and in time would adapt accordingly. No one was greatly concerned that a child of German extraction would say "zis" for "this." The dominant society "reinvented" and perpetuated a theory of racial inferiority to account for any deviations from standard exhibited in Black speech.

Constantly confronted by a system that condemned their speech as inferior, infantile, and incorrect, Blacks slowly began to accept this dogma as truth. Black children entering an elementary school soon became highly nonverbal as a result of the constant corrective interruptions of their speech. Obviously something was "wrong" with the way they spoke. At a point in the Children's development when they should have been receiving positive reinforcement and encouragement to grow, the Black children's language development was, in part, retarded. This provided confirming evidence for the lack of motivation, poor cognitive development, and a host of other educational maladies to which Black children were heir. The stigma which now accrues to Black English is as bad as it ever was.

Fortunately from time to time, rational thinking emerges. There is occasional recognition that such theories expressed above are not warranted. It has been pointed out that the presence of a prestigious standard among a host of other dialects is arbitrary. There is nothing necessarily intrinsic to that dialect such as it being more semantically sophisticated, more grammatically structured, or more euphoniously phonological.

Although a complete analysis of Black English remains to be done, studies already have demonstrated that Black English derives from a bona fide language system with its own semantic, grammatical, and phonological structures. While it is true that Black English has through the years assimilated somewhat to Standard, this is no excuse to label the speech of many Blacks are careless, incorrect, and haphazard. Differences should be treated as differences, for example, deriving from separate deep grammars, not as the deviations of a subdialect from the correct usages in the Standard.

Research has shown that many more African linguistic structures exist in American Black English than previously assumed. What is more important, those features which have tended to be highlighted as the most abusive syntactic deviations from standard, e.g., zero realization of genitives, lack of plurals, and use of be, have been shown to be structural vestiges traceable back from earlier Plantation Creole to the Proto-Pidgin to correspondences in the original African languages.

Black English, wherever it is spoken, is a systematic highly structured linguistic system which owes little, if any, to illogical or incorrect extensions of White dialect patterns over the past four centuries. Acknowledgment of this legitimacy is essential. Without such acknowledgment we shall be continually locked into a system which relies on racial inferiority. Ambrose Gonzales (1922), who was quoted at the very outset of this presentation, is a good example of what is not needed at this point in time. Though White, he learned to speak impeccable Gullah, and recorded and wrote Black folktales of the Gullah's with great appreciation for the "extraordinary richness of the oral tradition, the wit and charm of their dialect [Van Sertima, 1970, p. 2]." Such appreciation did not inhibit his reprehensible assertion. What should have been so obvious to him, the distinctively different linguistic system in which he was operating, was hidden by his already confirmed view that he was dealing with a people who were culturally and linguistically inferior.

So long as this attitudinal myopia continues, the long legacy of the Black–White linguistic confrontation will continue, and significant education for disadvantaged Blacks will remain a remote possibility.

CONCLUSION

Although it remains unacceptable, one can understand the fact that to Southern Whites Black English stood for something they wished to deny. At present, one need raise the question as to what threat Black English is now to the dominant linguistic group, especially in the Northern school system? Why the reluctance to recognize Black English as a language in its own right? Why have programs designed to approach Black children via Tesol methods rapidly degenerated into deficit models? Is it simply that the racial legacy is so dominant that the acceptance of facts strongly illuminating its vacuity is impossible? Is there the unexpressed fear that Black English will "corrupt" Standard English to the extent that the English-speaking world will hold the American speaker in contempt? Is it simply its association with a lower class or caste?

For whatever reasons the educational systems north, south, east, and west, have perpetuated the fallacies and myths of the Black linguistic experience, promulgated out of the times of slavery for the sake of the victims who continue to "reap the whirlwind" of that system, the time is ripe for a radically new approach to language skills development programs in our schools. If the stated objectives of education truly encompass social mobility and economic advancement, then such benefits should be made available to all who are subject to such an educational process. Standard English, like it or not, is *sine qua non* in our culture for economic, social, and vocational advancement. In order to afford many Black children the opportunity to acquire the expertise in Standard so essential, new methods of development are mandated. Requisite to such methods is the recognition of Black English as a legitimate linguistic system by the majority of American educators. Such recognition will provide for prideful Black recognition and positive reinforcement of the good inherent in the child's own culture. It will also help to develop comparable models of linguistic instructions of the two systems as equals, not as an inferior in relation to a superior. Such an approach will also help to put to rest the notions of impaired cognitive development, arrested grammatical awareness, and the rest of the racial pronouncements that have symbiotically existed with the proposed inferiority of Black English.

REFERENCES

Anonymous. Editorial, Black nonsense. *Crisis,* 1971, 78(3), 78.

Armstrong, R. G. *The study of West African languages.* Ibadan: Ibadan University Press, 1964.

Bailey, B. L. Toward a new perspective in Negro dialectology. *American Speech,* 1965, 40, 171–177.

Cesaire, A. *Cahier d'un retour au pays natal.* Paris: Présence Africaine, 1956.

Dalby, D. Black through white. In *Black–white speech relationships.* Washington, D.C.: Center for Applied Linguistics, 1971.

Dillard, J. L. *Black English.* New York: Random House, 1972.

Dunbar, P. L. *The complete poems of Paul Lawrence Dunbar.* New York: Dodd, Mead, 1913.

Dunn, E. F. African linguistic structures in black English. *Proceedings of the Conference on the Black Pluriverse.* Englewood, New Jersey: Emerson Press, 1974.

Fanon, F. *Black skin, white masks.* New York: Grove Press, 1967.

Gonzales, A. *The black border.* Columbia, S.C.: The State Printing Co., 1922. (Reprinted 1964.)

Greenberg, J. H. *The languages of Africa.* Bloomington: Indiana University Press, 1966.

Hall, R. A., Jr. *Pidgin and creole languages.* Ithaca: Cornell University Press, 1966.

Harrison, J. A. Negro English. *Anglia,* 1884, 8, 232–279.

Haskins, J., & Butts, H. F. *The psychology of black language.* New York: Harper & Row, 1968.

Hughes, L. *The Langston Hughes reader.* New York: George Braziller, Inc., 1958.

Hymes, D. Ed. *Pidginization and creolization of languages.* Cambridge, England: Cambridge University Press, 1970.

Johnson, H. P. Who lost the southern R? *American Speech,* 1928, 111, 377–383.

Johnson, J. W. *God's trombones.* (16th ed.) New York: The Viking Press, 1957.

Jones, L. (Imamu Baraka) *Blues people.* (6th ed.) New York: William Morrow, 1968.

Kemble, F. A. A Journal of Residence on Georgia Plantation. New York, 1863.

Koelle, S. W. *Polyglotta Africana.* Graz-Austria: Akademische Druck-A. Verlagsanstalt, 1963.

Krapp, G. P. The English of the negro. *American Mercury,* 1924, 2(5), 190–195.

Kurath, H. The origin of dialectal differences in spoken American English. *Modern Philology,* 1928, 25.

Loflin, M. D. Negro non-standard and standard English: Same or different deep structure?" *Orbis,* 1969, 18, 74–91.

Long, R. A. Towards a theory of Afro-American dialects. Atlanta: Atlanta University, CAAS Papers in Linguistics No. 1, 1970.

Matthews, M. M. *Some sources of southernisms.* Birmingham, Alabama: University of Alabama Press, 1948.

Meredith, M. Tall talk in America sixty years ago. *American Speech,* 1929, 4(3), 290–293.

Nichols, T. L. *Forty years of American life.* London, 1874.

Payne, L. W. A word list from East Alabama. *Dialect Notes,* 1903, 3, 279–328, 343–391.

Royall, A. *Sketches of history, life and manners in the United States.* New Haven, Connecticut: Yale University Press, 1926.

Senghor, L. *Poèmes,* Paris: Editions du Sevil, 1964.

Turner, L. D. *Africanisms in the Gullah dialect.* Chicago: University of Chicago Press, 1949.

Van Sertima, I. African linguistic and mythological structures in the New World. Unpublished manuscript for private circulation, 1970.

Welmers, W. E. Language change and language relations in Africa. *Language Sciences* 1970, **12**, 1–7.

Wolfram, W. Underlying representations in Black English phonology. *Language Sciences,* 1970, **10**, 7–12.

7

My Gullah Brother and I: Exploration into a Community's Language and Myth through Its Oral Tradition

Ivan Van Sertima

Douglass College, Rutgers University

I, for one, coming from the coastlands of Guyana in South America, have never met a Gullah Negro from South Carolina or the Georgia coast. A vast ocean lies between us which we have hardly crossed, my Gullah brother and I, since the days of the Middle Passage. Yet when I read Gullah in the folktales...something turns on in me like a second ear, something re-echoes the words and structures of that dialect within me like a submerged speaker and tongue. What, you may ask, is that something? What is really moving and playing, like a drummer in shadow, behind me? [Van Sertima, 1971, p. 13]

Those words are taken from an article I wrote four years ago when I first came to America. Since then I have visited the Sea Islands twice, in 1970 and 1971. I have recorded the voices of the Gullah of Johns Island in their homes, in their churches, in their workplaces, and on their farms. I have even sat in on the private councils of a revolutionary group centered in Charleston but spearheaded by men of Johns Island. I have listemed to the songs of the Gullah, to their stories of the vanished past, to the trickster tales of Rabbit and Tortoise which still runs like a river of legend across the banks of the Black world from the old Guinea coast to Guyana. I have looked closely at the relationships between their form of Black English and my own and the way in which we have both been profoundly affected by an African ancestral grammar. And through all these years I have been haunted by a sense of familiarity which I sometimes find strange and by a sense of strangeness which is oddly familiar. It is the way I feel when I come upon a member of my own family from whom I have been long separated, the strangeness that grows from distance in time and space, the familiarity that is native to a common brood and blood.

I use the terms native and familiar because their English is an English which is not far removed from the one I have used as an oral alternative in the Guyanas and which still runs subterraneously, surfacing occasionally from under the English I now formally speak and write. When I say, therefore, that the Gullah is my brother I am not merely being romantic and sentimental. Africa is not only the common womb out of which the Gullah and I have sprung. It is still, through the golden thread of the oral tradition, binding a chain of tenuous but persistent vestiges and roots. We are not yet fully severed—my Gullah brother and I—from that ancestral trunk or constellation of roots. Transplanted as we are, we have branched into what we have joined here, we have grown into what we have known here in this hemisphere, but through the veins of our psyche there circulates still an ancient and potent sap. Hence, as I follow the trail of the oral tradition in the Sea Islands, I am not simply seeking a forgotten pathway into exotic survivals but a master key into the maze of my own related past, the labyrinth of my complex inheritance, the half-buried roots and branches of my dismembered self.

For this purpose of exploration and recovery of the threads of traditions I could not have picked a better area than the Sea Islands. These islands off South Carolina and the Georgia coast are unique in all North America. Unlike the mainland states of the United States, they maintained a massive black presence throughout their history and absorbed and Africanized the Europeans rather than being absorbed and Europeanized by them. Thus there are Whites in the Gullah islands who have grown up speaking Black English.

So minimal in fact was this White presence that even in the early days of slavery some of the overseers had to be selected from the Blacks. Is it any wonder, therefore, that here, in these islands, stretching 300 miles across Atlantic space and 300 years across American history, we find the purest form of Afro-English and African-influenced art, craft, mythology, ritual behavior, religious music, motor habits, proverbs, chants and riddles, naming systems, family patterns, and even some economic associations with West African prototypes? What is even more significant but seldom recognized is that the language of the Sea Islands has affected not only the language of the Blacks in the South but that of the Whites also who owe not only some of the vivid proverbs and images, the lyrical sweep and speed of narrative (captured so powerfully by Twain and Faulkner) to these Black islands, but also some of the lilt and tonal quality of their curiously accented speech.

Research into the language and life of the Gullah has been going on for a long time. This research has spawned a stubborn brood of misconceptions. It would be interesting to list some of these, though they reveal more about the prejudice and ignorance of scholars and the racist climate of inquiry into Black life and culture over the past half century in these United States than they do about the Gullah themselves.

John Bennett was among the first of the researchers into the Gullah language. As early as 1908 he spoke of its "quick, crackling sounds" caused in part, he declared, "by excessive laxity of pronunciation, in part by the elision of every sound of which language may be shorn and still remain articulate." He compared the rapid-fire speech of the Gullah to the gabbling of ducks.

In 1939 George Krapp (and I think his surname is apt) dismissed any consideration of African influence on Gullah and merely echoed Bennett who saw all the peculiarities of the dialect traceable to the tongue of "low-bred redemptioners, humble Scotch, Scotch-Irish and Irish-English deportations." It would be folly to deny the influence of these immigrants, for it is true that it was their English that the Gullah first encountered on this continent and reworked and transformed, but it is amazing that this fiction of Gullah being simply a quaint preserve of the illiterate peasant English of the seventeenth and eighteenth centuries should have persisted to this day. As late as 1940, Mason Crum, author of the most comprehensive work on the Gullah before the coming of Lorenzo Turner (1939), remarked "Gullah is more truly English than much of the English spoken in America today." Again the surname Crum is apt, for in this major work *Gullah: Negro Life in the Carolina Sea Islands* he serves up the crumbs of both the old (Bennett, 1908; Krapp, 1939; Johnson, 1930; Gonzalez, 1922) as well as the new (Stoney & Shelby, 1930) theories of the Gullah. Stoney and Shelby, in their work *Black Genesis*, published in 1930, highlighted the African influence on Gullah language, although they could only come to grips with it at a superficial word level, which revealed very little since the African words in popular Gullah use are few. They, however, were the forerunners of Turner. But Crum, receptive though he was to what they had to say about the African influence, still spoke of Gullah as "a wreck of the King's English," albeit to him a fascinating and exotic wreck.

It is important to understand what is happening here. In Crum a new sentimental and parental–protective attitude toward the Gullah Negro emerges. Times had changed. He could boast in his book, with a proud and whimsical nostalgia, of having drank milk from a Black mammy's breast. What he was doing in making extreme claims for the Englishness of Gullah was what researchers were doing as late as the 1960's when equating Black dialects of America with those of lower-class Whites. I quote a statement from an earlier article of mine which helps to illuminate the latter day liberal motives behind this approach:

> It has been said that the forms of English spoken by black people in America owe nothing to Africa at all, that in fact Black forms of English are no different from dialects of English spoken by lower-class white groups, and that all the non-standard elements in Black English can be traced to an earlier English used and dropped by American settlers or still partly in vogue among lower-class American whites. Strangely enough, this theory was advanced in America by linguists who thought they were doing the blacks a great favor. They were putting forward this theory of the non-difference between white and black dialects of America to prove that, where language was concerned, the blacks were no different from the whites. This was their misguided but well-intentioned attempt to establish equality among the races. They believed that this could only be done by denying diversity among the cultural subgroups of America, as if the very existence of difference in the use of English by blacks indicated their inferiority, and only the denial of that difference could establish their claim to equality with the users of standard English. Integration of the black and white elements of America meant for them the standardization and uniformity of peoples, rather than the coexistence of diverse but equally valid culture-groups. They sought to negate ethnic and cultural plurality which is America's greatest heritage [Van Sertima, 1971, p. 16].

Let it be said in Crum's defence, however, for he is full of contradictions, that he was convinced of what he calls "the African spirit" behind the body of the dialect. In one breath he is saying "nowhere on this continent can a purer African culture be found," in another he presents a count made by Guy Johnson (1930) of standard, corrupted and archaic English words from a glossary of Gullah prepared by Gonzalez (1922) to prove that only one-half of 1% of Gullah is African. Even Stoney and Shelby (1930), who confidently proclaimed Gullah as "the strongest linguistic connection between America, the Caribbean, and Africa, linking two hemispheres and two eras" found themselves at a loss to prove their hypothesis when it came down to a count of surviving African words.

Turner (1939) discovered thousands of these words. He went beyond the popular speech of the Gullah to their secret naming systems which were modeled upon the West African tribes and language groups from which the Gullah came. But while it is true that these words may with diligence be unearthed from under the popular face of the dialect, it is not the real crux of the matter. It is in fact peripheral to our main concerns in any serious study of Gullah language and culture. For while I may show, through Richard Allsopp's study (unpublished), that there are scores of African words still in popular use in my Guyanese dialect, and through Lorenzo Turner's work, that there are thousands of African words secreted in the alternative names of the Gullah people, and while I may also point to a number of African words in popular American speech which we have come to take for granted as being of English derivation or indigenous Americanese, all I would be saying is that we were once in Africa and picked up a few things as tourists pick up hello's and goodbye's in foreign parlance, flitting through alien spaces like birds of passage. This would be far too obvious and too facile. Our inheritance is not, as Stoney and Shelby thought, a few rhymes, games, systems of counting, tricks of the tongue, or a sprinkle of African words in common use. These are in fact surface exotica—stones and shells. The African spirit behind the body of the Gullah dialect and culture is not so easily found and not so easily lost. I quote from myself again:

> ...forgetting these words, since it is true that the main vocabulary of American blacks is non-African, the crucial African element to watch is not vocabulary at all, but a grammatical base, a syntactical structure. It is the African structure underlying the top layer of Anglo-Saxon words which accounts for the peculiar combinations, patterns, and transformations in the speech of peoples as far apart as the Guyanese of South America, the Gambians of West Africa, and the Gullahs of Georgia [Van Sertima, 1971, p. 17].

Turner, of course, established this. He was the turning point in studies of the Gullah. He was the only linguist to take the trouble to acquaint himself with the West African linguistic background of these people. He could therefore speak with authority and authenticity on their language which no other linguist before him could do. He was also the first Black scholar to do serious work in this area and (racial considerations aside) his Blackness helped. To no White observer before him, for example, did the Gullah ever confess their non-English names. We may still go to Ambrose Gonzalez (1922) and Charles Colcock Jones (1888) for excellent recordings of Gullah folktales; for social studies of the Sea Islands in general we may still read Mason Crum (1940) with profit and for a Sea Island in particular—St. Helena—we should look again at Guy B. Johnson (1930). But for any genuine insight into the interaction between African memory and inheritance and the American reality, particularly with respect to language, we can turn to no one but Turner (1939).

It is also time to turn another road in Gullah studies and go beyond Turner. It is now 40 years since his first major field work was done in these Sea Islands. What has happened? Those of us who must follow

through have several tasks cut out. It is necessary to keep the work of
Turner up to date. Has the African influence on Gullah grammar changed
dramatically in these 40 years? In my own work I have asked myself
that question. It is necessary to probe beyond the syntax of the language
to the history and culture of the people, to use their oral tradition to
ask much larger questions. How did they see their own world, for so far
nearly all their social histories have been written by their masters, with
the perspectives and emphases of their masters? How did they work and
play and farm and fish and struggle and suffer and make love and rear
children and pass on their tales and beliefs and customs? What do they
think, not only of the vanished times but of the new day that is breaking
in the South? These questions are essential because, more than any other
people, our history, their history, lies in voices, oral treasuries, conversations, talking books. To go among the Gullah with one's ears wired
is to run a blind man's fingers across a history of islands written in
Braille.

I have tried to respond to all these questions and concerns, to see
the oral tradition in its sociocultural, mythological, and linguistic aspects.
My visits to these islands have been brief, my informants few, but the
time was intensively spent and the old men and women I spoke with well
chosen for the purpose. I try to trace, through the answers they gave
to my questions, aspects of their early lives which I feel go beyond the
personal and evoke the larger social background not only of the island
but of the era from which they have come. I then go on to deal with
their folktales of which there are many collections but few analyses.
Finally, and very importantly, I seek to demonstrate the African presence
in the Gullah language, not on a lexical but on a grammatical level, to
prove that on that level Gullah has not lost any of its significant elements
since the studies of Turner.

The old men and women of the islands were my informants. I ignored
the youth save the radical wing of young adults in Charleston who had
grown up on these islands. This was a deliberate choice on my part, for,
where the oral tradition is concerned, it is written on a wrinkled parch-
ment of skin and heard in a feeble voice. The vigorous shout, the smooth,
bright face of youth is an empty book.

One of my informants was a 70-year old man called Guinea. I thought
at first that this might be an African name and that it referred to the
Guinea coast. The truth was he had come by that name through an extraordinary circumstance that said as much symbolically of the Negro's life
as his own. He was so weak from malnutrition in his first years that
he could not carry his weight on his legs. He could not stand straight
or walk. His parents used to dig a hole in the ground (he showed us
the hole) and bury him up to the thighs. They did this in the hope that

it would make his legs grow firm and straight. As he stood there, half-buried in the ground, he watched the free and easy movement of the birds. He actually learned to walk by a close study of the guinea bird from which he took his name. But learning to walk was the beginning of a new disaster. He walked right into trouble. As soon as his legs grew strong they were clamped into chains. In an interview with Guinea, the story of his life in prisons and in a chain gang in the South began to unfold:

GUINEA: Looky heah, looky heah. I kin show all dese heah (lifts pants leg to reveal shackle scars). I wasn' no Uncle Chaalie, tho'. Ain' gonna be none uh dat. I radduh, I radduh all dis leg go. See ... shackle weah dat out, shackle weah dis out. Guard shoot me by duh head, try to get away. Evytime a slow train come in I try to ketch im, I have shackle on, but I try to ketch im, I wudden give up! ... Ah had duh shackle heah, den ah had a ball between muh leg, an den de shackle come ovuh heah, den I tote duh ball all day, walk ri' down wi' duh res' to prison. But I didden give up. I say, "I bawn a boy, Chaalie, an I suppose to catch hell, Ah reckon."

VAN: How long have you been in prison?

GUINEA: Oh, 'bout seventeen, eighteen yeah, sumpin like dat ... off an on. But evytime I do sumpin, I plan to go to jail because I know my people po an no need kill dem cuz dey ain' got fifteen cent, an' if I go to jail I foll up my aam an fine out what time deh feed . . . What I do make duh time, an try to make it back home. I don' write nobody no lettuh. You know what I write my people an say? "Doan sen me no hat. I take de hat off so fass. De white people doan like yuh weah no hat on. Juh sen me some long drawers an' some cigarette. S'all I need." De day I get home all the loving faces I leave I meet dem again.

VAN: Did you have any visitor, like your wife or your children?

GUINEA: O no, I doan know nuttin abow dat, nuttin abow dat.

VAN: You didn't? Why?

GUINEA: Weh, you see, people you love an' been roun' all togedduh, you haat break til dat take five yeahs off yuh life, mo den time you got. So if de Judge give you ten yeah, you be sho' make you ten yeah, doan leh none o' you close relation come see you. An I feel bettuh ... Doan wan' none o' duh people come heah, see me. What deh got, sen it deh. Doan come.

We found Guinea had remained militant and hardy in spite of nearly a century of extreme poverty and punishment. He was out there in the van with a group of young activists in Charleston, the members of COBRA, the Committee for Better Racial Assurance. It lived up to its name. It struck with a quick bitter force at racial injustice. Guinea had helped in the organization of a strike and he was in and out of jail but was now challenging the law with a just purpose, fighting for his civil rights. As Bill Saunders, the head of COBRA, put it, "Any time anybody needed to be arrested, Guinea was right there going to jail." Prodded

by Saunders, he recounted to us some of the highlights, or rather the
lowlights, of his boyhood. It seems, of all his deprivations it was his
crude, improvised clothing that humiliated him most. In his consciousness
it was a second skin he would have given a great deal to discard:

GUINEA: An I woiked wit croakuh suit on...my mudduh an fadduh din
          have no money. I have croakuh. Deh make duh croakuh pans, duh
          croakuh coat. If I wanna play I have to play in dat croakuh
          pans...you see dis bag? Is sack. I weh it.

SAUNDERS: What you people call burlaps.

GUINEA: Deh wash it off clean, deh wash it off clean. Den deh make a coat
          an' a pans fuh me. An I is duh ony chile my mudduh an' fadduh
          evuh'd. Deh din have no money atall. I leave home wen I was
          eleven yeah ole, doan know weh I going.

SAUNDERS: Tell them what you did after you left there, Guinea.

GUINEA: O, I went to stealing an' gambling an' doing evything else, selling
          tricks . . .

In his final lament for the life of hunger and denial he had led, Guinea
returned to the indignity of his croaker suit which he mentioned in the
same breath as the days he had wandered across the island like a stray
dog, foraging for food:

Now yuh know, I cudden suffuh no mo dan I was suffrin den, cudden suffuh
no mo dan I suffuh. I veah croakuhs. I eat today an' didden eat tomorrow.

Against this life one may contrast another—that of Alice Wine—also
of Johns Island, a life perhaps equally cruel and oppressive in some respects, but distinguished by a sense of proud independence and self-suffi-
ciency. Alice Wine nourished this spirit of pride and independence
through her proprietary relationship to the land. She worked it hard but
not as a labor hand or a servant of the White folks. Rather, unlike the
homeless and rootless Guinea, as someone who could say "is me own
place, me Daddy place." She was up from four in the morning to scrape
a living from this land:

ALICE WINE: I live on a faam, on me own place, me Daddy place . . . plan'
            potato, plan' peas, plan' cawn, plan' rice an' plan' mos' evyting . . .
            I wuk wit hoe, hoe potatos an' diffrin stuff like dat, you see.
            Hafta wuk. Wen I come home from school in de even time, I
            hafta wuk, an' befo' I go to school I hafta wuk, an' aftuh I come
            fum school I hafta wuk.

VAN: Did you ever have time to play games?

WINE: Weh doan know nuttin bow dat.

VAN: No kind of games?

WINE: No kinduh game.

VAN: It was all work, work, work?

WINE: All wuk.

VAN: You would get up very early in the morning?

WINE: Yes, lawd, fo' clock . . .

From Alice Wine, as old and sturdy as old Guinea, we learned a lot about the way the islanders struggled to make a living on the land, how they farmed and fished in the summer and lived off their bank of cured and corned provisions in the winter:

WINE: We doan nevuh wuk wen wintuh comes. We nevuh come out in wintuhtaam.
VAN: So where would the food come from?
WINE: Come fum ow   gaaden, my Daddy, we raise evyting. We raise rice, cawn, an de cawn bring you grits an flowuh an cawnmeal, des right. Hocks go anyway you wants em to go. An das tree paat right deh. An is grits an cawnmeal (no, das two paat fo to sell) an duh hocks go someplace else. We raise rice an rice an uh nex i' be peas an nex it be potato an you have you turnip an you cut off duh leaf an bank it like potatos an yuh have dat in yuh baan. Din you go to duh creek an den you get plenty fish an you cawn dem an you put it to dry an wen deh done dry yuh out it in a barrel, den you have yuh fish, den yuh have yuh fish. Den yuh have yuh cow, 'e give yuh milk. Den yuh have yuh chicken, 'e give you eggs. an' den wheel on back, you take yuh cow milk an make buttuhs. Den you wheel on back again, you kin kill a cyaf an' cyo' it. Den you wheel on back, you kill a hog an' make buttsmeat out of it . . .

At one stage she compared this food-banking operation to the winter planning of the ants:

WINE: We reduce food jes like de ants reduce dem own in de summuh. In de summuh de ants reduce dey food an bank em in de urt an wen cole day come, deh doan come out. So dats wat de ole people was doin wi' deh children. Dey plant plenty uh potatos an bank it up, an peas, an put em in duh barrel, an turnup, dey sweeten dat in duh bank, an duh hog, deh cyo' it, an Daddy go in de crick an git duh fish an cawn em. We dry em out on duh bode (board). We nevuh buy nuttin . . . I injoy my life coming but not now. Kuh dis is no good now.

We found this insistence that *time-comin* (the Gullah phrase for youth and the past) was in every way better than the new times, the recent times, strange. We felt that this was an ultraconservative judgment and that it had to do with age, which looked back to its youth through eyes softened by nostalgia, however filled with terror and anguish the past had been. Also, we felt it was a defence against her children who were departing from cherished customs and traditions. We questioned her closely on this:

VAN: So what about those hard days in the fields getting up at four in the morning?
WINE: I radduh do dat kuz you doan wuk in sunhot but is vip an strappin vip behine you now kuz dese people put you in de feel rung seven o'click in de mawnin, knock off you a' twelve, putch you back deh one, knock

off you six. Dat ain no business fuh me, see. I caan larn nuttin like dat . . . In my time coming, usetuh git fawty cent a day an five dolluhs in de white people kitchen.

VAN: How much is it now?

WINE: O, deh git eight uhr nine dolluhs a day now but wat good it is? Ain' a bit mo bettuh den I make my fawty cent a day kuz duh tings ah so high. Das right. Din you cud git a yaad o' clawt jes only fuh tree cent uhr five cent a yaad win now you hafta pay a dolluh an' two dolluh a yaad. So I radduh go back dan dis time.

I radduh go back dan dis time! Alice Wine was not unique in this, of course, but none of our other informants felt so strongly that the young people of the islands had fallen away completely from ideals they cherished, that the world had changed for the worse.

Isabella Simmons did complain of the "seeing story" (television) competing with the "hearing story" in the same tone of regret as Alice Wine had complained of "you be laughing at me wen you see buttsmeat an' grits." But many were open to the winds of change blowing across these islands and did not see it as a necessary threat to what was essential in their traditions. Some were out there in the vanguard with the young, fighting their new battles, like Guinea for example, one of the fangs of COBRA, who could boast at 71, "way I feel now its a fo'ty seven, good as I feeling." Some tolerated considerable movements in consciousness toward a new life in their young, while continuing to initiate them into some of the styles and values of the old, into what was still relevant and crucial in their oral and cultural inheritance. Such was the case of Jane Hunter, the great grandmother of Johns Island. It was in the Hunter home, surrounded by her grands and great-grands, who listened to her every word intently, that we felt a renewal of faith in the perpetuity of these traditions.

We sat for hours as she spun tale after tale of Brer Rabbit and Brer Cooter, the ancient Bantu tricksters Hare and Tortoise, which the oral tradition had for centuries preserved. They were still the popular tales of these islands and were told in an English nearer to the original Gullah than we had heard so far in conversations. I quote from one of these—Bruh Rabbit an Mistuh Wolf:,

Duh Rabbit an duh Wolf was fren, dey was two fren, an deh was a big dance. Mistuh Wolf girlfren was havin a big dance da night an Bruh Rabbit had love duh Wolf girl more den he does his girl. So Rabbit go an tie up he leg lukkuh e got a broke leg an e kun walk.

(Wolf) 'e say "Ol fren," say, "you going to duh dance tonight?"

(Rabbit) e say, "O man, I doan tink I make it, kuh I go a' fall an hurt me leg an I haaly kin walk." 'E say, "I tell you sumpin, ol fren," 'e say, "if you let me ride you back paa duh way, en wen I ah-us (almost) get to duh house . . ."

"Den you get off quick. Doan let my girl see you ride my back now."

All dat time duh Rabbit done gone tell duh Wolf girl dat he gonna ride Mistuh Wolf to duh dance tonight. Duh girl say, "O no, not Mistuh Wolf, not Mistuh Wolf. You nevuh ride my boyfren back."

Well duh Rabbit doan tell, doan say he give im ride cause 'e had a sick leg, an he say (to Wolf) "Yeah, I promise, datsa promise. Yeah, I promise yuh dat I get off yuh back befo yuh get to my girlfren house."

An duh Rabbit put two what yuh call spur on 'e foot an he jump on duh Wolf back an'e say, "Walk slow now".

"Now mine me yuh promise, get off my back fo yuh git to dat girl house."

"Datsa promise, Mistuh Wolf." An all dat time de music was playin, an duh Wolf an Rabbit way till dey mos' get but a few step from duh Wolf do' an 'e put duh two spur in duh Wolf side and 'e push right in duh do'.

An all duh girl say, "O no, o no dat ain't Mistuh Wolf dat ain't Mistuh Wolf" say "you no muh boyfren. Come on, Mistuh Rabbit, dance wit me." An Rabbit had duh whole houseful uh girl.

Brer Rabbit in this story outwits Brer Wolf, riding on his back to ultimate possesion of all they both desire. In the real world it would be Wolf who would win out in this struggle but in the world of dream the defencelessness of the Rabbit and the inherent predatory viciousness of Wolf are reversed. It is important to understand the profound relationship between the Rabbit's act and the slave's dream. It is important also to understand how it is that the Rabbit in Black American mythology is associated not only with mischievous and immoral but even criminal acts which would normally outrage but awaken instead in his listeners an enormous fascination and respect. This is not, as would appear on the surface, simply a child's story told for a child's amusement. Behind the disarming naivéte of the tale lies the complex psychology of the oppressed.

These trickster figures, of course, were born in another world, not a world of the slave and the free but a world, nonetheless, which like all societies is composed of the rulers and the ruled, the strong and the weak, the powerful and the powerless. These tales owe their original inspiration to the mythological imagination and architecture of fantasy in Africa. The surface features or motifs that appear (objects, creatures, incidents) in the new geographic and cultural environment of the South give the traditional African bones of the tale a new fleshing. The underlying structures, however, are the same. Why have these African animal archetypes survived and persisted in these islands? What new function do they serve and in what new forms and shapes are the African tale types expressed among the Gullah and the Blacks of the South?

An analysis in depth of the main elements in African folktales will show that the animals are involved in a shadow drama of the human world. They are dream figures through which personality traits, values, or power relations of groups—commoner and king, slave and master, the weak and the strong, the powerful and the suppressed—may be reflected in a dreaming drama of the social world, within which dream and drama the figures are invested with a fluidity and metamorphic quality denied them in the more rigidly structured social world, so that they often seem to reverse and overturn their given social role or condition. It is this capacity of the dream figure (animal archetype) to overleap and overturn an oppressive social condition that makes the personae of the tales (Rabbit, Tortoise, etc.) take on a heroic cast and revolutionary function.

This role reversal and revolutionary function of certain African folk heroes account for their enormous popular appeal among the Black communities of the New World. Like the Caribbean Annancy, the Gullah Rabbit plays the role of outlaw and con-man. Neither subscribes to the laws and moral values of their society. Secretive, elusive, cunning, deceptive, sometimes cruel and treacherous, they are in the role of the Transcendent Criminal, avoiding through their legendary agility of wit the onerous and unfair burdens imposed upon their fellows, always one step ahead of Brer Wolf and Brer Tiger, the predatory lords and overseers of the jungle.

The amoral character of these folk heroes do not represent in any sense the character of the Gullah or the Blacks of the Caribbean. In the Gullah Rabbit and the Caribbean Annancy we are face to face with what I would call a Black innocence. Whatever they may do in the tales can never outrage us, not because they are simply tales, not because their nonhuman personae remove us from an easy identification with their personality, but because theirs is an evil that liberates rather than oppresses. We love them in spite of their evil; we may even love them for their evil, for they assume aspects of evil in order to elude and conquer a condition of evil.

In their original African home and culture these figures took on other functions that are ignored, minimized, or forgotten among the Gullah and the Blacks of the New World. Their functions in this hemisphere have become restricted to a treachery and guile aimed at transcendence over impotence and servility within a highly oppressive order of relationships. It would be interesting to look at some of these functions and the reasons why they have been neglected or ignored in transplantation. The trickster in Africa is not only involved in tricking the lords of the jungle—Tiger, Elephant, Lion—the class of the mighty and powerful. He is involved in playing tricks on the rulers of Heaven itself, stealing fire or food for his fellows under the noses of the Gods. We seldom find him in such a role in the New World. Trickster is also involved in a revolt against the mores of his own group—committing taboo acts, acts of outrage which release him from the confines and boundaries laid down and observed by his peers. Here, he is the Individual in revolt against the Collective. Rarely do we find him in such a role among Afro-Americans.

Such functions of the Trickster were a luxury in a slave and colonial society, for the lords of the plantation were the Gods themselves, in terms of the laying down of the boundaries of behavior, and the individual personality was a remote probability within a dehumanized and deracinated collective.

So deep, so intense, so total indeed was this negation in real life that the role of the Trickster in the life of dream among Afro-Americans was nearly always recreative, transcendent, overpowering, and triumphant, rarely self-destructive, regressive, or anarchistic in a primal sense. We could hardly afford this. We, Afro-Americans, needed no vision of chaos to relieve our impatience with stable structures and immemorial orders. What we needed (at least in the past) was a new order through Black lawlessness which would negate the old order of White lawlessness that had negated and outlawed us.

But the Trickster figure has a duality of function in other societies. To put it in Paul Radin's words, "He is at one and the same time creator and destroyer, giver and negator, being duped as often as he dupes [Abrahams, 1968, p. 171]." In only one or two tales among Afro-Americans is the trickster tricked or duped. A rare example of this comes from tales told to us by Jane Hunter in our Gullah field trip of 1971:

Duh Rabbit en Duh Patrid (Partridge)—1971

Duh Rabbit en duh Patrid, dey was two great fren. So one day Patrid take her head en stick he head unduh he wing, went to Rabbit house.
[Rabbit] say, "Ol fren, watcha doin?"
Say, "Oh, I ain't doin nuttin but sittin in duh sun."
Say, "Oh, wheahs you head?"
Say, "Man, I leave my head home fuh my wife to shave."
All dat time he had his head unduhnea' his wing. Rabbit run in duh house, say, "Ol Gal," he say, "Come on to chop my head off."
'E say, "No, Mistuh Rabbit. If I chop yuh head off, you'll die."
Say, "No, I won' eidduh, cause Mistuh Patrid leave he head home fuh his wife to shave en so why caan I leave my head fuh you to shave?"
So all his wife, all duh res uh (what) he wife tell him, (he) say, "If you doan chop my head off, I'll chop you head off."
So das two fren now. Das why you fren in duh one who gets you, enemy who come en accoshu (accost you). Buh if yuh get hurt, it (you) kin get hurt from fren. So he go en bawl his wife, bawl. Duh wife take duh big knife en chop 'e head off 'en 'e chop 'e head off.
So Patrid had a pretty girlfren. Rabbit had a very pretty girl, en Patrid wife wasn' as goodlookin as Rabbit wife. Patrid had a love fuh Rabbit wife, see? En dats duh only way he coulda get Rabbit wife by doin im some haam. So when duh lady gone en chop duh Rabbit head off, Rabbit pitch off yonduh en die.

En duh Patrid take 'e head from unduhnea' he wing, say, 'Wing, nuh foolin, nuh fun. En wing, no lovin, no gettin love." En den she had two wife, had his wife en duh Rabbit wife.

What has seldom been remarked upon is the fact that West African archetypes, like Annancy, are almost the exclusive inheritance of the Caribbean and the Guyanas whereas East African or Bantu archetypes (Hare, Tortoise) feature largely in tales of the Gullah and the American South. Speculation on the reasons for this have led into all kinds of blind alleys but it is at least clear why these African folk figures play the roles of trickster and underdog.

Observe closely the qualities of Hare (Rabbit). He occupies a disadvantageous position in the animal world. Extremely vulnerable, without a heavy hide, claws, beak, or sting, his fragility is counterbalanced by an extraordinary sensitivity (huge antennae for ears) and a lightning nimbleness (fleetness of foot). Though he may seem, therefore, an easy prey to the larger animals, the potential for outmaneuvering them belies his apparent fragility. In the body and spirit of Hare, therefore, is crystallized a subtle and delicate radar for scanning the potential peril (which he averts) and the potential possibility (which he exploits) in a given situation—a situation usually (in those tales most native to the tradition) of menace from the Mighty. A typical tale told by Uncle Remus is that of Brer Rabbit and Brer Lion, in which Rabbit is invited to offer up his life for Lion's supper and is so adept in his survival strategy that Lion dies wrestling with his own fearful shadow.

In a review of the Uncle Remus tales, Bernard Wolfe (1949) sees these not only as manifestations of the Black man's protest against the system and his sadistic delight in sabotaging the schemes or outraging the morality of his overlords, but also as manifestations of the White man's guilt and his masochistic delight in seeing the Black man (in his guise as the Rabbit) overcome, outrage, or negate him. Wolfe observes that the little White boy, Marse John, listens to Uncle Remus, the old Negro, with a mixture of fear and admiration and that this admiration (which he finds to be particularly strong in Joel Chandler Harris, the Southern White collector of the tales) corresponds to a certain vicarious identification of the White man with the Black: "For Harris as well as for many white Americans the Negro seemed to be in every respect the opposite of his own anxious self: unworried, gregarious, voluble, muscularly relaxed, never a victim of boredom ... unashamadly exhibitionistic, devoid of self-pity in his condition of concentrated suffering, exuberant ... [Wolfe, 1949, p. 896]."

Wolfe, however, feels there is an ambivalence in the feelings of Whites in the South about these stories. They are not only harassed by guilt accompanied by a desire to revel in the Negro's hatred of themselves, but also by a protective instinct to shield themselves from their own masochistic unconscious. They have, therefore, attempted to drain these stories of their own aggressive potential, saying, for example that "the Black man makes all the animals behave like a lower order of human intelligence" as the Black man feels "he is in closer touch with the lower animals than the White man."

Wolfe sums this up in his article "L'Oncle Remus et son lapin" *Les Temps Modernes*, May, 1949:

> The Remus stories are a monument to the ambivalence of the South. Harris, the archetype of the Southerner, went in search of the Negro's love and claimed that he had won it (the eternal grin of Uncle Remus). But at the same time he was striving for the Negro's hatred (Brer Rabbit) and he revelled in it, in an unconscious orgy of masochism—punishing himself .... Certainly no one is *compelled* to read stories of Negroes who make love to white women (*Deep are the Roots, Strange Fruit, Uncle Remus*), of whites who learn they are Negroes (*Kingsblood Royal, Lost Boundaries, Uncle Remus*), of white men strangled by black men (*Native Son, If He Hollers Let Him Go, Uncle Remus*) ... [p. 898].

Franz Fanon (1952) also sees these fables as "working off the black man's aggression" and this aggression being justified by "the white man's unconscious [which] gives it worth by turning it on himself." What I find rather strange is that this aggression is of a gentler nature in America than what we find in the Caribbean tales of Annancy. Is it diluted by passing through (most of it anyway) the filter of Chandler Harris, the Southern White collector, and his creation, the old gentle Negro, Uncle Remus? Is it that the contradiction between the White man's masochism and his protective instinct did in fact temper the heat of the Black man's aggression in the figure of Rabbit? There is no easy answer to these questions. But it has often been remarked that while Brer Rabbit in the American South is merely mischievous, Annancy in the Caribbean is a venomous and malignant creature.

Assuming this to be the case, I venture to suggest that the spider in the folk mythology of the Caribbean has taken on the configuration of the mudcrab (whom he so closely resembles). He can be as vicious as the crab struggling in a barrel of crabs to get out of his cramped position. He must move against all and everything in order to free himself. Whereas in Africa we sometimes see Annancy functioning on behalf of the collective we often find this creature in the Caribbean callously following his individual bent, his very attempt to free himself of the system involving an outrageous assault on both the oppressor and the oppressed. The collective had some functional reality in traditional Africa but in the colonial limbo the common mass had no relationship to the sources of social control and power. Like the crab coming out of the barrel one could only succeed at times by climbing with a relentless viciousness upon the backs of other crabs.

The tortoise is another symbol of the underdog in Bantu mythology. In fact he is more popular than the hare in some parts of East Africa. His main virtue is his capacity to endure for he can live longer without food than any other animal. He moves with a painstaking slowness, but with the sureness of the sun in motion across the streets of the world, and this impresses itself upon the Bantu mind as the unrelenting and invincible doggedness of an elemental force. The brooding silence and secrecy of the tortoise also invest him with a suggestion of craft and cunning and mystery. He hides his innards under a shell in the way the Black had to hide his true face and feelings in the Americas under shells and veils and masks of deception in order to carry and conceal the horror at the heart of his daily life.

In the final section of this presentation I would like to deal with the linguistic aspect of our Gullah research. Lorenzo Turner has done the definitive job in this field, establishing the African background for most of the features in Gullah which distinguish it from Standard English. Our task, therefore, has been made much easier. We were concerned to discover whether these distinctions were still in force, whether Gullah had appreciably changed between Turner's tape-collecting expeditions in the late 1920's and early 1930's and ours nearly 50 years later in the early 1970's. A list of distinctions between Gullah and Standard English is presented hereunder, their African origins outlined, and these distinctions are illustrated by sentences or phrases from our 1970, 1971 tape transcriptions. The list clearly shows that, whatever surface transformations in Gullah may have occurred through urban impact upon the islands in the past half century, the important African influence—the influence on grammar—remains the same as in Turner's day.

These distinctions, it should be borne in mind, are not only of relevance to the Gullah dialect of the Sea Islands but may be found also for the most part in forms of Black English throughout the Caribbean and Guyana and other areas of Black America. Obviously, there are not as many such distinctions preserved in the urban Black dialects of North America, where only half of them are still in popular use, but in the English-speaking Caribbean and Guyana the parallels are as many and as close and establish Gullah as a crucial link in the interhemispheral chain of Black English forms. This list, therefore, though primarily prepared as an index of distinctions between Gullah and Standard English, may in fact be viewed as a tentative outline of a Black English grammar.

1. In Gullah there is an absence of gender distinction, that is, the distinction between masculine, feminine, and neuter is not expressed in the

pronouns "he," "she," and "it." Thus Jane Hunter, in her story of the Rabbit and the Partridge, uses *his* and *her* indiscriminately to refer to the Partridge: "so one day Partridge take *her* head an' stick *he* head unduh *he* wing." Also, in her story of *Mannuhs an' No-Mannuhs*, when the old lady calls on the bad boy (No-Mannuhs chile) to cut her some firewood, we find the referents "e" and "im" for the Standard English "she." Thus, "so dehs two brudduh en *a ole lady* live way pon duh hill en *'e* say, *im* say 'Son . . . ah . . . comere, cut piece o' wood fo me.' "

West African languages have other methods of indicating gender rather than relying on pronoun case. In both of the examples just quoted it is obvious from the context that the Partridge is feminine and that it is the old lady, not one of the boys, who is speaking. Sometimes, as in Ga and Yoruba, a word meaning "woman" or "man" would be prefixed to the noun (or in Kimbundu, Mandinka, and Fante, added to specific nouns) to indicate gender. We find this practice carried forward both in the Caribbean (one day Brer Annancy sen *gal Annancy* fe go a Brer Deat' yaad) and in Gullah (de snake gone en structid dis *chillun gal*).

Gender distinction by reference to pronouns is also absent from Bantu languages. In Swahili, for example, *a-na-kuja* could mean he, she, or *it* (an animal) is coming. The prefix *a*, which is equivalent to the English pronoun *he, she, it* would vary to indicate the class of the subject—living creature or tree, something large or long (giant/snake), something expressing a collectivity (teeth/eyes), an abstract quality (beauty/folly), an inanimate object (chair), or a very small thing (baby)—all these sophisticated niceties of distinction, but *not* gender. Turner says practically nothing about Bantu in his study but it should be noted here that, while the West African linguistic influence is the most relevant the Bantu complex cannot be completely ignored. Many Black slaves of North America came from the Lower Congo, which is within the Bantu culture complex. In fact, the Gullah examples quoted above are taken from tales which have their origin in Bantu folklore.

2. In Gullah, the plural marker used in Standard English is absent. Almost all Gullah nouns have the same form in the plural as in the singular. Plurality may be expressed by number only, as in the following examples:

(a) "an' das *tree paat* right deh . . . no, das *two paat* fo' sell (Wine)."

(b) "den you cud git a yaad o' clawt jes only fuh *tree cent* uhr *five cent* (Wine)."

Plurality may also be expressed by a qualifier (like the pronoun "dese" or "dem") or a type of phrase (houseful o' gyurl) that indicates clearly that more than one of something is involved:

(a) "each one *dem milepos'* you get to, you breaken ah egg an' it tun a blessing fa you (Hunter)."

(b) "I forget all *dem ting* now (Wine)."

Many West African languages use the same noun form for plural and singular as Gullah does. Ibo and Kongo are among these. Ga and Yoruba form plurals by adding qualifiers (like the pronouns *these* and *them*) or numerical adjectives (*two,three*) before or after the noun. Another method of indicating the plural is found in Ewe where the third person pronoun (them) comes after the noun. This is quite frequent in the Caribbean (an *Crab dem* cudden hear Annancy at all). Our tape expedition turned up examples also in the Gullah islands ('an each one *dem milepos'* you git to, you break *one dem* egg).

3. In Gullah there is no possessive marker. Possession is expressed by the juxtaposition of the possessor to the thing possessed:

(a) " 'an Rabbit have love de *Wolf gyul* mo dan he does his gyul (Hunter),"

(b) "De gyul say, 'Not Mr. Wolf, not Mr. Wolf, you nevuh ride my *boyfriend back'* (Hunter)."

Several West African languages, such as Ibo, do not use possessive markers. In Ibo the noun's position in the sentence shows whether it is in the possessive case. Ewe has no possessive case in the names of relationships. Again, where Standard English makes a distinction between nominative (he, she) and possessive (his, her) forms of personal pronouns, the nominative and possessive forms in Gullah are the same. Thus we have

(a) all duh res' wuh *he wife* tell im;

(b) duh Patrid take *'e head* from unduhnea' *he wing*.

This sameness in nominative and possessive pronouns may be found in Ibo, Ga, Yoruba, and Ewe. A qualification, however, should be noted here. Miss Hunter shifted from Standard to Gullah frequently in her use of personal possessive pronouns. Even when she did this, however, the primary rules of Gullah emerged strongly. Thus in her sentence—*Patrid take her head stick he head undernea' he wing*—the initial pull to Standard English as she began her story gave way to the stronger inner drift toward Gullah, which not only canceled out the use of a personal possessive pronoun like *her* but also the gender distinction implicit in its use.

4. Gullah frequently does not display the same past tense marker used in Standard English. A Gullah verb is often the same in both present and past tenses. Standard would have given us, in the following sentence,

the past tense forms *got, broke, jumped, shot,* and *killed:* "Nex milepos' he get dere, he break de egg, a man jump out, shoot im an' kill im. Das wat he get fo be bad (Hunter)."

Other clues in the Gullah sentence may indicate the past tense. Phrases like "in my time-comin" or "yestuhday" and "lass mont" may carry the time information or a Gullah word like *binnuh* may be placed before the verb to indicate the past tense (as well as the perfect and pluperfect). Thus, *You binnuh walk een briah patch since you bawn.*

Looking to Africa again for grammatical roots, one finds that tense may be expressed not by something added to the verb, as is usual in English (jump-*ed*, kill-*ed*), or an alteration in the form of the verb (got,broke,shot), but by another verb or noun in what we may call a "verbal complex." This is the case in Ewe. We also find a number of West African languages, like Yoruba, where the past and present verb forms are the same.

5. In Gullah there is the absence of the third person singular present tense marker: "*What bark heah bite yonder?* (Hunter)" for "What bark(s) here and bite(s) there (Standard)."

Ewe, Fante, Yoruba, and Ga are among West African languages where the verb forms remain unchanged through the singular and plural number.

6. In Gullah the definite article is often absent. It is usually used to indicate something specific or to refer back to something previously mentioned. This use of the definite article almost exclusively for specificity and referentiality is characteristic of many African languages. Examples in Gullah are the following:

(a) "*Shackle wear dis out. Shackle wear dat out* (Guinea)."

(b) "*Das why you fren is duh one who gets you, enemy who come an accosh you* (Hunter)." Note here the presence of the definite article in the first half of the sentence and its absence in the second half. It is your friend who is the one to be careful of (specific); Enemies will attack you (general). It is your friend, of course, who is the enemy but that is already implied and needs no emphasis through the use of the definite article.

(c) "*Is de same dance ri' now ... they jes change rung, diffrunt name ... Mash Potato, yes it is, das Charleston, Mash Potato das Charleston* (Hunter)."

7. There is a frequent absence of the copula—the verb "to be"—where it would normally occur in Standard English. The absence of the copula occurs in several types of constructions. I shall confine myself to a discussion of one of these, the construction which contains what is known as a predicate adjective:

(a) "I know my *people poor*. I doan need kill 'em (Guinea)."

(b) "Das why he *tail white* (Hunter)."

(c) "Das why *you weak* today ... *you wise* alright, *you wise*, got plenty o' sense (Wine)."

In these constructions, what in Standard would be called adjectives, "poor, white, weak, wise," are not linked by the copula "are" or "is" to the nouns "people, tail" or to the pronoun "you." In some West African languages "to be white" or "to be weak" would be one word in itself. The verb "to be" and the adjective "white" or "weak" etc. would be compounded. One word serving both functions of verb and adjective—*the verbal adjective*—cancels out the need for a link word or copula. Thus, in Fante the word *hwa* means "to be white," in Yoruba *dũ* means "to be sweet," and in Mandinka *kidi* means "to be lonely." Within these verbs the concept expressed by *copula plus adjective* in Standard English is fully contained. This can account for most copula deletions in Gullah.

8. Gullah has no passive voice. Black English verb forms are always active. Take the following sentence from Alice Wine's description of preparations for winter: "Deh plant plenty o' potato an' bank it up an' peas an put 'em in de barrel an' turnip, deh sweeten dat in de bank an' potato, deh sweeten dat in de bank an' de hog, deh cyo' it (Wine)." In Standard this would in most cases be expressed thus: "Plenty of potatoes and peas and turnips are planted and banked in barrels. Potatoes are sweetened in the barrel banks and the hog's meat is also stored and cured there."

West African languages which have no distinctions in voice include Ewe, Yoruba, Twi, Fante, and Ga.

9. The Gullah use a number of words which, although they resemble English words in sound, function in Gullah in the way their African equivalents would function. For example, the word *go* means "to" or "toward" after a verb of motion (Rabbit, he jump off an' *run go* home). In Ewe the word for go (yi) when following a verb of motion also means "to" or "toward." Also, in both Ewe and Fante, the word for *go* or *go away* means "and" or "in order to" if it connects two verbs. The same is found in Gullah. Thus, "Once a man have tree daughter. Dem go *go* pick wacky."

The word *fa*, which is sometimes confused with the dialect distortion of *for* (fo', fuh), is from the Twi language and may be translated as "intend to, choose to, must" according to its context. It is another word in this category of English-looking words with African-type functions in Gullah but we can quote no good examples of this from our tape transcriptions though they abound in Turner's work.

The use of sɛ, however, even after the word "say" or "tell," which would seem to the untrained ear to be simple duplication occurs in several of Jane Hunter's stories: " 'E give bote o' em fo' eggs an' *tell em say,* 'On duh way going, dehs fo' milepost, an' each one dem milepos' you git to, see, yuh break one dem egg.' "

Sɛ (or say) here really means *that.* The sound sɛ, when occurring in Gullah after a verb of saying, thinking, or wishing, always means "that." This use of sɛ is common in some West African languages, including Twi and Ibo. Its resemblance to an English word explains why it has been retained in common speech while functioning in the way a similar sound functions in certain African languages.

10. Gullah uses what may be called the double negative or the multiple negative, that is, negation is expressed not once, as in Standard English, but twice or several times at various parts of the sentence. Thus,

(a) "Dat *aint no* business fo me. *Cyaan* learn *nuttin* like dat (Wine)."
(b) "I *doan* write *nobody no* letter (Guinea)."
(c) "Jesus *didden* need *no* baptize but he let John baptize im in de river (Hunter)."

The double or multiple negative arises out of the presence of several negatable elements in the verb or verbal complex in African languages. Negative inversion is also another feature of Gullah which has its roots in African languages but our tape expedition turned up no example. *"Don't nobody know* wat Nixon got on dose tapes" would be an example of this but it is not a very common construction.

11. Gullah frequently duplicates words also in conversation and, particularly in narrative, words and phrases are often repeated. This may be done, as in West African languages, for emphasis, for rhythm, and in sermons, testimonials, and prayers, as an oratorical device.

(a) "O yeah, *looky heah, looky heah,* I kin show all dese heah (Guinea)."
(b) *"You eat it, you eat it, you eat it* kuz you dere an' you cyaan get nuttin from home ... you eidduh take dat or jes *lay down dere, lay down dere* an' die (Guinea)."
(c) *"He driving, he driving going* home an' he didden pay no attention, look back in de cart at de fish an' dat rabbit put everyone dat ole man fish *in de bush, ri' in de bush* (Hunter)."

12. Gullah sometimes places the adjective after the noun as in West African languages, like Fante, Ewe, and Twi: "I radder do dat kuz you doan wuk in *sunhot* (Wine)."

13. Gullah maintains the same order in interrogative and declarative sentences. A shift in intonation, as in West African languages (such as

Ibo, Kikongo, and Efik) is all that is needed to indicate that a question is being asked as against a statement being made. Thus:

(*a*) "O, deh give you eight uhr nine dollah a day now but wat good it is? (Wine)"

(*b*) "Why 'e say dat? I askin you a question now, why the Bible say, 'weak an' wise?' (Wine)"

14. The subject or object is stated in Gullah, then repeated by the use of a personal pronoun, then a statement is made about the subject. This word order is common in Yoruba, Ewe, Kimbundu, and Kongo languages:

(*a*) "Then you *cow, he* give you milk . . . you *chicken, he* give you egg (Wine)."

(*b*) "So old *Rabbit, he* jump off and run go home (Hunter)."

15. In Gullah we find the use of groups of words for the Standard English equivalent of a noun, verb, or adverb:

(*a*) "In my *time-comin* all chillun have a sutten 'mount o' work to do evvyday (Guinea)."

(*b*) "But is bettuh time *down yonder* dan is dere now (Wine)."

This is particularly true of phrases expressing time, as the above for the past, and *rebel time* (a Turner example) for the era of slavery. Others, like *crack e teet* (smile) *jes az it come out 'e mout* (verbatim) are concrete images as opposed to more formal abstractions. To what extent this greater tendency to image-making is African influenced and to what extent it is a natural preference and response to an unfamiliar word or a too formal or impersonal a concept it would be hard to say. In Guyana, for example, even in fairly formal parlance, I would prefer to say "I'm going to see 'the eye-man' " rather than the oculist or optometrist. This is not only preferable on grounds of simplicity but a concrete image is immediately projected. Image-making on a far more extended scale than one would find in Standard English is a feature of Gullah and all Black English dialects.

16. Gullah makes use of the habitual tense which has no equivalent in Standard English. It indicates an habitual action. To convey the same concept in Standard English would necessitate the addition of a qualifying word or phrase:

(*a*) "*We be out trying* to keep up with everything that's going on (Bill Saunders)."

(*b*) "De 'umble chile, das da one *be honorable* (Hunter)."

(*c*) "I doan feel like *be going* to the barber all da time so's I leave me head home for my wife to shave (Hunter)."

The habitual tense has its roots in West African languages and in the Bantu languages of East and South Africa. These languages place more emphasis on the "mode of action" than on the "time of action." Rather than focusing on whether a verb tense (time) is past, present, or future they focus on whether the action indicated is habitual, completed, conditional, or obligatory.

There are a number of other distinctions which may be noted, such as the way the comparative and superlative degrees of the adjective are formed in Gullah, the basic or indicative form (big, for example) remaining unchanged in the comparative (big mo'nuh or mo'dan) and the superlative (big 'pass alla). No good, illustrative example from our field trip is available but Turner has noted the basic form of the adjective does not change in certain West African languages and the verb meaning to surpass ('pass) is used with the basic form of the adjective to express comparative and superlative degrees in Ewe, Twi, Fante, Ibo, Kimbundu, Mandinka, and Kikongo.

We could also point to other features of Gullah like the elision of sounds at the end of some words (doan instead of don't, cyan instead of can't, for example) because of the tendency of African languages to follow a vowel/consonant/vowel pattern and to avoid a clustering of consonants, particularly in final position. These, however, are phonological rather than syntactic considerations and take us into an entirely new field.

While in the Gullah Sea Islands we observed African influence in the art and craft of basketmaking, walking sticks, iron cooking pots, fishing nets, and stools, and African influence on cuisine, herbal medicine, folk beliefs, and riddles. We observed also the impact of African music and motor behavior on the rituals of the church, but these observations we feel were far too brief and superficial to form the basis for any authoritative statement or analysis. Other investigators, like Dr. Herman Blake, head of the Kinte Oral Tradition Project on Dafuskie Island, are now conducting extended and intensive investigations into these and other cultural areas. On a recent visit to St. Helena island as a consultant for the Kinte Project, I learned of plans for the development of a Gullah museum to preserve the history and tradition of these islands. We need not fear, therefore, the total loss of Gullah art and artifact which have been kept fairly intact over the last three centuries. No museum, however, is needed for the oral tradition. It is a tradition very much alive in the way the Sea Islanders speak and in the way also many of them think, a tradition enshrined in the language and mythology of the folk, a tradition which, in spite of its many locations and variants in the Black world, has a common root, a common ground in the linguistic and mythological structures of Africa.

ACKNOWLEDGMENTS

Tape recordings upon which this work is based were done on Johns Island and James Island, and in Charleston, South Carolina in the fall of 1970 and 1971. These trips were financed by the Dean's Fund, Douglass College, Rutgers University.

The tape recordings were put into broad and phonetic transcription by my research assistant, Mrs. Elizabeth Farrah, a speech therapist and phonetician, with the help of a grant awarded me by the Rutgers Research Council in 1972.

REFERENCES

Abrahams, R. Trickster, the outrageous hero. *In* T. Coffin (Ed.), *Our living traditions*. New York: Basic Books, 1968. P. 171.

Bennett, J. Gullah: A negro patois. *The South Atlantic Quarterly*, 1908, **7**, 332–347.

Crum, M. *Gullah: Negro life in the Carolina sea islands*. Chapel Hill, N.C.: Duke University Press, 1940. Reprinted by Negro University Press, 1968.

Fanon, F. *Black skin, white masks*. (Translated by Charles Markmann.) London: Paladin, 1970. P. 125. Originally published as *Peau noire, masque blancs,* Paris: Editions de Seuil, 1952.

Gonzalez, A. *The black border*. Columbia, S.C.: The State Company, 1922. Reprint, The State Printing Company 1964.

Johnson, G. B. *Folk culture of St. Helena Island, South Carolina,* Chapel Hill, N.C.: University of North Carolina Press, 1930.

Jones, C. C. *Negro myths from the Georgia coast*. Boston: Houghton-Mifflin, 1888. Reprinted by The State Co., Columbia, 1925. Reissued by Singing Free Press, Book Tower, Detroit, 1969.

Krapp, G. P. The English of the American negro. *American Mercury*, 1939, **2**, 190–195.

Stoney, S. G., & Shelby, G. M. *Black genesis*. New York: Macmillan, 1930.

Turner, L. D. *Africanisms in the Gullah dialect*. Chicago: University of Chicago Press, 1939. Reprinted by Arno Press, New York, 1969.

Van Sertima, I. African linguistic and mythological structures in the new world. In R. Goldstein (Ed.), *Black life and culture*. New York: Thomas Crowell & Sons, 1971. Pp. 12–35.

Wolfe, B. L'Oncle Remus et son lapin. In *Les temps modernes*. Paris, 1949.

Part III
USE

8

The Sounds of Black English

William G. Moulton

Princeton University

1. INTRODUCTION

In this chapter we shall discuss the sound systems of Black English, and how they differ from the sound systems of Standard English—the English usually spoken, for example, by radio announcers, whether black or white. We cannot speak of either "the" sound system of Black English, or "the" sound system of Standard English, because in each case there are several of them. Furthermore, though speakers of Black English may use sound systems rather different from those of Standard English when they speak informally, their pronunciation may come closer and closer to that of Standard English as they speak more and more formally. Black English therefore shows two types of variation: first, a variation within itself, from system to system; and second, a variation between these systems and those of Standard English.

Paradoxically, we shall devote more time to Standard English than to Black English. For this there are two reasons. First, this is the best way of making clear to you, the reader, what is meant by "sound systems," and how one can go about analyzing and describing them. Second, as you investigate a variety of Black English, you will inevitably use your own sound system as a point of departure. You will want to note the differences between your system and that of the Black English you are investigating; and the most efficient way of doing this is to start off with a good understanding of your own system. Our discussion of Black English will consist largely of alerting you to some of the differences you should watch out for and may expect to find.

149

2. PHONEMES

When we try to figure out the sound system of a language, or of a variety of language, our first task is to try to identify those differences in sound which correlate with differences in meaning. For example, the words *pit* and *bit* obviously differ in sound; they obviously differ in meaning; and this difference in sound (*p* versus *b*) correlates with this difference in meaning (the meaning of *pit* versus the meaning of *bit*). The same thing is true of such a pair of words as *rip* and *rib*. Here again a difference in sound (*p* versus *b*) correlates with a difference in meaning (*rip* versus *rib*).

In cases like these we say that the initial sounds of *pit* and *bit* represent different PHONEMES, and so also with the final sounds of *rip* and *rib*. To distinguish them from the letters of ordinary spelling, we write symbols for phonemes between slant lines: the phoneme /p/ (as in *pit, rip*) the phoneme /b/ (as in *bit, rib*).

We must speak of "phonemes" rather than of "sounds" because a given phoneme such as /p/ can be realized in sound in different ways. First, if any one of us pronounces a word such as *pit* five times in a row, no two of our pronunciations are absolutely identical; there are always slight differences. (We can compare this with handwriting. When any one of us writes the word *pit* five times in a row, no two of the marks we make on paper are absolutely identical; there are again always slight differences.) Second, when two people pronounce a word such as *pit*, their pronunciations are different (just as their handwritings are different); if nothing else, the differences in sound will tell us whether it was John Smith or Jack Robinson who was speaking. Third, phonemes are often realized in sound quite differently depending on what precedes and/or follows them. At the beginning of a word (as in *pie*), English /p/ is realized in sound with a following outflow of air called "aspiration" that is strong enough to blow out a match (try it!); but after /s/ (as in *spy*) there is no such aspiration, and a match flame will hardly even flicker (try it!). (We can again compare this with handwriting. When we write *tap*, the initial stroke of the *p* begins on the line—because it follows *a*; but when we write *top*, the initial stroke of the *p* begins above the line—because it follows *o*.)

We must distinguish symbols for phonemes from the letters of ordinary spelling for three reasons. Our English spelling system is basically phonemic, as in *pit, bit, rip, rib*, which are also phonemically /pit bit rip rib/. Yet our ordinary spelling is often quite unphonemic. First, one and the same spelling often symbolizes different phonemes. The spelling *gh* symbolizes /g/ in *ghost*, /f/ in *tough*, /p/ in *hiccough*, and nothing at all in *though*. Second, different spellings often symbolize the same phoneme.

The words *pear*, *pair*, *pare* are spelled differently, but they are phonemically the same. Finally, our English alphabet contains only 26 letters, but all varieties of English contain more than 26 phonemes. Hence we shall have to go beyond the regular alphabet in order to symbolize the additional phonemes. We shall use such special symbols as /č/ for the initial phoneme of *chin*, /ī/ for the vowel of *see*, etc. See below.

With a little experimenting we can determine the number of phonemes in any given word. Consider again the word *pit* /pit/. There are three places in this word where a change in sound will correlate with a change in meaning. A change in the initial segment will give such different words as *bit* /bit/, *chit* /čit/, *mitt* /mit/. A change in the middle segment will give such different words as *peat* /pīt/, *pat* /pæt/, *pet* /pet/. And a change in the final segment will give such different words as *pig* /pig/, *pick* /pik/, *pill* /pil/. Since each of these three changes in sound correlates with a change in meaning, *pit* contains at least three phonemes; and since there are no further places where a change in sound correlates with a change in meaning, *pit* contains no more than three phonemes.

3.   THE CONSONANTS OF STANDARD ENGLISH

Once we have identified the phonemes of a language, our next task is to figure out the SYSTEM which they form. We can illustrate this notion of "system" by examining the consonants of Standard English.

Consider first the phonemes /p t č k/, as in the following set of words:

pin /pin/   tin /tin/   chin /čin/   kin /kin/

All four of these phonemes share the same MANNER OF PRONUNCIATION. We make a closure somewhere in the mouth; we then build up air pressure behind this closure; and we then break the closure, letting the breath stream flow out with an audible noise. Sounds produced in this way are called STOPS, because the breath stream is momentarily "stopped."

Though these four phonemes share the same manner of pronunciation (they are all "stops"), they have different PLACES OF PRONUNCIATION. For /p/ the closure is at the lips, and this is therefore a LABIAL STOP. For /t/ the closure is between the tip of the tongue and the area at or above the upper teeth; this is therefore a DENTAL STOP. For /č/ the closure is between the front of the tongue and the front of the hard palate; this is therefore a PALATAL STOP. And for /k/ the closure is between the back of the tongue and the soft palate or velum; this is therefore a VELAR STOP.

Before we consider some further consonant phonemes of English, we need to introduce the notion of "voice." Try the following experiment. Stick a finger in each ear and pronounce first the phoneme /z/ (as in *buzz*) and then the phoneme /s/ (as in *bus*). Try going back and forth from one to the other: /z/—/s/—/z/—/s/. Every time you pronounce /z/ you will hear a loud buzzing in your ears, but the buzzing disappears every time you pronounce /s/. This buzzing is technically called VOICE, and it is produced by vibration of the vocal cords. When we pronounce /z/ the vocal cords are held loosely together, and as the breath stream flows out between them it makes them vibrate. When we pronounce /s/, on the other hand, the vocal cords are pulled wide apart and the breath stream has no effect on them as it flows out.

The stop phonemes /p t č k/ that we considered above are all VOICE-LESS. That is to say, they are pronounced without any buzzing of the vocal cords. But what would be the result if, to these voiceless stops, we added the buzzing that is called "voice"? The answer is that we would get the VOICED STOPS /b d ǰ g/, as in the following examples:

bet /bet/   debt /det/   jet /jet/   get /get/

This device of adding voice is very ingenious. It immediately enables us in English to double the number of stops. We now have not only the four voiceless stops /p t č k/, but also the corresponding voiced stops /b d ǰ g/.

We can summarize the system of English consonant phonemes consid-ered thus far in the following diagram:

	Labial	Dental	Palatal	Velar
Stops	p, b	t, d	č, ǰ	k, g

The eight consonant phonemes listed above are all "stops" because in their pronunciation the breath stream is momentarily stopped as it flows out. This is one manner of pronunciation. A second manner or pronuncia-tion is that of forcing air through a narrow opening so as to produce audi-ble friction. Sounds produced in this way are called FRICATIVES. Standard English has eight consonant phonemes of this type. There are four voice-less fricatives: /f θ s š/, as in *fin* /fin/, *thin* /θin/, *sin* /sin/, *shin* /šin/. And there are four corresponding voiced fricatives: /v ð z ž/, as in *clove* /klōv/, *clothe* /klōð/, (*to*) *close* /klōz/, *azure* /æžər/. We can diagram them as follows:

	Labial	Dental	Palatal	Velar
Plain fricatives	f, v	θ, ð	( )	( )
Sibilant fricatives		s, z	š, ž	

Plain fricatives are produced by forcing air through a slit-shaped opening: voiceless /f/ and /θ/, voiced /v/ and /ð/. Sibilant fricatives are produced by forcing air through a groove-shaped opening: voiceless /s/ and /š/, voiced /z/ and /ž/. Sibilant fricatives are always either dental (/s/

and /z/) or palatal (/š/ and /ž/). Plain fricatives, on the other hand, may be labial (/f/ and /v/), dental (/θ/ and /ð/), palatal, or velar. English does not happen to have any plain palatal or velar fricatives, but many other languages do. In German, for example, the sound spelled *ch* in *ich* 'I' is a voiceless plain palatal fricative; and the sound spelled *ch* in *ach* 'oh' is a voiceless plain velar fricative.

All of the English consonants considered thus far are ORAL: the breath stream flows out only through the mouth, because the exit at the back of the mouth that leads out through the nose has been closed off. There is, however, still another manner of pronunciation: that used for the types of sounds that are called NASALS. English examples are: the /m/ of *ram*, the /n/ of *ran*, and the /ŋ/ of *rang*. In this type of sound, (1) there is a closure somewhere in the mouth (labial for /m/, dental for /n/, velar for /ŋ/); (2) the exit at the back of the mouth that leads out through the nose is open, and the breath stream flows out through it; and (3) the vocal cords vibrate (that is to say, the English nasals /m n ŋ/ are voiced—though some languages also use voiceless nasals). We can now diagram the system of English consonant phonemes as follows:

	Labial	Dental	Palatal	Velar
Stops	p, b	t, d	č, ǰ	k, g
Plain fricatives	f, v	θ, ð	( )	( )
Sibilant fricatives		s, z	š, ž	
Nasals	m	n	( )	ŋ

Though English does not happen to have a palatal nasal, many other languages do. Examples are Spanish, where it is spelled *ñ*: *español* 'Spanish', *señor* 'Mr.'; and French, where it is spelled *gn*: *agneau* 'lamb', *digne* 'worthy'.

We now have three manners of articulation: (1) stops (/p, b t, d č, ǰ k, g/); (2) fricatives (plain /f, v θ, ð/), sibilant /s, z š, ž/); and (3) nasals (/m n ŋ/). A fourth manner of articulation is that of the LIQUIDS—sounds like our English /l/ (as in *leaf* /līf/, *feel* /fīl/) and our English /r/ (as in *reef* /rīf/, *fear* /fīr/). Liquids are pronounced not by stopping the breath stream momentarily (as for stops), not by forcing the breath stream out through a narrow opening (as for fricatives), and not by letting the breath stream flow out through the nose (as for nasals). Instead, the breath stream flows out freely through the mouth but is "steered" in special ways. In the case of /l/, it is steered out along one or both sides of the tongue, and sounds like /l/ are therefore called "laterals" (i.e., "side sounds"). In the case of /r/, it is steered along a constriction of the tongue, and the tongue tip is often curled up toward the roof of the mouth. The pronunciation of liquids is very similar to that of vowels: they differ from vowels only in the special "steering" that is given to the breath stream. If this special steering is given up, the liquids are "vocalized" and become vowels. As we shall see later, /l/ and /r/ are both commonly vocalized in Black English. And /r/ is vocalized in the Standard English of those speakers who pronounce *fear* as "fea-uh", *four* as "fou-uh," etc.

A fifth manner of pronunciation is that of the SEMIVOWELS, i.e., the /y/ of *yet* /yet/ and the /w/ of *wet* /wet/. These differ from true vowels only in that they do not form the centers of syllables. For example, if say *to itch* at normal speed it is /tū ič/, with two syllables; but if we speed it up so that it gives only one syllable, the result is *twitch* /twič/. That is to say, /w/ is the (nonsyllabic) semivowel that corresponds to the (syllabic) vowel /ū/. Similarly, if we say such a nonsense form as *key oot* at normal speed it is /kī ūt/ with two syllables; but if we speed it up so that it gives only one syllable, the result is *cute* /kyūt/. That is to say, /y/ is the (nonsyllabic) semivowel that corresponds to the (syllabic) vowel /ī/.

We have now accounted for 23 of the 24 consonant phonemes of Standard English: 4 voiceless stops (/p t č k/), 4 voiced stops (/b d ǰ g/), 4 voiceless fricatives (/f θ s š/), 4 voiced fricatives (/v ð z ž/), 3 nasals (/m n ŋ/), 2 liquids (/l/ and /r/), and 2 semivowels (/y/ and /w/). The twenty-fourth consonant phoneme is rather special: it is the /h/ of *hit* /hit/, *hat* /hæt/, *ahead* /əhed/, etc. In terms of manner of pronunciation it is a fricative: the breath stream flows out through an opening and produces audible friction. It differs from all other fricatives, however, in two ways: (1) the opening is not narrow, (2) the opening is not "localized," i.e., it is neither labial, dental, palatal, nor velar. We can best describe it as a NONLOCALIZED FRICATIVE, comparable to the sound that is produced by blowing air through a pipe.

We can diagram the full system of consonant phonemes in Standard English as follows:

	Labial	Dental	Palatal	Velar
Stops	p, b	t, d	č, ǰ	k, g
Plain fricatives	f, v	θ, ð	( )	( )
Sibilant fricatives		s, z	š, ž	
Nasals	m	n	( )	ŋ
Liquids		l r		
Semivowels		w y		
Nonlocalized		h		

4. THE CONSONANTS OF BLACK ENGLISH

All varieties of Standard English have the system of 24 consonant phonemes just described. In the variety of Black English which you are investigating, you will probably find again this same system—though with two variations. These concern voiceless /θ/ (the *th* of *thick, thin, tooth, south*) and voiced /ð/ (the *th* of *this, that, brother, rather*). This variation between Standard English and Black English is not random and unpredictable, however. Instead, it is highly systematic. We can diagram it as follows:

	Labial	Dental	Palatal	Velar
Stops	p, b	t, d	č, ǰ	k, g
Plain fricatives	f, v	← θ, ð		

Voiceless /θ/

You will probably find that this is frequently replaced by the corresponding voiceless dental stop /t/, so that *thick* is pronounced as "tick," *thin* as "tin," etc. Or that it is replaced by the corresponding voiceless labial fricative /f/, so that *tooth* is pronounced as "toof," *south* as "souf," etc.

Voiced /ð/

You will probably find that this is frequently replaced by the corresponding voiced dental stop /d/, so that *this* is pronounced as "dis," *that* as "dat," etc., or that it is replaced by the corresponding voiced labial fricative /v/, so that *brother* is pronounced as "bruvver," *rather* as "ravver," etc.

It is worth noting that the replacement of /θ/ by /t/ or /f/, and the replacement of /ð/ by /d/ or /v/, are by no means unique to Black English. Pronunciations such as "tick" and "tin" (for *thick* and *thin*) and "dis" and "dat" (for *this* and *that*) are common among nonstandard white speakers in New York City, for example. (This is part of what is often called a "Brooklyn accent.") And pronunciations such as "toof" and "souf" (for *tooth* and *south*) and "bruvver" and "ravver" (for *brother* and *rather*) are common among speakers of London "cockney" English.

A second difference that you will probably find concerns the velar nasal /ŋ/. Though Black English has this phoneme in such words as *ring, hang, wrong, sung,* you will probably find it is frequently replaced by the dental nasal /n/ in the second syllables of such words as *ringing, hanging, stocking, cutting,* giving what is often spelled as *ringin', hangin', stockin', cuttin'.* This replacement can be diagrammed as follows:

	Labial	Dental	Palatal	Velar
Nasals	m	n ←——————————— ŋ		

This replacement of velar /ŋ/ by dental /n/ is again not unique to Black English. It occurs in many other varieties of nonstandard English. And it occurs in the speech of many persons, both in the United States and in Great Britain, who otherwise speak a fully "Standard" English.

5.   CONSONANT CLUSTERS IN STANDARD ENGLISH

The phonemes of every language show two types of "system." One is the type of system that we have just shown: that formed by such consonantal features as Labial, Dental, Palatal, Velar; Voiceless and Voiced; Stops, Fricatives (plain and sibilant), Nasals, Liquids, and Semivowels.

The second type of system concerns the sequences of phonemes within words. In English, for example, words may begin with a vowel: *if* /if/; or with one consonant: *rip* /rip/; or with two consonants: *trip* /trip/; or with three consonants: *strip* /strip/; but never with *more* than three consonants. Furthermore, if a word begins with three consonants, the first is always /s/, the second one of the set /p t k/, and the third one of the set /l r w y/; examples: /spl-/ in *split,* /str-/ in *strip,* /skw-/ in *squint,* /spy-/ in *spew.* Or, to consider another type of example, the so-called FREE VOWELS of English occur not only before consonants but also at the ends of words. For example, the free vowel /ī/ occurs not only before consonants as in *beat* /bīt/ and *bead* /bīd/, but also word-finally as in *be, bee* /bī/. On the other hand, the so-called CHECKED VOWELS of English occur only before consonants and never at the ends of words. For example, the checked vowel /i/ occurs before consonants as in *bit* /bit/ and *bid*/bid/; but English has no words of the type /bi/. Still another type of example is provided by the phoneme /r/. In some varieties of English, /r/ occurs not only before vowels (as in *red* /red/, *berry* /berī/), but also before consonants (as in *cart* /kārt/), and word-finally (as in *car* /kār/). But in other varieties of English, /r/ still occurs before vowels (*red* /red/, *berry* /berī/); on the other hand, it does not occur before consonants (*cart* is /kāt/), and it does not occur word-finally (*car* is /kā/).

When two or more consonants occur in sequence, they are said to form a CONSONANT CLUSTER. We need to consider consonant clusters in some detail, because the cluster system of Black English is in part rather different from that of Standard English. Let us consider first three types of

double consonant clusters that occur word-finally: (1) Voiceless +
Voiceless; (2) Voiced + Voiced; and (3) Voiced + Voiceless; examples:

Voiceless + Voiceless			Voiced + Voiced			Voiced + Voiceless		
/-sp/	wasp	/wasp/	/-bd/	rubbed	/rəbd/	/-mp/	jump	/ǰəmp/
/-pt/	apt	/æpt/	/-ǰd/	judged	/ǰəǰd/	/-nt/	pint	/paint/
/-čt/	reached	/rīct/	/-gd/	tagged	/tægd/	/-nč/	lunch	/lənč/
/-kt/	fact	/fækt/	/-vd/	lived	/livd/	/-ŋk/	sink	/siŋk/
/-ft/	lift	/lift/	/-zd/	raised	/rēzd/	/-ns/	sense	/sens/
/-st/	test	/test/	/-md/	aimed	/ēmd/	/-lp/	help	/help/
/-št/	washed	/wašt/	/-nd/	find	/faind/	/-lt/	belt	/belt/
/-sk/	desk	/desk/	/-ld/	cold	/kōld/	/-ls/	false	/fɔls/

When speakers of Standard English speak "sloppily" (i.e., informally),
they often simplify such word-final clusters as these in interesting and
systematic ways:

1. *Voiceless + Voiceless.* The second consonant is often dropped.
This is most common when the second consonant is part of the word stem,
as in *fact* ("the *fac'* that he came") or *lift* ("*lif'* the cover"). It is less
common when the second consonant is an ending, as in *reached* ("they
reach(ed) the end") or *washed* ("I *wash(ed)* my hands"). It is least
common when a word beginning with a vowel follows immediately, as in
"the *fact is* that . . . ," "*lift it* up," "they *reached a* decision," "he
washed it."

2. *Voiced + Voiced.* The second consonant is again often dropped.
Again, this is most common when the second consonant is part of the
word stem, as in *find* ("I can't *fin'* my keys") or *cold* ("it's *col'* today").
It is less common when the second consonant is an ending, as in *rubbed*
("I *rubb(ed)* my hands") or *lived* ("he *live(d)* next door"). It is least
common when a word beginning with a vowel follows immediately, as in
"to *find it* out," "*cold or* hot," "he *rubbed it* out," "he *lived in* Boston."

3. *Voiced + Voiceless.*   In this type of double cluster the second consonant is generally *not* dropped. For example, speakers do not pronounce
jump the gun as "*jum'* the gun," or *pint bottle* as "*pin'* bottle," etc.

The Voiceless + Voiceless clusters of Type (1) above all end in voiceless
stops (/p/, /t/, or /k/). And the Voiced + Voiced clusters of Type 2
above all end in a voiced stop, namely /d/. (The /b/ and /g/ of the
Voiced + Voiced clusters /-mb/ and /-ŋg/ were dropped long ago in
Standard English, though the letters *b* and *g* are still kept in spelling.

Cf. *lamb* /læm/, *sing* /siŋ/, etc.) In addition, Standard English also has
many (4) Voiceless + Voiceless clusters ending in /s/: /-ps/ in *rips*,
/-ts/ in *hits*, /-ks/ in *looks*, /-fs/ in *reefs*, etc. And it also has many (5)
Voiced + Voiced clusters ending in /z/: /-bz/ in *ribs*, /-dz/ in *beds*,
/-gz/ in *bugs*, /-vz/ in *leaves*, /-mz/ in *rims*, /-nz/ in *pans*, /-ŋz/ in *rings*,
/-lz/ in *bells*, etc. However, unlike double clusters ending in stops (Types
(1) and (2) above), double clusters ending in fricatives (the types (4) and
(5) just given) are generally *not* simplified in Standard English. (The
one Voiced + Voiced cluster ending in /z/ that is commonly simplified
is the /-ðz/ of *clothes* /klōðz/, etc. Here, however, it is not the second
consonant that is commonly dropped but rather the first consonant:
clothes /klōz/, just like (*to*) *close*.)

In addition to the above double consonant clusters in word-final position, English also has triple consonant clusters (such as the /-ŋks/ of
banks and the /-mpt/ of *jumped*), and even quadruple consonant clusters
(the /-mpst/ of *glimpsed*). One voiceless triple cluster that behaves like
the voiceless double clusters of Type (1) above is the /-kst/ of *next* etc.
Here the final /t/ is often dropped, as in *next morning* /neks mōrniŋ/,
though it is usually kept if it is immediately followed by a word beginning
with a vowel, as in *next evening* /nekst īvniŋ/.

Six triple consonant clusters which deserve special mention are the
following:

/-skt/ asked /æskt/	/-fts/ lifts /lifts/	/-ndz/ hands /hændz/
/-kts/ facts /fækts/	/-sts/ lists /lists/	/-ldz/ fields /fīldz/

Here it is not the *last* consonant that is often dropped, but rather the
middle consonant. Examples: "that's what he *asked*" (/æst/); "tell me
the *facts*" (/fæks/); "he *lifts* it" (/lifs/); "show me the *lists*" (/liss/);
"wash your *hands*" (/hænz/); "out in the *fields*" (/fīlz/).

If we are trying to describe the sound system of Standard English,
how should we handle examples like those given in the preceding para-
graphs—where various consonant clusters are "simplified" in various
ways? One useful method is to assume that each of the word types discussed has a basic, unsimplified, UNDERLYING FORM; and then to give the
VARIABLE RULES by which the consonant clusters of these underlying
forms can be simplified. These rules will be "variable" in two senses.
First, they will vary depending on the *style* in which a person is speaking.
In formal style, a speaker of Standard English will generally keep the
final /t/ of *fact* and say "the *fact* that he came." Only in informal style
will he drop the final /t/ of *fact* and say "the *fac'* that he came." Second,
the rules will vary depending on the *environment* in which a given underlying form occurs. A speaker of Standard English will often drop the
final /t/ of *fact* if it is immediately followed by a word beginning with a

consonant: "the *fac'* that he came." But he will generally not drop it if it is immediately followed by a word beginning with a vowel: "the *fact is* that. . . ."

6. CONSONANT CLUSTERS IN BLACK ENGLISH

By and large, Black English has the same underlying forms for words with final consonant clusters as Standard English; and it also has the same variable rules for the simplification of final consonant clusters as Standard English. Yet there is a big difference. We can perhaps express this best by saying: (1) whereas these variable rules are optional for Standard English, they come far closer to being obligatory for Black English; and (2) whereas these rules are relatively restricted as to style and environment in Standard English, they are far less restricted as to style and environment in Black English. Furthermore, (3) the variable rules for cluster simplification in Black English can be "cumulative." For example, a first rule in Black English (as in Standard English) may reduce the /-fts/ of *lifts* to /-fs/, giving "he *lif's* it"; and then a second rule in Black English (unlike any rule in Standard English) may reduce the /-fs/ of *lif's* to /-f/, giving "he *lif* it."

1. *Voiceless + Voiceless.* In Black English, final stops are generally dropped. The /-sp/ of *wasp* is then simplified to /-s/, giving *was'*; the /-pt/ of *apt* is simplified to /-p/, giving *ap'*; the /-čt/ of *reached* is simplified to /-č/, giving *reach'*; the /-kt/ of *fact* is simplified to /-k/, giving *fac';* and so on. This simplification is made (a) nearly always when the second consonant is part of the word stem ("the *fac'* that he came"); (b) very commonly when the second consonant is an ending ("they *reach'* the end"); and (c) commonly even when a word beginning with a vowel follows immediately ("the *fac' is* that . . . ").

2. *Voiced + Voiced.* In Black English, final stops are again generally dropped. The /-nd/ of *find* is then simplified to /-n/, giving *fin'*; the /-vd/ of *lived* is simplified to /-v/, giving *live'*; the /-ld/ of *cold* is simplified to /-l/, giving *col'*; and so on. This simplification is made (a) nearly always when the second consonant is part of the word stem ("I can't *fin'* my keys"); (b) very commonly when the second consonant is an ending ("he *live'* in Boston"); and (c) commonly even when a word beginning with a vowel follows immediately ("*col' or* hot").

3. *Voiced + Voiceless.* In Black English, as in Standard English, clusters of this type are not generally simplified. For example, *jump* remains /jəmp/, *lunch* remains /lənč/, and so on. An exception is the

cluster /-nt/, from which /t/ may be dropped. Underlying *bent* /bent/ is then simplified to /ben/ (like *Ben*); underlying *meant* /ment/ is then simplified to /men/ (like *men*); etc.

4. *Voiceless + Voiceless /s/.* Unlike Standard English, Black English often shows simplification of this cluster type. The /-ks/ of *six* may be simplified to /-k/, giving /sik/ (just like *sick*); the /-ks/ of *Max* /mæks/ may be simplified to /-k/, giving /mæk/ (just like *Mack*); and so on. However, the plural ending /-s/ is generally *not* dropped. The cluster /-ps/ is kept in *pipes*, /-ts/ is kept in *boots*, /-ks/ is kept in *books*, etc.—though not always.

5. *Voiced + Voiced /z/.* Unlike Standard English, Black English may again show simplification of this cluster type. Because /z/ in this position serves nearly always as ending, however, this type of simplification is less common. But the /-bz/ of *ribs* may be simplified to /-b/, giving *rib'*; the /-dz/ of *beds* may be simplified to /-d/, giving *bed'*; and so on.

6. *Triple clusters.* It is here that the simplification rules of Black English often apply "cumulatively." A first rule may (as in Standard English) delete the middle /k/ of *asked* /æskt/ to give /æst/, as in "he *as't* me to come"; and a second rule may then delete the final /t/ of /æst/ to give /æs/, giving "he *as'* me to come."

In the preceding section we noted that speakers of Standard English often delete the middle /t/ of the cluster /-sts/: the plural of *list*, namely *lists*, is often pronounced as *lis's* /liss/. In Standard English this deletion of /t/ is of course optional. In formal style *lists* is pronounced /lists/— that is to say, it consists of the full underlying form /list/ plus the plural ending /s/.

Black English has this same deletion rule; but in its use of this deletion rule it differs from Standard English in two ways. First, whereas this deletion rule is optional in Standard English, it is just about obligatory in Black English. Many black children who have been tested find it almost impossible to pronounce the triple cluster /-sts/. Second, this deletion rule applies in Black English not only to the cluster /-sts/, but also to the clusters /-sps/ and /-sks/, as in *wasps* and *desks*. That is, *all* word-final clusters of the type /s/ + voiceless stop (/p t k/) + /s/ are simplified by deletion of the voiceless stop. This means that *wasps* is pronounced as *was's* /wass/, *lists* is pronounced as *lis's* /liss/, *desks* is pronounced as *des's* /dess/, and so on.

In addition to the plural forms *was's*, *lis's*, *des's*, many speakers of Black English also use the plural forms *wasses* (for *wasps*), *lisses* (for *lists*), *desses* (for *desks*), etc. How are we to account for these plural forms —which seem so strange to speakers of Standard English? The answer is quite simple, and quite systematic. By the "Voiceless + Voiceless" deletion rule (Number (1) above), *wasp* becomes *was'*, *list* becomes *lis'*, *desk* becomes *des'*, and so on. For speakers of Standard English, *was'*, *lis'*, *des'* are "simplified" forms—and the underlying forms remain *wasp*, *list*, *desk*. For many speakers of Black English, however, *was'*, *lis'*, and *des'* serve as "underlying" forms, which we might now rewrite as *wass*, *liss*, *dess*. Such speakers then apply the usual rules for plural formation in English, whereby noun stems ending in /s/ take the plural ending in the shape /-iz/: *dress* /dres/, plural *dresses* /dresiz/; *kiss* /kis/, plural *kisses* /kisiz/; etc. Hence, quite systematically, the plural of *wass* /was/ is *wasses* /wasiz/, the plural of *liss* /lis/ is *lisses* /lisiz/, the plural of *dess* /des/ is *desses* /desiz/, and so on.

7. THE LIQUIDS /l/ AND /r/

In Section 3 above we noted that the pronunciation of the liquids /l/ and /r/ is very similar to that of vowels. Liquids are like vowels in that the breath stream flows out freely through the mouth; they differ from vowels only in that the breath stream is "steered" in special ways—out along one or both sides of the tongue in the case of /l/, and out along a constriction of the tongue in the case of /r/. If, in words where /l/ and /r/ follow vowels (such as *soul* and *sore*), this special "steering" is not maintained, then /l/ and /r/ themselves become vowels of a sort—the type of non-syllabic vowel often called a "glide." *Soul* /sōl/ then becomes something like /sōw/; and *sore* /sōr/ becomes what we shall symbolize as /sōə/ ("so-uh"). As a further change, these glides may then no longer be pronounced. When this happens, *soul* and *sore* are both simply /sō/.

In the history of Standard English, /l/ has been vocalized and then lost in a number of environments. Examples are such words as *half*, *calm*, *talk*, *folk*. Though we still write *l*'s in such words, we no longer pronounce them. *Half* is /hæf/ (or /hāf/), *calm* is /kām/, *talk* is /tɔk/, and *folk* is /fōk/.

Black English often shows a still more extensive vocalization and then loss of /l/. In the variety of Black English that you are investigating, you may find that /l/ is often lost before consonants, so that *help* is pronounced as /hep/, and *fault* is pronounced as /fɔt/ (just like *fought*). You may also find that /l/ is lost word-finally, so that *all* is pronounced as /ɔ/ (just like *awe*), *toll* is pronounced as /tō/ (just like *toe*), and *tool* is pronounced as /tū/ (just like *too*). Furthermore, this optional rule for *l*-loss may be cumulative with one of the rules for cluster simplification.

For example, by Rule (2) (in the Voiced + Voiced section above) the word *told* /tōld/ may be simplified to /tōl/; and the optional rule for *l*-loss may then in turn simplify this still further to /tō/.

The vocalization and loss of /r/ before consonants (*fierce* = /fīəs/, *cart* = /kāt/) and word-finally (*fear* = /fīə/, *car* = /kā/) is very widespread in Black English, as also in many varieties of Standard English. Because it has profound effects on the vowel system, we shall postpone a discussion of it until the next section. We must mention here, however, a loss of /r/ that is frequent in some varieties of Black English but does not generally occur in Standard English: the loss of /r/ where it occurs between vowels. In Standard English, the intervocalic /-r-/ of such words as *Carol, Paris, terrace* is generally pronounced. In the variety of Black English which you are investigating, however, you may find that it is often lost. *Carol* is then *Ca'ol*, often just like *Cal; Paris* is *Pa'is*, often just like *pass;* and *terrace* is then *te'ace*, often just like *tes'* (*test*).

8.   THE VOWELS OF STANDARD ENGLISH

It is far more difficult to describe the vowels of Standard English than to describe the consonants of Standard English—for three reasons. First, vowels as such are more difficult to analyze: they cannot be described in terms of such obvious places of pronunciation as Labial, Dental, Palatal, and Velar. Second, there is no single vowel system used by all speakers of Standard English; instead, speakers in different areas use different systems. Third, the vowel systems of Standard English differ in particular depending on whether or not their speakers pronounce so-called "postvocalic /r/," that is to say (1) /r/ after a vowel and before a consonant (e.g., *cart* as /kārt/ or as /kāt/), and (2) /r/ after a vowel and at the end of a word (e.g., *car* as /kār/ or as /kā/). Those varieties in which postvocalic /r/ *is* pronounced (/kārt/, /kār/) are customarily referred to as "*r*-ful"; those varieties in which postvocalic /r/ is *not* pronounced (/kāt/, /kā/) are customarily referred to as "*r*-less." By and large, Black English is "*r*-less."

In order to describe the vowel systems of Standard English, let us start off with three "anchor points"—three basic vowels in terms of which we can locate more or less accurately the remaining vowels in the many varieties of Standard English.

(1) /ā/.   Open your mouth wide, keep your tongue flat at the bottom of the mouth, and relax the vocal cords so that they vibrate as the breath stream flows out through them. This gives the vowel that most of us use in *father* /fāðər/, in *pa* /pā/ and *ma* /mā/, and in *car* (*r*-ful /kār/, *r*-less /kā/). This is a LOW vowel, i.e., the body of the tongue is low in the

mouth. It is also a CENTRAL vowel, i.e., the body of the tongue is neither pushed toward the front of the mouth nor pulled toward the back of the mouth. It is also a FREE vowel, i.e., it can occur word-finally as in *pa*, *ma*, and (*r*-less) *car* /kā/. We shall symbolize the fact that it is a free vowel by writing a macron over it, i.e., /ā/ rather than (without a macron) /a/. The macron will also symbolize the fact that free vowels are generally somewhat longer than corresponding checked vowels.

(2) /ī/.   Open your mouth very slightly, push the body of the tongue up toward the front, keep your lips spread, and say the vowel of *tea* /tī/. This is a HIGH vowel, i.e., the body of the tongue is high in the mouth. It is also a FRONT vowel, i.e., the body of the tongue is pushed toward the front of the mouth. And it is again a FREE vowel, i.e., it can occur word-finally as in *tea* /tī/.

(3) /ū/.   Open your mouth very slightly, push the body of the tongue up toward the back, round your lips, and say the vowel of *too* /tū/. This is a HIGH vowel, i.e., the body of the tongue is high in the mouth. It is also a BACK vowel: the body of the tongue is pushed toward the back of the mouth. And it is again a FREE vowel, i.e., it can occur word-finally as in *too* /tū/.

The three "anchor points" /ī/, /ā/, /ū/ (as in *tea*, *pa*, *too*) now give us three vowel types in terms of which we can plot the approximate places of pronunciation of all other vowels. The basic scheme can be diagrammed as follows:

	Front	Central	Back
High	ī		ū
Mid			
Low		ā	

The vowel system described in the pronunciation sections of most dictionaries of American English can be diagrammed as follows:

System 1:

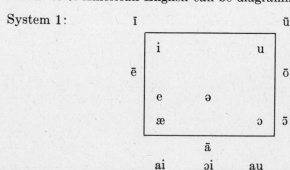

The six symbols inside the rectangle (all written without a macron) symbolize CHECKED vowels: /i/ as in *pit*, /e/ as in *pet*, /æ/ as in *pat*, /ɔ/ as in *pot*, /u/ as in *put*, /ə/ as in *but*. The nine symbols outside the rectangle (written either with a macron or with two symbols) symbolize FREE vowels: /ī/ as in *tea*, /ē/ as in *pay*, /ā/ as in *pa*, /ɔ̄/ as in *paw*, /ō/ as in *toe*, /ū/ as in *too*, /ai/ as in *pie*, /ɔi/ as in *boy*, /au/ as in *now*. The vowel phoneme symbolized as /ə/ sounds somewhat different depending on whether or not it is followed by /r/: simple /ə/ in *putt* /pət/ and *bud* /bəd/, but /ər/ in *pert* /pərt/ and *bird* /bərd/. It also sounds somewhat different depending on whether or not it is stressed (symbolized as /ə́/) or unstressed (symbolized simply as /ə/). Examples: stressed /ə́/ in *putt* /pə́t/, *bud* /bə́d/; unstressed /ə/ in *ago* /əgṓ/, *sofa* /sṓfə/; unstressed and stressed in *above* /əbə́v/. In ordinary spelling, stressed /ə́/ is usually written *u*: *but*, *putt*, *bug*, etc. (but it is written *o* in *other*, *mother*, *brother*, and in *above*, *love*, *glove*, etc.). Unstressed /ə/ is written in many different ways: *a* in *sofa* /sṓfə/, *e* in *item* /áitəm/, *i* in *edible* /édəbəl/, *o* in *gallop* /gǽləp/, *u* in *circus* /sə́rkəs/; and with no vowel letter at all in *rhythm* /ríðəm/.

This vowel system given in dictionaries of American English is actually not used by most speakers of Standard American English. Instead, they use systems with the following changes:

System 2, merger of /ɔ/ and /ā/. In Standard British English, checked /ɔ/ is used in *bother* and *Tom*, and free /ā/ is used in *father* and *calm*. In most varieties of Standard American English, however, /ɔ/ has merged with /ā/; and this /ā/ is used in all four of these words (and others like them). *Bother* then rhymes with *father*, and *Tom* rhymes with *calm*.

System 3, merger of /ɔ/ and /ɔ̄/. In Standard British English, checked /ɔ/ is used in *cot* and *tot* and free /ɔ̄/ is used in *caught* and *taught*. In much of eastern New England, however, /ɔ/ and /ɔ̄/ have merged in a low back vowel customarily symbolized as /ō̞/. This /ō̞/ is used in *cot* and *caught*, in *tot* and *taught*, in *Boston*, and also in *bother* and *Tom*, etc. It is still distinct from the /ā/ of *father*, *calm*, *pa*, however, since this vowel has moved a bit toward the front. (This is the vowel often made fun of in "*pa*hk your *ca*h in the H*a*hvuhd Yahd," i.e. "park your car in the Harvard Yard.")

System 4, merger of /ā/, /ɔ/, /ɔ̄/. In an area around Pittsburgh, in much of Canada, and in much of the northwest of the United States, one and the same vowel phoneme is used not only in *bother* and *father*, *Tom* and *calm*, but also in *cot* and *caught*, *tot* and *taught*, *pa* and *paw*. That is, /ā/, /ɔ/, /ɔ̄/ have all merged in a single vowel phoneme; and since this is again a low back vowel, it is again customarily symbolized as /ō̞/.

System 5, split of /æ/ into /æ/ and /ǣ/. In part of the mid-Atlantic seaboard (roughly, from New York to Philadelphia) there is not only a checked (and short) /æ/, but also a free (and long) /ǣ/. This /ǣ/ is just barely "free," since it appears word-finally only in such special words as *yeah*. Nevertheless, it is clearly a different vowel phoneme from checked /æ/. For example, free /ǣ/ is used in (*tin*) *can* /kǽn/ and *Ann* /ǽn/; but checked /æ/ is used in (*I*) *can* /kǽn/ and *an* /ǽn/.

The above presentation of the various vowel systems of Standard English will sound confusing to you. For this there is no help. It is simply a brute fact that Standard English has at least these five different vowel systems (with still more to come). In order to understand these various systems, it may be useful to consider your own pronunciation:

1. Do you make a difference between *bother, Tom* (with /ɔ/) versus *father, calm, pa* (with /ā/)? If so, you use System 1.
2. Do you use the same vowel /ā/ in *bother* and *father*, and in *Tom, calm*, and *pa*? If so, you use System 2.
3. Do you use the same vowel /ō/ in *bother, Tom, cot, caught, tot, taught*, but a different vowel /ā/ in *father, calm, pa*? If so, you use System 3.
4. Do you use the same vowel /ō/ in *bother* and *father, Tom* and *calm, cot* and *caught, tot* and *taught, pa* and *paw*? If so, you use System 4.
5. Do you make a difference between (*tin*) *can* and *Ann* with /ǣ/ versus (*I*) *can* and *an* with /æ/? If so, you use System 5.

Phonetic Differences

Two varieties of Standard English may use the same system of vowel phonemes, but may pronounce them in phonetically different ways. Of particular importance to us here is the fact that the glide [i] of /ai/ may be reduced or even eliminated in "Southern American English." Such words as *pie, my, shy* may then be pronounced as "pah, mah, shah," with the usual /ai/ changed phonetically to [ā]. This [ā] may then still be phonemically distinct from the /ā/ of *pa, ma, shah;* or it may have merged with this /ā/, so that *pie, my, shy* sound just like *pa, ma, shah*. This reduction and even loss of the glide [i] in /ai/ is of importance to us because it is widespread in Black English.

9. POSTVOCALIC /r/

Most speakers of Standard English in the United States and Canada pronounce so-called "postvocalic /r/," that is to say /r/ before a consonant (as in *cart* /kārt/) and /r/ word-finally (as in *car* /kār/). Along the eastern seaboard of the United States and in much of Great Britain, however, there are millions of persons who speak a variety of Standard English in which postvocalic /r/ has been "vocalized." It has then undergone three different developments: (1) after some vowels it has changed to the glide [ə] (much like the /ə/ of *sofa* /sófə/); (2) after other vowels it has been lost; and (3) it has combined with stressed /ə́/ to give the free vowel /ə̄/. Examples are:

(1) Change to a glide

fear is not /fír/	but /fíə/	*fierce* is not /fírs/	but /fíəs/
tour is not /túr/	but /túə/	*toured* is not /túrd/	but /túəd/
scare is not /skér/	but /skéə/	*scarce* is not /skérs/	but /skéəs/
soar is not /sór/	but /sóə/	*soared* is not /sórd/	but /sóəd/
fire is not /fáir/	but /fáiə/	*fired* is not /fáird/	but /fáiəd/
sour is not /sáur/	but /sáuə/	*soured* is not /sáurd/	but /sáuəd/

(2) Loss

car is not /kár/	but /kā́/	*cart* is not /kárt/	but /kā́t/
for is not /fór/	but /fɔ́/	*fort* is not /fórt/	but /fɔ́t/
river is not /rívər/	but /rívə/	*rivers* is not /rívərz/	but /rívəz/

(3) The free vowel /ə̄/

sir is not /sə́r/	but /sə̄́/	*bird* is not /bə́rd/	but /bə̄́d/
her is not /hə́r/	but /hə̄́/	*heard* is not /hə́rd/	but /hə̄́d/
fur is not /fə́r/	but /fə̄́/	*word* is not /wə́rd/	but /wə̄́d/

Because of these changes, speakers of this variety of "*r*-less" English may have the following vowel system:

System 6:

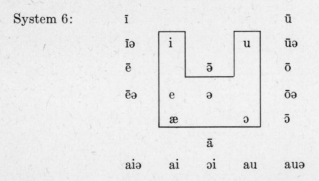

Examples of the six checked vowels: *pit* /pít/, *pet* /pét/, *pat* /pǽt/, *pot* /pót/, *put* /pút/, *but* /bə́t/. Examples of the sixteen free vowels: *bee* /bī́/, *beer* /bī́ə/, *bay* /bḗ/, *bare* /bḗə/, *pa* /pā́/ and *car* /kā́/, *saw* /sɔ́/ and *for* /fɔ́/, *soar* /sóə/, *toe* /tó/, *tour* /túə/, *too* /tú/, *fur* /fə̄́/, *hire* /háiə/, *high* /hái/, *boy* /bɔi/, *sow* /sáu/, *sour* /sáuə/. Examples of unstressed /ə/:

father /fáðə/, *mother* /mə́ðə/, with the same word-final /ə/ as *Cuba* /kyúbə/, *Russia* /rášə/.

This is, by and large, the vowel system of Standard British English. But there is one frequent modification. The /ɔ/ of *saw* and *for* is often higher than indicated in the above diagram. There is then not sufficient "room" for both /ɔ/ and /ōə/ at the same height. This higher /ɔ/ is then used not only in *saw* /sɔ́/ and *for* /fɔ́/ but also in *soar* /sɔ́/ and *pour* /pɔ́/, etc. (instead of /sóə/, /póə/, etc.).

In *r*-less varieties of Standard English, word-final /r/ (as in *fear, fair, far, for, four, tour, fur, fire, sour, father*) is regularly vocalized to [ə] or lost in two environments: (1) before a pause, as in *we have nothing to fear* /fíə/, or Franklin D. Roosevelt's famous *I hate war* /wɔ́/; and (2) before a following word beginning with a consonant, as in *to fear nothing* (with /fíə/), *war for freedom* (with /wɔ́/ and /fɔ́/), *bitter defeat* (with /bítə/). Yet it is clear that such "*r*-less' speakers retain underlying forms with /r/, i.e., *fear* /fír/, *war* /wɔ́r/, *for* /fɔ́r/, *bitter* /bítər/. The evidence for this is the fact that such speakers pronounce this underlying /r/ in two environments: (1) they pronounce it quite regularly before a vowel in the same word, as in *fearing* /fíriŋ/ (versus *fear* /fíə/), or *forever* /fɔrévə/ (versus *for* /fɔ́/), or *bitterest* /bítərəst/ (vs. *bitter* /bítə/), and (2) they pronounce it more or less regularly before a following word beginning with a vowel, as in (again a famous quote from Franklin D. Roosevelt) *we have nothing to fear but fear itself* /fír itsélf/, or *war against fascism* /wɔ́r əgénst fǽšizəm/, or *father and mother* /fáðər ən mə́ðə/.

It is an interesting fact that *r*-less speakers often have more words with underlying word-final /r/ than do *r*-ful speakers. For an *r*-less speaker, the word *soar* has an underlying form with /r/, namely /sɔ́r/. This /r/ is regularly dropped before pause or a consonant, giving /sɔ́/; but it is more or less regularly kept before a following vowel, as in *soaring* /sɔ́riŋ/ or *soar over* /sɔ́r óvə/. For the same type of speaker, the word *saw* is also /sɔ́/ before pause or a consonant; and it may therefore be analogically reinterpreted as also having an underlying form with /r/, namely /sɔ́r/. This /r/ is again regularly dropped before pause or a consonant, giving /sɔ́/; but it is again regularly kept before a following vowel, as in *sawing* /sɔ́riŋ/ or *saw it* /sɔ́r it/.

This analogical use of underlying /r/ is probably not fully acceptable in truly "Standard" English, yet it is very widespread among *r*-less speakers. The following are some further examples. Word-final /īə/ in *idea* /aidíə/, like *fear* /fíə/; hence also prevocalic *idea of it* /aidír əv it/, like *fear of it* /fír əv it/. (Underlying form: *idea* /aidír/, like *fear* /fír/.) Word-final /ɔ/ in *law* /lɔ́/, like *war* /wɔ́/; hence also prevocalic *law and order* (lɔ́r ən ɔ́də/, like *war and peace* /wɔ́r ən pís/. (Underlying form: *law* /lɔ́r/, like *war* /wɔ́r/.) Word-final /ə/ in *Cuba* /kyúbə/, like *father*

/fáðə/; hence also prevocalic *Cuba and Russia* /kyúbər ən réšə/, like *father and mother* /fáðər ən mə́ðə/. (Underlying form: *Cuba* /kyúbər/, like *father* /fáðər/.) The late President John F. Kennedy (born and raised in Boston, an *r*-less area) was an inconsistent *r*-less speaker. He sometimes dropped /r/ in the "right" places, sometimes pronounced /r/ in the "right" places, and sometimes introduced /r/ in the "wrong" places—as in his famous *Cuba and Russia* /kyúbər ən ŕəšə/.

10. THE VOWELS OF BLACK ENGLISH

You will probably find that the vowel system of the variety of Black English that you are investigating is basically *"r-less"*—though perhaps inconsistently so. Like the late President Kennedy, your speakers may usually drop /r/ in the "right" places, may sometimes pronounce /r/ in the "right" places, and may sometimes introduce /r/ in the "wrong" places. At the same time, you will probably find one big and important difference. Whereas *r*-less speakers of Standard English often have *more* words with underlying /r/ than do *r*-ful speakers, speakers of Black English often have *fewer* words with underlying /r/. An example is the word *pour*. For *r*-less speakers of Standard English this is /póə/ or /pɔ́/ before pause (*it won't pour*), before a consonant in a following word (*pour the milk*), and before a consonant in the same word (*pours, poured*); but it is /pór/ or /pɔ́r/ before a vowel in a following word (*pour it*), and especially before a vowel in the same word (*pouring*). That is, to say, the underlying form is /pór/ or /pɔ́r/. In Black English, on the other hand, you may find that *pour* is /pó(ə)/ or /pɔ́/ not only before pause (*it won't pour*), before a consonant in a following word (*pour the milk*), and before a consonant in the same word (*pours, poured*), but also before a vowel in a following word (*pour it*), and even before a vowel in the same word (*pouring*). That is to say, the underlying form is /pó(ə)/ or /pɔ́/, with no /r/ at all.

Some other special developments in Black English that you may find are the following:

/i/ and /e/ before nasals. Though the distinction between these two vowels is kept in most environments (*bit* versus *bet, miss* versus *mess,* etc.), you will probably find that it has been given up before nasals. *Pin* and *pen* then sound alike, *him* and *hem* sound alike, *since* and *sense* sound alike, etc. (This development is not unique to Black English; it is also found in the Standard English of much of the American South.)

Lowering of /īə/ and /ūə/. The /īə/ of *cheer, steer,* etc. is often lowered to /ēə/, so that these words sound just like *chair, stair,* etc.

Correspondingly, the /ūə/ of *poor, sure,* etc. is often lowered to /ōə/, so that these words sound just like *pour, shore,* etc. (These developments— especially the lowering of /ūə/—are again not unique to Black English, but are widespread in the Standard English of the American South.)

Loss of the glides [i] and [u]. These glides in /ai au ɔi/ may be lost, so as to give /ā ā ɔ̄/, respectively. *Find* is then not /fáind/ but /fā́nd/, just like *fond;* and *time* is then not /táim/ but /tā́m/, just like *Tom.* *Found* is then not /fáund/ but /fā́nd/, again just like *fond;* and *pound* is not /páund/ but /pā́nd/, just like *pond. Boil* is then not /bɔ́il/ but /bɔ̄́l/, just like *ball;* and *oil* is not /ɔ́il/ but /ɔ̄́l/, just like *all.* (These developments are again not unique to Black English, but may occur in the Standard English of the American South.)

Loss of the glide [ə]. In System 6 above there are three pairs of vowels with the glide [ə]: /īə ūə/, /ēə ōə/, /aiə auə/. The "lowering of /īə/ and /ūə/" may eliminate these two vowels, since they have merged with /ēə/ and /ōə/ (/ēə/ in both *cheer* and *chair,* /ōə/ in both *poor* and *pour*). And the "loss of the glides [i] and [u]" may have changed /aiə/ to /āə/ (*tire* = /tā́ə/) and /auə/ to /āə/ (*tower* = /tā́ə/). That is to say, the system now contains only three vowels with the glide [ə]: /ēə ōə/ and /āə/. As a further development, the glide [ə] in /ēə ōə āə/ may now be lost, giving /ē ō ā/. The vowel /ē/ may be used not only in *stay* but also in *stair* and *steer. (Stay, stair, steer* all = /stḗ/.) The vowel /ō/ may be used not only in *show* but also in *shore* and *sure. (Show, shore, sure* all = /šṓ/.) And the vowel /ā/ may be used not only in *tar* but also in *tire* and *tower. (Tar, tire, tower* all = /tā́/.)

11. CONCLUSION

As was explained at the beginning of this chapter, it is not possible to describe "the" sound system of Black English, any more than it is possible to describe "the" sound system of Standard English. In each case there are several systems rather than a single one. Furthermore, each such system may show a considerable amount of variation within itself. An example is provided by the variable rules for the presence versus absence of /r/ in *r*-less types of Standard English. Black English also has its own variable rules, such as the variable lowering of /īə/ to /ēə/ in words like *cheer, steer.* In addition, like other types of nonstandard English, Black English also shows a second type of variation. Depending on the style which a speaker uses, he may pronounce forms which are now more like those of Standard English, now less like those of Standard

English. Black English is therefore doubly varied: both within itself, and in its closeness to Standard English.

Our purpose in this chapter has been threefold. First, it has been to present the sound systems of the commonest types of Standard English. One of these systems is probably the system which you yourself use. It will therefore serve as your point of departure when you investigate any variety of Black English. And you can best understand this variety of Black English by noting the ways in which its sound system differs from your own sound system. Second, our purpose has been to alert you to some of the differences between your own sound system and that of the Black English you are investigating. Without the hints we have tried to give, you might have missed many of the characteristic features of this variety of Black English. With these hints we hope, at least, that you will be able to identify and understand these characteristic features. Third, our purpose has been to show that the differences between the sound systems of Standard English and Black English are not random and haphazard, but highly systematic. For example, if a speaker of Black English does not use the voiceless /θ/ of Standard English for the *th* of *thick* and *south*, he does not replace this /θ/ with just any old sound. Instead, he uses either the nearest available dental phoneme (the stop /t/, giving "tick"); or the nearest available labial phoneme (the fricative /f/, giving "souf").

Human language, in whatever variety, is never haphazard and capricious. It is always governed by systematic rules. Our task, as investigators, is the fascinating one of trying to identify and describe these systematic rules.

SOURCES

Our knowledge of Black English is still quite inadequate. Trying to find out more about it will be a laborious, painstaking, but rewarding task for the future. Though the data in this chapter were taken from many sources, they are based primarily on the following work: William Labov, *Language in the Inner City: Studies in the Black English Vernacular*, Philadelphia: University of Pennsylvania Press, 1972.

9

Is There a Correspondence between Sound and Spelling? Some Implications for Black English Speakers

Verley O'Neal

Stanford University

Tom Trabasso

Princeton University

Since the middle of the 1960s, there has been considerable speculation about the relation of language to educational success, particularly with respect to minorities. If the language spoken by the teacher does not match that spoken by the child, then potential sources of miscommunication arise through a state of mutual ignorance. The teacher may not understand the child, may penalize the child on irrelevant grounds of pronunciation during oral reading, or may fail to appreciate variations in spelling or writing which are consistent with the child's speech. These represent situational and interactional problems in the classroom. On the other hand, the child may not understand the teacher's lect, either spoken or written, and the child's reliance upon how he or she pronounces words may make it difficult for him or her to recognize or to spell words. This problem may be a personal source of difficulty, independent of situational sources involving the teacher (Labov, 1967).

This chapter is concerned with the latter problem. Since our written forms of language involve an alphabet, there appears to be a

171

correspondence between the written symbols we use as letters and spoken forms of the words. This correspondence, sometimes referred to as the alphabetic principle (Smith, 1972), relates the written and spoken forms through the orthography of printed English and phonology of spoken English (cf. Moulton, Chapter 8 of this volume, for a discussion of phonology). The problem of interest is whether one can find empirical evidence that phonology and orthography are related by examining how speakers of different lects spell words. Putting the question another way: Would speakers of Black English spell words differently than speakers of other lects? If so, can we account for these variations in spelling by the differences in phonology?

One can readily accept the assertion that many speakers of Black English differ in pronounciation from other Americans. Labov (1967) provides several examples which contrast Black and White speakers in similar geographic locations, particularly inner-city youth in northeastern cities in the United States. Whether these phonological differences lead to other differences in behavior, such as spelling, is a matter of empirical research.

The exact basis for how one relates a spoken to a written word is not clearly understood and is still a matter of debate. Hodges (1972) gives a readable account of several viewpoints which are linguistic in nature; Smith (1972) challenges this relation and provides some additional psychological insight. We shall postpone discussion on these matters, however, until after we have presented our empirical research.

We began our study by assuming that a speaker might, under some circumstances, rely upon how he pronounced a word to spell that word. We assumed further that the pronunciation or the speaker's phonological representation could be described systematically using the symbols of the International Phonetic Alphabet; that is, at some abstract level in the speaker's head, there exists a representation for the word *take:* / / tek / / and it is this representation which may be used to spell a word. This idea follows from the alphabetic principle. By this is meant that when we read we go from the print (the "orthographic" representation) to sound (the "phonological" representation) to meaning (the "semantic" representation). When we write, we do the reverse, namely, we go from meaning to sound to spelling (or semantics to phonology to orthography). A representation is a symbol system used by the person to stand for experiences or ideas and it is common among psychologists and others interested in mental activity to assume some kind of symbolic representation for the content of these mental processes.

In order to bring to bear some empirical evidence on the alphabetic principle, we adopted Labov's (1967) description of phonological differences in Black English. Labov's characterization suggests that there are a large number of words that would be treated as homonyms by

Black English speakers but would be heard as different words by Standard English speakers. Suppose, then, that these speakers are asked to spell words which are either nonhomonymous for both kinds of speakers or homonymous for one lect but not the other. Might not a Black English speaker confuse acoustically these words and render them into the same, homonymous spellings? That is, if the phonological representation was the same for a pair of words, one might then use common spellings to write these words. These spellings might be conventional and be realized as homonyms or not be conventional and be considered incorrect. For example, for a speaker of Black English, *door* or *dough* may be either substituted as spellings or spelled *doo* or *dou*; that is, a Black English speaker might hear these words as // do // whereas a Standard English speaker would hear them as // dɔr // and // do // respectively.

In addition to confusing two words acoustically and rendering them as homonyms, it is also possible that the phonological representation may lead to spellings which are correct as far as this representation is concerned but incorrect with respect to the conventional spelling. Among these words for Black English speakers, one finds, *these, brother, tooth, protest, poor, boil, right, plenty,* and *wasps.* (See Table 2 for possible unconventional spellings of these words by Black English speakers.)

Upon this argument, it seemed to us that a developmental study was required. Younger speakers of Black English (who also would be less skilled readers) may either rely more upon a phonemic level of representation than older children or be lacking in the rules of correspondence between phonological and orthographic representations and consequently make more confusions or unconventional spellings.

To test these ideas, we asked children at two grade levels, the third and the fifth, to spell a set of 128 words. The words, listed in Table 1, were selected so that (1) they would not be confused by speakers of different lects, (2) they would be confused by speakers of Standard English, (3) they would be confused by speakers of Black English, and (4) they would have phonological changes for Black English speakers but not for Standard English speakers. The words in Table 1 were developed by use of Labov's (1967) categories and several of them are his examples (see Table 2 and the discussion below).

We note that in Table 1 the words have been grouped into four classes of 16 pairs each. In what we call Lect Neutral, the words in each pair rhyme but are not likely to be confused phonologically by either speaker, especially since the initial segments differ. The words in the pairs in the Standard English Confusable category should be homonymous for speakers of Standard English whereas those in the third column, labeled Black English Confusable, should be homonymous for Black English speakers. Finally, the right-most column lists pairs of words which should, within

TABLE 1
The Set of Words Used in the Study

		Word category		
Pair	Lect Neutral	Standard English Confusable	Black English Confusable	Black English Changes or Deletions
1	away tray	are or	ball boil	booth tooth
2	blue glue	ate eight	coal cold	brother mother
3	book look	bare bear	door dough	cashed finished
4	brain train	do due	garden guarding	coldest wildest
5	brick stick	fair fare	guess guest	enter winter
6	crumb thumb	knight night	half have	farmer army
7	gave save	meat meet	hold hole	floor more
8	knee tree	new knew	jar jaw	golf wolf
9	plant can't	pair pear	mind mine	mouth south
10	saw raw	peace piece	pitcher picture	nothing something
11	side ride	sail sale	poor pour	professor protest
12	tear year	son sun	rat right	rest test
13	talk walk	steal steel	roar row	there these
14	toy boy	tale tail	send sin	throw throat
15	try sky	wait weight	show sure	twenty plenty
16	wall tall	weak week	win wind	wasps ghosts

each pair, undergo similar phonological changes or deletions by Black but not Standard English speakers.

Using Labov's (1967) descriptions, we were able to identify five categories of possible phonemic transformations: (1) / /θ/ /, (2) r-lessness, (3) vowel changes, (4) nasal confusion, and (5) final consonants. In Table 2, we have regrouped words from columns 3 and 4 of Table 1 according to these categories. In addition to listing the words appropriate to the critical phoneme, the possible alphabetic symbol is given as well as actual examples of spelling variations obtained in our study. We shall discuss these when we present the results of our study.

In each classroom where we conducted the experiment (two classrooms per age group in an urban and suburban school district were used), we asked each child to first listen to a certain word that was spoken over tape by a White, middle-class teacher, and to then repeat the word to himself five times, making a check mark on his answer sheet for each repetition and, after the fifth repetition, to spell the word on his answer sheet. The idea behind this delayed procedure was to assure that the children imposed their pronunciations on the words despite the fact that they heard the words spoken by someone else. This should maximize the chances that they would use their, and not the teacher's, pronunciation.

The words were heard in two contexts, either alone or in a sentence. Table 3 gives some examples of the sentence contexts. Note that in the sentence context condition the target word was said first alone, then in a sentence and the child was asked to begin his rehearsal after the sentence was read. When one hears a word alone or out of context, one does not know which of the possible homonyms one should spell. Hence we would expect many homonymous spellings in the single word context. Which words are spelled depends upon which words are treated as homonyms and are preferred by the speakers. When a word occurs in a sentence context, however, the person can use the meaning of the word established by that context. This should reduce the confusion produced at the phonological level. Thus, the word-alone condition serves as a kind of control and asks if words are in fact treated as homonyms; the sentence context allows meaning to play a role. The expectation was that for the Standard English Confusable words of Table 1, Standard English speakers would make more homonymous spellings than would Black English speakers; the reverse was expected for the Black English Confusable words. Thus, we expected an interaction between the two word categories and two kinds of speakers. We also expected the sentence context to reduce confusions at the phonological level and consequently reduce differences between the kinds of speakers for both word categories.

About half of the children heard the words alone while the other half heard them in sentence context. There were a total of 149 children in

TABLE 2
Phonemic Classification of Black English Words

Category	Word	Possible alphabetic symbol	Observed example
1. /θ/	there	d, v	ver
a. initial	these	d, v	veace
	throw	t	toh
	throat	t	trought
b. medial	brother	d, v	brave
	mother	d, v	none found
	nothing	f, t	nifing
	something	th deletion	someing
c. final	booth	th deletion,	boot
	tooth	f, t substitution	too
	south		sowf
	mouth		mout
2. vocalic r, /ɪ/	army	r deletion	amy
a. initial	farmer		famer
	professor		pofusar
	protest		potes
	throw		thought
	throat		thot
	garden		ganeden
	guarding		gaten
b. final	door	r deletion	dool
	floor		flooh
	pour		none found
	poor		none found
	sure		she
3. vowel shifts	golf	vowel elongation	goff
	wolf	and letter change	wofe
	boil	in following con-	boll
	half	sonant	have
	right		rat
	jar		jaw
	picture		pichter
4. nasal confusion, /ɛ/ and /ɪ/	winter	e or i substitution	wenter
	enter		intear
	sin		sen
	send		sin
	win		when
	wind		wend
	plenty		pliny
	twenty		twiny

(continued)

TABLE 2 (*continued*)

Category	Word	Possible alphabetic symbol	Observed example
5. final consonants			
a. /t/	coldest	t deletion	coldes
	wildest		wilds
	protest		prostes
	rest		rise
	test		tese
	guest		guess
b. /t/ past tense	cashed	ed deletion	caes
	finished		finsh
c. /sps/ or /sts/	wasps	ps or ts deletion or es addition	was
	ghosts		ghostes
d. /d/	cold	d deletion	cole
	hold		hole
	mind		minn
	send		sin
	wind		win
e. /nt/	twenty	t deletion	wtery
	plenty		plenny

the study. They were from two grade levels, third and fifth, and ranged in age from 7 to 11 years. Table 4 gives a summary description of these characteristics of the children.

In an effort to contrast racial origin and geographic (as well as socioeconomic class) differences, the children were either Black or White from an inner-city school district or White from a suburban school system.[1] We did not, unfortunately, have the resources or time to assess independently each speaker's linguistic competence or phonology. We operated on the assumption that our sample was representative of those studied by Labov (1967), and that his observations would generalize and their implications be tested. Obviously, a stronger experiment would be one where one knew and could maximize contrasts in the speakers' lects. We also used only a White, middle-class teacher to pronounce the words,

[1] The authors wish to thank the school districts of Poughkeepsie and Arthington, New York, and William S. Hall for assistance in providing facilities and children as subjects for the research.

TABLE 3
Examples of Sentence Contexts

(1) *Look* as in: Do not *look* directly at the sun!
(2) *Plant* as in: Let us *plant* a vegetable garden.
(3) *Knight* as in: A *knight* in King Arthur's round table was a strong man.
(4) *Wait* as in: *Wait* for me on East State Street.
(5) *Door* as in: Please close the *door*.
(6) *Guest* as in: Bill will be a *guest* at my house.
(7) *Test* as in: Did you pass the reading *test*?
(8) *Plenty* as in: There is *plenty* of fruit in the basket.

TABLE 4
Number, Age, and Sex of Children from Each Group and Grade Level

	Inner City				Suburban White	
	Black		White			
	3	5	3	5	3	5
Grade						
Number of						
Boys	13	15	7	6	17	16
Girls	9	11	4	9	23	19
Median age (year, month)	8,4	10,6	8,7	10,4	8,4	10,8

in part because we felt that most teachers would speak some standard form of American English. We wonder, however, what would be the effect of having Black English speakers saying the words, both for the Black and White children. Such a contrast would allow a kind of bilingual cross comparison. We also did not have any independent data on socioeconomic class. Therefore, we felt it best to use the regional terms, urban and suburban, since they, in fact, describe the school districts we visited.

HOMONYM ANALYSIS

Our first main analysis is on the question as to whether or not the children treated the words homonymously. This analysis was carried out on the second and third word categories of Table 1, called Standard and Black English Confusable, respectively. We calculated the number of spellings that were homonyms of the "intended" word and found what

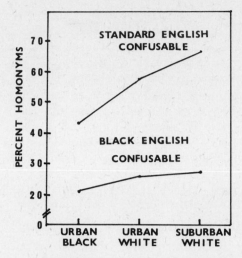

FIG. 1. The percentage of homonymous spelling variations for Standard English Confusable and Black English Confusable words by the three main groups of children. Note that the calculations exclude the conventional spelling of the intended word and blank answers.

percentage these homonyms constituted relative to the total number of spellings other than those that were correct or left blank.

If the children confuse words and render them as homonyms in spelling according to the phonological representation of different lects, then we would expect the White children to spell more homonyms for the Standard English Confusable words and the Black children to spell more homonyms for the Black English Confusable words. Figure 1 gives the main data on this hypothesis.

Figure 1 shows that the children indeed gave a large proportion of homonyms in spelling. This is *prima facie* evidence for a sound-to-letter correspondence. However, the data do not support the idea that the Black and White children had different phonological representations. All groups show more homonyms for the Standard English Confusable words and the White groups spelled proportionately more homonyms for the Black English Confusable words than did the Black children. The latter finding was contrary to our expectations. The fact that both curves show parallel trends suggests that the children share knowledge on these words at some phonological level. An analysis of age and context effects on homonymous spellings sheds light on this interpretation. Figure 2 summarizes this analysis.

In Fig. 2, one can readily see that the sentence context was very effective in reducing homonymous spellings. This was true for all groups and grades. These data suggest that *meaning* plays a major role in reducing dependence upon the phonological level to spell the word. The sentence

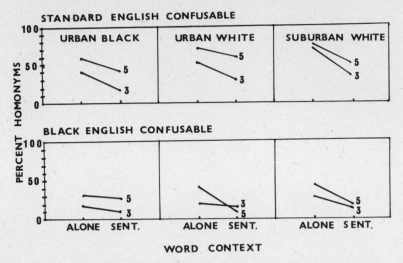

FIG. 2. The percentage of homonymous spelling variations for Standard English and Black English Confusable words as a function of context and grade level.

allows one to disambiguate the word at the phonological level and to find other means to spell the word. They also suggest that, while individual words may be semantically processed when heard, context effects are extremely important in accessing other information about the word. We note that context did not seem to interact with reading experience since the reduction (about 50% across the groups) was virtually identical for third and fifth graders.

The main developmental finding is that the amount of agreement among the speakers as to the spelling increases with age; that is, older children who give unconventional spellings approximate more closely the correct spelling of the word, at least at the phonological level. Since this result holds for all the children, we have additional evidence of code sharing (cf. Hall, Chapter 11 of this volume) and bilingualism (cf. Riegel and Freedle, Chapter 2 of this volume) for both Black and White children.

UNCONVENTIONAL VARIATIONS

We next analyzed the data with respect to the number of unconventional variations. We first noted that there were large individual differences among the children and that the girls made fewer variations than the boys. The latter factor posed some problems since sex was not equally distributed across the groups in Table 4. In order to control statistically for these individual differences, we performed what is known as an analysis of covariance. This analysis allows one to remove the effect of a factor

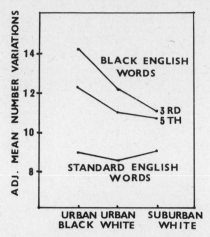

FIG. 3. Adjusted mean number of unconventional variations for Standard English Confusable words with Lect Neutral performance covaried and for Black English words with Standard English Confusable and Lect Neutral performance as covariates.

to the extent that it correlates with one's measures. We decided to use the number of unconventional spellings per child for the Lect Neutral words as a covariate. The first analysis of covariance was then done on the SE Confusable words with context, grade, and group as factors. The main finding here was that there were *no* differences among the racial and regional groups when we covaried performance on the SE Confusable words [$F(2, 47) < 1$]. The adjusted means are shown in Fig. 3.

The covariance on the SE Confusable category words did show grade and context effects in the expected directions [$F(1, 27) = 8.71$ and 15.51, $ps < .01$, respectively]. Thus, with individual differences in performance controlled, the groups did not differ according to race or region. However, the context and grade factors had effects in reducing variations over and above individual differences in spelling ability as evidenced by performance on the Lect Neutral words. These are clear environmental influences on performance and their effects, independent of individual spelling ability, have obvious practical significance.

We then asked whether there would be phonological effects on spelling, over and above individual differences in spelling ability. To answer this question, we carried out a similar analysis of covariance on unconventional spellings of the Black English Confusable and Change/Deletion words using spelling performance on the first two word categories as covariates. We examined the contribution of grade, context, and racial and regional factors.

Figure 3 shows the main results of interest where one can see that the Black children gave more unconventional spellings for the BE Confusable and Change/Deletion words than did the White children $[F(2,$ 127) = 4.27, $p < .01]$. The number of unconventional spellings was reduced by grade $[F(1, 127) = 7.51, p < .01]$, and the fifth grade, Black, urban children more closely resembled the other White groups. Thus, with individual differences in spelling controlled, we found an increase in the number of unconventional spellings by Black children which correlates with phonological differences. This result suggests that children who speak Black English may have a phonological problem in spelling (and, possibly, reading) certain classes of words.

PHONEMIC FACTORS

In order to provide a more detailed analysis of possible sources of the spelling variations observed above, we then carried out an analysis of the variations per se in terms of the sound-to-letter correspondences that seemed to follow Labov's (1967) paper. Two analyses were performed. In the first, we asked whether there would be any spelling differences in various *word segments* which contain phonemes that were likely to undergo phonological transformations by Black but not by White speakers. We broke each word in the BE Confusable and Change/Deletion categories into consonatal and vocalic segments and noted which segment contained critical phonemes. We then scored the spellings as to whether or not variation occurred in that segment. If a variation occurred, we considered it as "predictable" by Labov's phonological descriptions.

We should illustrate our procedure on a set of words to avoid misinterpretation. Consider the following words whose phonological representation is symbolized $//$ $//$, indicating that it is abstract. Our symbols are those from the International Phonetic Alphabet and these representations are those supposedly used by Standard English speakers:

	Word	Phonological representation	Segmentation
(1)	throat	$//\theta\textrm{.\!\textsc{r}ot}//$	$C_1C_2 \cdot V_1C_3$
(2)	enter	$//\varepsilon\textrm{nt\textgamma}//$	$V_1C_1 \cdot C_2V_2C_3$
(3)	these	$//\theta\textrm{iz}//$	$C_1 \cdot V_1C_2$
(4)	army	$//\textrm{a\textsc{r}m\textsc{i}}//$	$V_1 \cdot C_1 \cdot C_2V_2$
(5)	farmer	$//\textrm{fa\textsc{r}m\textgamma}//$	$C_1V_1 \cdot C_2 \cdot C_3V_2C_4$
(6)	pen	$//\textrm{pen}//$	$C_1 \cdot V_1 \cdot C_2$
(7)	wasps	$//\textrm{wasps}//$	$C_1V_1 \cdot C_2C_3C_4$
(8)	ghosts	$//\textrm{gosts}//$	$C_1V_1 \cdot C_2C_3C_4$
(9)	south	$//\textrm{sa\textsc{u}\theta}//$	$C_1V_1 \cdot C_2$

In this list above, words (1), (2), and (3) should manifest spelling differences corresponding to lect differences in phonology in their *initial* segment, separated off by the dot; likewise, words (4), (5), and (6) should show spelling variations in the medial segments and words (7), (8), and (9) in their final segments. Following this procedure, the 59 words in Table 2 were segmented and scored for unconventional variation in spelling in the initial, medial, or final segments according to prediction. Then the proportion of predicted variations was obtained for each word in each context. Following this, the predicted proportions for the 118 words were compared on the urban third graders and urban fifth graders. These comparisons showed that the Black children made statistically significant *more* spelling variations in the predicted segments than did the White children. Specifically, of the 118 comparisons, urban, third-grade Black children made more predicted variations in 42 words while the White children showed more in only 28 words; the urban, fifth-grade Black children showed similar trends: 41 words had more and 25 words had fewer predicted variations than their White counterparts. These proportions of 60 and 62% were statistically reliable by sign tests ($z = 1.65$ and 1.95, $p < .05$, respectively).

Similar comparisons on White urban and suburban children showed no reliable differences for third graders but the fifth-grade urban Whites showed more predicted variations (66%, $z = 2.39$, $p < .01$).

The nature of these differences will become clearer in our subsequent phonemic analysis. Suffice it to say at this point that the observed variations in unconventional spellings were correlated with possible differences in phonology and for the Black children, these correlations were consistent with that predicted from Labov's (1967) descriptions of phonological differences.

In our second phonemic analysis, we attempted to specify further the phonological source of the spelling variations. The spellings for each of the 59 words listed in Table 2 were scored as to whether or not they conformed to the letter changes specified in the table. Again, these changes assume a close correspondence between phonology and orthography and represent our interpretation of Labov's (1967) classification. The examples and scoring rules listed in Table 2 serve as examples of our criteria.

For each of the subcategories of Table 2 and for each grade level and group of children, we found the percentage of unconventional spellings that conformed to the sound-to-spelling rules of Table 2. A summary of these percentages is given in Table 5.

We compared urban Black and White children and suburban White children within each grade level on percentages for the 13 categories listed in Table 5. Of these four comparisons, only the third-grade urban Black

TABLE 5
Percent of Unconventional Spellings Conforming to
Expected Sound-to-Letter Correspondence for Black English Speakers

		Third grade			Fifth grade		
		Urban Black	Urban White	Suburban White	Urban Black	Urban White	Suburban White
1.	Initial /θ/	3	0	5	1	10	6
	Medial /θ/	14	15	11	28	25	8
	Final /θ/	(37)	15	15	13	17	15
2.	Initial /ɪ/	13	18	10	14	17	13
	Final /ɪ/	2	0	2	0	0	0
3.	Vowel transformation	17	17	18	22	9	20
4.	Nasal /ɛ/, /ɪ/ confusion	(12)	1	(40)	28	(45)	21
5.	Final consonants						
	/t/	(20)	13	5	(26)	21	17
	/ɛ/, /ɛd/	34	33	22	(66)	54	51
	/ps/, /ts/	(28)	10	11	10	12	9
	/s/	34	(47)	40	62	(82)	58
	/d/	(43)	29	27	35	(59)	38
	/ti/, /pi/	3	0	0	5	0	(12)

children showed reliably higher proportions across the categories (sign test, $z = 1.92$, $p < .05$). The differences, then, between groups reside in some but not all assumed phonological differences.

In Table 5, we have circled those percentages which reached statistically reliable levels in pairwise contrasts, and some trends are discernable. The younger urban Black children made a higher percentage of predicted spelling variations for final //θ//, confusion between //ɛ// and //ɪ// before nasal consonants and for several final consonants and consonant clusters, // t, ts, ps, d // when compared to White urban third graders. With the exception of the final consonant //t//, these differences are not maintained by urban Black fifth graders.

These children show only a slight increase in past tense //ɛd// reductions. There are some differences between urban and suburban White speakers. Older urban White children show a higher proportion of nasal confusions, an exceptionally high incidence of plural //s// deletion, and a high percentage of final consonant //d// deletion. This set of facts helps clarify the phonological source of differences between fifth grade Whites found in the segment analysis above. Finally, since urban children, regardless of race, show more final consonant cluster simplification and medial //θ// transforms than do suburban children, one may assume phonological code sharing by these groups.

In overview, our results show that phonological representations do correlate with spelling and that, to some extent, phonological differences in lect lead to differences in spelling. The homonym data clearly show that words which are confusable at the phonological level will be substituted as spellings even when meaningful contexts are provided. However, we did not find evidence that urban Black children confused words expected to be homonymous for speakers of Black English more than White children. Black children, particularly those in the 8 to 9 year range, made more unconventional spelling variations for words that have different sound-to-letter correspondences for speakers of Black English.

When spelling ability was controlled, Black children did not differ from Whites in terms of the number of spellings for words that would be confused by Standard English speakers. However, using similar controls, Black children made reliably more variations on words which have allegedly different phonological representations for Black English than Standard English speakers. Again, meaning, as established by sentence contexts, and schooling had significant effects in reducing these unconventional spelling variations.

A consonatal and vocalic analysis of the segments in which phonemic differences between Black and Standard English speakers predicted spelling differences showed that Black children made reliably more spelling variations in these segments than did Whites. A subsequent, phoneme-to-letter analysis showed that younger urban Black children made reliably more unconventional spellings of the type predicted by Labov's (1967) phonological description of Black English speakers in northeastern cities of the United States. However, older urban Blacks did not maintain these differences in their unconventional spellings. On the basis of these results, we conclude that Smith (1972) erred in claiming that there is little or no relation of the alphabetic principle to writing.

THE ALPHABETIC PRINCIPLE: LINGUISTIC CONSIDERATIONS

We indicated in our introductory comments that the formal relation between sound and spelling (phonology and orthography) is not clearly understood. The debate is about the alphabetic principle which assumes some correspondence between spoken and written symbols. The question seems to be: What level of representation has psychological relevance?

A word may be represented phonologically by several different symbol systems. These systems have been treated as "levels," moving from a detailed phonetic description to a systematic phonemic representation to a deeper, underlying phonemic level which is "closer" to the written form. For example, the word *take* may be represented:

    (1)   phonetic: //tʰɛéɪk//
    (2)   phonemic: //tēɪk//

or

    (3)   underlying phonemic: //tēk//

Linguists (e.g., Fasold, 1969) have discounted the phonetic level as a direct source of the sound-to-letter correspondence since it requires too many symbols. Smith (1972) treats it as "epiphenomenal" in the sense that the "sound," including stress, follows knowing the word, not vice versa. The issue thus has focused on the second and third alternatives.

The phonemic position has been questioned by Fasold (1969) who favors a more abstract level of representation stemming from Reed (1965) and Chomsky and Halle's (1968) generative phonology. The latter theory argues that English orthography is optimal, at least for skilled readers, and that one would not expect lect differences to produce differences in spelling. Our data with the older Black children tend to support this expectation. There would be, as Fasold (1969) notes, no reason to develop a special spelling system for Black English speakers. In the main, conventional English orthography is considered to be as adequate for Black English speakers as for other speakers of American English. This does not, given our findings, mean that there is no necessity for teachers to make special adjustments for interpreting and teaching conventional spellings or reading by Black children whose lect differs from that of the teacher.

English orthography may be considered optimal for speakers of different lects only if the children have been able to acquire some knowledge about the morphemic similarities among words, for example, *telegram* and *telegraph*. These kinds of similarities give rise to rules by analogy which overcome differences in phonological representation, but they have to be acquired. Thus, even though a child marks lect differences in the underlying representation, if he or she has not been able to acquire some knowledge about the morphemic similarities among words, then differences in spelling between speakers who differ in pronunciation may occur. We believe that this is the case for our younger Black children and that the teaching of these correspondences through examples may promote the development of these analogic and other rules.

The issue as to whether the Black English speaker has (1) a different underlying form than the White Standard English speaker but has not acquired the rules to compensate for the differences or (2) the same underlying form but has acquired a different set of rules of correspondence between sound and spelling is not resolved here. It may be the case that the distinction between systematic phonemic and underlying phonemic (systematic phonetic) levels is not real psychologically. Rather, if we interpret Steinberg (1973) correctly, the differences in spelling we observed, especially for the younger inner-city Black children, stem from surface phonemic differences. Our data are certainly consistent with this assertion but do not discriminate between the other alternatives which assume different or common underlying representations between Black English and Standard English speakers.

OTHER FACTORS AND PROCESSES

In this section, we would like to consider other factors that are psychologically significant in order to temper conclusions that phonological factors alone account for our results. We began by asking ourselves what other factors besides phonological ones might be important. An analysis of the frequency of occurrence (Thorndike & Lorge, 1944) and length of the words in Table 1 revealed a correlation with number of unconventional spellings. Table 6 gives a summary of these word characteristics.

In Table 6, note that the Black English words were both *longer and less frequent in occurrence* than were the words in the first two categories. The number of unconventional spellings was thus positively correlated with these confounding factors, making interpretation of our data in terms of phonological factors alone quite difficult.

TABLE 6
Frequency and Length Characteristics
of Words Used in the Study

Frequency	Lect Neutral	SE Confusable	BE Confusable	BE Transformation
AA	24	23	19	20
A	1	8	8	7
10-50 per million	7	1	5	5
Mean number of letters	4.06	4.00	4.32	5.72

One would expect schooling and reading practice to be helpful in learning the spellings of less familiar and longer words; that is, one's immediate memory for a word as well as one's retrieval of information related to it should be enhanced by practice in spelling and reading these words. Can we assume such differences between the groups of children in our study? We think so but do not have independent corroboration.

Smith's (1972) arguments on strategies for spelling and reading words strike us as very plausible and avoid the overemphasis on linguistic accounts for language performance. In spelling, Smith suggests that the child may use more than the phonological level as a cue to spell a word. He, the child, can rely upon learned, organized, integrated movement sequences which are derived from experience in rote spelling and writing. The child may also have stored spelling lists derived from rotely memorized letter sequences or stored visual patterns. He may also develop analogic strategies to spell novel words based upon their morphemic or printed similarities. *Telegraph* and *telegram* are similar not only morphemically but visually as they share the first seven letters. Information from visual configurations and sequences of letters has been by and large ignored in linguistic accounts of spelling.

The above arguments suggest that we have much more information available to use than phonology to decipher a word's orthography. This information, when represented in memory, may be organized at some deeper, more abstract level, but it is deducible from sensory input which is visual, acoustic, or motoric in nature and is decodable into all three forms of expression. When differences in pronunciation exist, educational emphasis on tracing or copying letters as well as some version of "whole word" reading *may be preferred* since these *may* accomplish the result of efficiently recognizing and writing words without penalizing the child for differences in phonology.

As a final test of one's accuracy in conventional spelling, Smith's (1972) description of what he does in spelling a word is insightful. In the act of spelling, Smith indicates that there are really several optional strategies. Which strategy one uses depends upon whether one is satisfied that the spelling matches some internal standard; that is, one may write a word with little or no reflection—it emerges directly as a string of letters. Then one checks the *visual* pattern achieved as in the act of reading: "Does it *look* right?" one asks. If the answer is "yes," one continues on. If "no," then one can use other strategies. Among these are rules to handle exceptions ("*i* before *e*, except after *c* or when sounded like *a* as in neighbor or weigh"), morphemic analogies (psych*ological* and soci*ological*), vowel shift rules (sane and sanity, profane and profanity), and so on. When these fail, one may be satisfied with spelling equivalences at a phonemic level.

The majority of words may be handled as lists of rotely learned spellings from which regularities may be easily discerned. With reading and writing practice, words may become idiograms in the sense that they form unique patterns, and we apparently have a considerable capacity for storing a large number of such instances. The problem is that they take time and experience to obtain. The acquisition of these patterns and strategies would appear to overcome any total reliance upon phonology to spell.

It may be that phonology plays a role in novel situations where one does not already have a stored representation of the word. For young children or persons learning another language, this, of course, is more likely. For adults, the one example which illustrates this is the learning of surnames. If one heard [solzánitsn], one would be hard put to spell it. If one read *Solzhenitsyn*, one would be hard put to say it to oneself and, therefore, might rely upon the visual pattern for recognition. However, if one both hears [solzánitsn] and sees *Solzhenitsyn*, one has two ways to begin remembering a Russian writer's name.

ACKNOWLEDGMENTS

This chapter is based upon a Senior Thesis by the first author, Princeton University Psychology Department, 1974. The research was supported, in part, by Grant MH-19223 to T. Trabasso by the National Institute of Mental Health. The chapter was written while the second author was a Visiting Professor at the University of Edinburgh. He wishes to thank the Department of Psychology and Professor David Vowles for their generosity. In addition, we wish to thank Deborah Harrison, Margaret Donaldson Salter, and Phillip Smith for their constructive comments on an earlier version of the manuscript.

REFERENCES

Chomsky, N., & Halle, M. *The sound pattern of English.* New York: Harper, 1968.
Fasold, R. Orthography in reading materials for Black English speakers. In J. C. Baratz & R. W. Shuy (Eds.), *Teaching black children to read.* Washington, D.C.: Center for Applied Linguistics Urban Language Series, 1969. Pp. 68–91.
Hodges, R. E. Theoretical frameworks of English orthography. *Elementary English,* 1972, 8, 1089–1097.
Labov, W. Some sources of reading problems for Negro speakers of nonstandard English. In A. Frazier (Ed.), *New directions in elementary English.* Champaign, Illinois: National Council of Teachers of English, 1967. Pp. 140–167. Reprinted in J. C. Baratz & R. W. Shuy (Eds.), *Teaching black children to read.* Washington, D.C.: Center for Applied Linguistics Urban Language Series, 1969. Pp. 29–67.
O'Neal, V. Underlying phonological structures and dialect differences: A preliminary psycholinguistic investigation. Unpublished Senior Thesis, Department of Psychology, Princeton University, 1974.

Reed, D. W. A theory of language, speech, and writing. *Elementary English,* 1965, **42,** 845–851.

Smith, F. Phonology and orthography: Reading and writing. *Elementary English,* 1972, **8,** 1075–1088.

Steinberg, D. Phonology, reading and Chomsky and Halle's optimal orthography *Journal of Psycholinguistic Research,* 1973, **2,** 239–258.

Thorndike, E., & Lorge, I. *The teacher's wordbook of 30,000 words.* New York: Teachers College, Columbia University, 1944.

10

Techniques for Eliciting Casual Speech Samples for the Study of the Black English Vernacular

Deborah Sears Harrison

University of Kansas

Do all Black Americans speak a Black English vernacular? Is there more than one variety of Black English? Are there sufficient differences between Black English and Standard English to justify treating them as separate languages in the educational system? These and related questions deserve serious study because the answers will have important and far-reaching social, economic, and educational consequences, not only for Black Americans, but also for any American who speaks an ethnic, social, or regional dialect of English. Answers to these questions will come from careful analysis of actual speech samples of Black Americans representing all the many age, educational, economic, occupational, and regional variations found in the Black community.

However, to date, many of the studies of Black English have worked with speakers drawn from restricted and unrepresentative samples of the Black community. The speech patterns of teenaged gang members, representative of the Black street culture, have been studied extensively (e.g., Labov, Cohen, Robbins, & Lewis, 1968). Other studies are based on speech data generated by mother–child interactions or adult authority figure–preschool child interactions (e.g., Englemann, 1970). One experimental study (Baratz, 1969) tested Black and White school-aged children using Black English "translations" of Standard English sentences generated by the experimenter, which may or may not have accurately reflected Black speech patterns. These and other studies have tapped an extremely limited segment of the immensely varied Black American culture and many socioeconomic and demographic groups have been largely ignored. Yet, Black men, women, and children from all educational, occupational, income, and age groups must contribute to the language data base for an accurate picture of Black speech patterns to emerge.

A major obstacle to collecting the appropriate data base has been the inability of linguistic techniques to successfully and consistently elicit high-quality casual speech samples. This is even a greater problem when the researcher is unfamiliar with the casual speech patterns of the language group he is studying. This is frequently the case when members of certain Black socioeconomic groups are interviewed by linguists. This contribution explores techniques which will allow linguists and Black speakers to work together in collecting these important missing data.

The problem of how to collect casual speech samples is a crucial one for the study of the language of speakers of Black English. The vernacular is, by definition, the most casual of speech styles and most varieties of Black English are best characterized as vernaculars. They usually occur in informal situations where the speakers feel little need to monitor their speech flow. It is that speech style in which a person "argues with his wife, scolds his children, or passes the time of day with his friends [Labov, 1972, p. 85]." Because the lack of monitoring helps to eliminate "hypercorrection" of speech and the resulting irregular phonological and grammatical patterns, observation of the vernacular, or the most casual speech style, provides probably the richest source and least biased data for the analysis of the structure of a language.

Since the vernacular is usually reserved for use in informal situations, it is generally not used by a linguistic informant when he is taking part in a linguistic interview. This creates what Labov refers to as the Observer's Paradox:

> The aim of linguistic research in the community must be to find out how people talk when they are not being systematically observed; yet we can only obtain these data by systematic observation. The problem is of course not insoluble: we must either find ways of supplementing the formal interviews with other data, or change the structure of the interview situation by one means or another [Labov, 1972, p. 209].

Labov (1972) suggests several ways for the linguist to overcome the constraints of the interview situation. These methods are all calculated to help divert attention away from speech per se and to allow the vernacular to emerge. The methods may be grouped into three categories.

The first category involves language recordings made in situations well removed from the traditional linguistic interview. They may invoke role playing by the informant and observer or direct observation in real-life situations. For example, the informant may be a department store employee responding to a request for directions from a "customer." Or, the linguist can clandestinely record the speech of people in public places, such as lunch counters or zoos. In these situations, the speakers are completely unaware that their speech patterns are being observed or recorded. In fact, they are functioning as linguistic informants unknowingly and, therefore, unself-consciously.

Because the unsystematic and candid observation of speech in public places may contain many biases in the sample of persons or situations obtained, Labov (1972) feels that these data should be used primarily as a corrective to the bias toward formal speech found in the interview situation. On the other hand, he foresees an important role for the rapid and anonymous method illustrated by asking for directions in a department store. This method controls the behavior of subjects yet avoids the bias of the experimental context as well as the irregular interference of prestige norms.

The second class of methods moves closer to the formal interview, but relies on the peer group interaction to control the speech flow, thereby eliminating the formal effects of an interviewer versus the subject. This method involves recording the speech of persons participating in the activities of a group that was formed naturally and whose members are voluntary or self-selected. Though the group members may be aware of the linguist's interest in what they are saying and doing (each member wears a Lavaliere microphone), their attention is not focused on their speech, and the effects of systematic observation appear to be reduced, especially with time. The linguist thus functions as a participant–observer in this method, but he allows or tries to allow for most of the interaction to take place between the members of the group. However this does not necessarily yield good quality data on individual speech patterns.

The third category contains contexts which can occur within the formal linguistic interview, but which increase the probability of the informant using the vernacular. Three of these contexts can be introduced into the interview by the linguist himself, or be encouraged and exploited by him when they occur spontaneously. In the first two contexts, the interviewer asks questions which recreate strong emotions the interviewee has felt in the past or he brings up topics which cannot easily be talked about in a formal style. These two contexts were incorporated in the questionnaire designed for the Detroit Dialect Study (Shuy, Wolfram, & Riley, 1968). The interview included questions about games and leisure activities, most-hated or most-loved teachers, and the interviewees were asked to tell about situations they had been in where there was danger of being killed or dying. The staff of the Detroit Dialect Study report that these topics were productive and reached nearly all but the most reserved or hostile informants.

Since these two contexts occur within the interview session, the informant is well aware that he is being interviewed, but the subject matter seems to be successful in overriding the control or editing of casual speech which is normally associated with the linguistic interview.

A third context for the elicitation of casual speech occurs when the informant discusses subjects not in direct response to questions asked by the interviewer. The linguist, in this situation, encourages the informant to digress, hoping that discussion of favorite points of view, rambling replies, or outbursts of rhetoric will facilitate the shift from formal to casual speech.

Labov (1972) discusses two final contexts which may occur during various intervals and breaks in the interview. These time periods can, at an unconscious level, lead the person to believe that he is not being interviewed at that moment and he is more likely to be relaxed, informal, and casual. If, before, after, or during a break in the interview session, the interviewee perceives that the role and speech constraints of the interview are not in force, he may tend to address the linguist in a more casual speech style. If the interview session is interrupted by a third person, such as a member of his family or a neighbor, the informant is more likely to speak to him in the vernacular. These latter events cannot be initiated by the linguist, however, and thus may or may not occur during the course of the interview. They depend either on the unexpected interruption of an outsider or on the informant's own perception of the situation.

As fruitful as these methods may be for the elicitation of casual speech, they cannot yield a complete set of language data for the linguist to analyze. At best, the data collected by these methods are used in conjunction with other data generated in a regular interview session, or as supplementary evidence on speech patterns. The linguist who wishes to study speech patterns using casual speech samples as his primary data must have at his disposal a more reliable and systematic method for the elicitation of the vernacular. This method must consistently provide good data and, as Labov points out:

> No matter what other methods may be used to obtain samples of speech (group sessions, anonymous observation), the only way to obtain sufficient good data on the speech of any one person is through an individual, tape-recorded interview: that is, through the most obvious kind of systematic observation [Labov, 1972, p. 209].

Thus, we once again find ourselves face-to-face with the "Observer's Paradox."

It seems reasonable, therefore, to consider ways of restructuring the interview situation so that it will be conducive to casual speech. A start in this direction can be made both by analyzing the nature of the traditional linguistic interview and also by exploring the possible changes that could be incorporated into a restructured interview, and some implications of those changes.

There are many important psychological and social factors at work in an interview session. The interview is a special subset of the many possible forms of verbal communication between people, and many factors distinguish it from an ordinary conversation. Usually, in our society, there are distinct status and role differences separating the interviewer and interviewee, the flow of information is one-sided, and the technique of obtaining this information involves sustained questioning by the interviewer. This form of communication is accepted by the interviewee because he hopes the interview will prove beneficial to him in some way. Samarin (1967) calls this the "assistance interview," for the person goes to a medical, legal, or mechanical expert for help with the understanding that the expert must ask questions to achieve his—the client's—own goal.

The person acting as the interviewer is doing so in an official capacity and his role is formally defined within a legal, institutional, or social context. The range of questioning and the type of information exchanged are directly related to the particular kind of assistance or benefits the interviewee is seeking and the interviewer is able to render through his position as the agent of a social institution. Occupations which frequently involve interviewer–interviewee interactions are college admissions officer, welfare case worker, personnel manager, and psychiatrist, to name but a few.

In general this type of interview is characterized by the well-defined roles of both interviewer and interviewee and the assumption that this unusual form of verbal communication is justified by the potential it has for realizing the personal goals of the interviewee.

The research interview has surface similarities to the "assistance" interview, but it incorporates some important differences. Like the assistance interview, the exchange of information as well as the actual amount of talking done is vastly unequal. The statuses of the interviewer and interviewee are dissimilar, with the research interviewer usually representing some establishment institution. In terms of who asks the questions and who supplies the answers, the roles of the two parties involved in the research interview are the same as the two parties involved in the assistance interview. But, significantly, the subject areas to be covered have generally been determined beforehand by the interviewer, with little or no input from the interviewee. In fact, it is often considered desirable to conceal the true research goals from the interviewee to minimize the possibility of his giving socially desirable responses or answers which he feels will help "prove" the researcher's hypothesis.

One extremely important difference between the two types of interviews is that the research interview is not conducted for the benefit of the interviewee. Although he may be reimbursed for services rendered with money or some other form of payment, the interviewer is the one who actually benefits. Blauner and Wellman (1973) point out that, ironically, social research tends to widen the material and status gaps between subjects and social scientists. The scientist receives research grants and a salary and the resulting publications advance him in income and rank. The subject, on the other hand, gives his time, energy, and trust, yet receives almost nothing from his participation.

The linguistic interview is, of course, a research interview. But once again we find some interesting and important differences. In the linguistic interview it is an accepted practice to acquaint the interviewee with the goals of the research. Quite often he is even given some simple linguistic training so that his responses may prove even more valuable. In linguistic jargon, the interviewee is referred to as the informant, because his role is to inform the linguist about his (the informant's) language. This is made clear to the informant, and so we find that both the linguist and the informant share knowledge, not only about the goals of the interview, but also about the subject matter to be covered. Although the linguist guides the progress and direction of the interview session by skilled questioning of the informant, the informant is encouraged to actively contribute additional relevant material, even if unsolicited. The informant derives little, if any, personal benefit from the linguistic interview, though often he is paid for his time.

But, there are some aspects of the traditional linguistic interview method which make it particularly unsuitable for studying Black English. Over the years, linguists have developed and refined this method to effectively elicit information about the structure of a language and the informant is free to convey this information by speaking in the language being studied or in some other language spoken by both the informant and the linguist. In fact, the informant usually uses both languages, perhaps generating examples of speech patterns in the language being studied, but elaborating on the meaning and usage of those examples in a different language.

However, this method has not been successfully extended to deal with the research situation where the linguist and the informant both speak the same language, and the linguist is interested in studying a *dialect* of that same language which is spoken by the informant but not by the linguist. As stated earlier, it is important in this type of research for the informant to speak unself-consciously in his own dialect and not any other dialect of the language. The informant is not required to talk about the structure of his dialect, but simply to talk about anything, and the essential thing is for him to use his dialect as he would in everyday speech interactions. While the question–answer format of the traditional linguistic interview works well when the informant's task is to supply information about his language, it can hinder the collection of casual speech data for several reasons. First, it forces the informant to focus his attention on his speech patterns, which may cause monitoring, hypercorrection and distortion of the dialect. Second, a mismatch between the dialects of the linguist and the informant can also affect the informant's speech, especially if the dialectical differences correspond to status and prestige differences. If the informant perceives the linguist's dialect as being more prestigious than his own, his speech will tend to approximate the dialect spoken by the linguist, thus creating additional distortion of his own dialect. Third, Labov points out that the longer an informant digresses the more likely he will begin using his natural speech patterns. For these and other reasons the question–response format, characteristic of the traditional interview, should perhaps be abandoned when studying dialects. A change from this format to another which facilitates the elicitation of high-quality casual speech samples could prove beneficial to linguists for several reasons.

One of the most unpleasant aspects of an interview is its similarity to an interrogation. If the linguist is relieved of the duty of eliciting data by direct questioning of the informant, this might facilitate the evolution of a discussion format which would be more appropriate for casual speech not only for the informant, but for the interviewer as well. A discussion format would also help eliminate the constraints created by the well-defined roles associated with the research interview. The role of questioner could be assumed by either the linguist or the informant as a consequence of natural communication requirements. This, in turn, would help to balance the one-sided nature of the interview and allow both parties to be involved in the exchange of information, opinions, and beliefs.

It should also be assumed that the informant, and not the linguist, is the best judge of the topics which are appropriate for discussion in a casual speech style. The discussion format would work well here because the informant would have as much or more influence than the linguist in determining what they would talk about. This shared control over the subject matter could be crucial, especially since a discussion conducted in a casual speech style will more likely center on matters of personal interest and concern to the informant. If he feels that the conversation is becoming a little too personal, he is free to move on to other areas. Also, an informant is more likely to freely discuss a personal topic that he introduces into the conversation than he is to talk about that same subject when it was asked about by an interviewer.

Equalizing the roles of the interviewer and the informant as well as the amount of control each has over what happens in a one-to-one, face-to-face situation may be two of the keys to successfully eliciting casual speech. The interviewer, no longer able to hide behind the "neutral" mask of the researcher, will become a participant in a discussion, perhaps using his most casual speech style to help set the tone of the conversation. The informant, hopefully, will respond appropriate to this style cue, maintaining a greatly increased amount of control over the subjects to be discussed, and at the same time supplying the linguistic researcher with the data of interest.

Up to this point, the terms linguist and interviewer have been used interchangeably. However, an especially beneficial characteristic of a discussion format is that it eliminates the need for a trained linguist to collect the data and, therefore, adds flexibility to the data collection stage of language research. A member of the dialect group being studied could replace the linguist. Since the emphasis is on eliciting casual speech, he would require no specialized linguistic skills and his cultural, racial, and dialectical similarity to the informant should help eliminate barriers to the free flow of speech. A dialect group member would likely be more sensitive to the topics that would stimulate casual speech and would be less likely to arouse the suspicions or hostilities of informants wary of speaking freely with a culturally or racially different interviewer. Given that the relationship between social scientists and the Black community has long been uneasy, the use of community members might be particularly advantageous in the study of Black English. This might also increase access to previously unrepresented groups in the Black community.

The linguist can expect the causal speech samples collected by community members to provide him with systematic and representative dialect data for formal linguistic analysis. Labov (1972) discusses methods for verifying that the speech samples actually do represent the speaker's most casual style. The community member could also aid the linguist at this stage by commenting on the casualness of the recorded speech samples and by clarifying grammatical structures and semantic usages unfamiliar to the linguist. These recordings would also be useful in selecting, for future studies, topics which are most conducive to eliciting the vernacular. The growth of a systematic data base should also illuminate language patterns which require further study.

In concluding, the importance of studying Black English should be reemphasized. It is the dialect of the largest minority group in the United States and has greatly influenced the language of all Americans. Linguists, educators, and the general public are becoming increasingly aware that, far from being a collection of poor speech habits, Black English is a highly systematic dialect, which has important implications for teaching reading skills and understanding interpersonal and intercultural communication. The techniques presented here will, hopefully, provide an initial means for developing the representative data base necessary for scientific study of this rich and varied dialect and lead to further efforts to construct a sound methodology for the elicitation of casual speech patterns.

REFERENCES

Baratz, J. C. A bidialectical task for determining language proficiency in economically disadvantaged children. *Child Development,* **40,** 1969, 889–901.

Blauner, R. & Wellman, D. Toward the decolonization of social research. In J. A. Ladner (Ed.), *The death of white sociology.* New York: Vintage Books, 1973.

Englemann, S. How to construct effective language programs for the poverty child. In F. Williams (Ed.), *Language and poverty.* Chicago: Markham Publ., 1970.

Labov, W. *Sociolinguistic patterns.* Philadelphia: University of Pennsylvania Press, 1972.

Labov, W., Cohen, P., Robbins, C., & Lewis, J. *A study of the non-Standard English of Negro and Puerto Rican speakers in New York City.* Final Report (1968), Cooperative Research Project 3288. 2 vols. Philadelphia: U.S. Regional Survey, 204 N. 35th St., Philadelphia, Pennsylvania, 19104.

Samarin, W. J. *Field linguistics: A guide to linguistic field work.* New York: Holt, Rinehart & Winston, 1967.

Shuy, R., Wolfram, W., & Riley, W. *Field techniques in an urban language study.* Washington, D.C.: Center for Applied Linguistics, 1968.

11

Black and White Children's Responses to Black English Vernacular and Standard English Sentences: Evidence for Code-Switching

William S. Hall

The Rockefeller University

Several professional investigators of diverse disciplines have recently become more interested in the facility with which children whose "parent" lect is either Black English Vernacular (BEV) or Standard English (SE) can switch between such codes. This ability to use different lects in appropriate contexts is a cognitive skill common to bilingual or polyglot speakers and the linguistic, psychological, or educational implications of these abilities are only dimly realized.

Data from a large-scale language study (Hall & Freedle, 1973) conducted by the author and a colleague in the northeastern part of the United States may throw some light on the question. The study included 240 children distributed over ages 8 and 10 years. Equal numbers of boys and girls were included. One-half of the children were from the lower socioeconomic group; the other half were from the middle socioeconomic group as determined by the Hollingshead scale (Hollingshead & Redlich, 1958). Using an individual testing format, the interviewer asked the children to listen to sentences, one-half of which were spoken in BEV and the other half in SE, and to repeat them. The repetitions were recorded

TABLE 1
Some Examples of Syntactic Differences between
Standard English and the Black English Vernacular[a,b]

	Variable	Standard English	Black English Vernacular
1.	Linking verb (copula)	He *is* going	He_____ goin'.
2.	Possessive marker	John*'s* cousin.	John___ cousin.
3.	Plural marker	I have five cent*s*.	I got five cent___.
4.	Third person singular (verb agreement)	He live*s* in New York.	He live___ in New York.
5.	Past marker	Yesterday he walk*ed* home.	Yesterday he walk___ home.
6.	"If" construction	I asked *if he did it*.	I ask *did he do it*.
7.	Negation	I *don't* have *any*.	I *don't* got *none*.
8.	Use of "be"	Statement: He is here *all the time*.	Statement: He *be* here.
9.	Subject expression	John moved.	John, *he* move.
10.	Verb form	I *drank* the milk.	I *drunk* the milk.
11.	Future form	I *will go* home.	I*'ma go* home.
12.	Indefinite article	I want *an* apple.	I want *a* apple.
13.	Pronoun form	*We* have to do it.	*Us* got to do it.
14.	Pronoun expressing possession	*His* book.	*He* book.
15.	Preposition	He is over *at* John's house.	He over *to* John house.
		He teaches *at* Francis Pool.	He teach___ Francis Pool.
16.	Use of "do"	Contradiction: No, he *isn't*.	Contradiction: No, he *don't*.

[a] Data from Hall and Freedle (1973).
[b] This table is adapted from one presented by Joan Baratz (1969, pp. 99–100).

on tape (Table 1).[1] The expectations were that the child would (1) perform better on sentences given in his parent lect, and (2) translate from his parent lect into a nonparent one, depending upon his ability to switch between the lects.

---

[1] Examples of the criteria used in scoring the children's response for BEV and SE are given in Table 1. It should be noted that the grammatical forms listed in Table 1 by no means exhaust all of those that one might find in either SE or BEV. But as far as BEV goes, research results from various sections of the United States suggest that these occur with great frequency (see, for example, Hall & Freedle, 1973; Labov, 1973; Mitchell-Kernan, 1969).

EVIDENCE FOR CODE SWITCHING

We will now discuss the results of the study, beginning with how well the children responded to Standard English sentences. Our measure of interest is the proportion of correct repetitions of sentences.

First, there was a relationship between level of correct performance on SE sentences and socioeconomic status (SES). The higher the child's SES, the greater was his proficiency in correctly repeating Standard English sentences. Therefore, White middle-class children were the most proficient; Black middle-class children, the next most proficient; White lower-class children followed the Black middle-class children in degree of proficiency; and Black lower-class children were the least proficient.

The reverse was the case with respect to correct repetitions of BEV sentences; that is, the higher the children's SES, the more ineptly they performed. The only exception to this finding was for White children, and here the middle-class children reversed positions with the lower-class ones. But these particular findings do not tell us what we need to know about the extent to which children code-switch. To get a better insight into the question we must look at data on the translation behavior of the children (see Table 2).

Before discussing this question, we must first make clear what we mean by *translation*. When a child furnishes a grammatical form in BEV for an SE sentence, we say that a translation has occurred. Similarly, when a BEV sentence is the stimulus and the child restates it in grammatical forms from Standard English, we again say that a translation has occurred. When we apply this definition to the data we are discussing, an interesting phenomenon is apparent. When the group tested was given sentences in SE, the results show a relationship between race, SES, and translation activity. Black lower SES children were more inclined to translate SE sentences into BEV, whereas the other groups hardly translated at all (although middle SES children engaged in this activity to a slight degree). On the other hand, when the children were given BEV sentences, we found a relationship between race, SES, and translation, but in a different way. Lower SES Black children translated the least and middle SES White children the most.

The question that should now be asked is to what degree do the patterns of correct repetition of sentences and translation provide evidence for code-switching among Black and White children? The answer seems to be that the data affirm the presence of code-switching; that is, children frequently responded by using a language code different from the one in which the original stimulus was stated. To understand more precisely

TABLE 2
The Effect of Race and SES Levels on Proportion of
Correct Repetitions and Proportion of Translations for
Standard English and Black English Vernacular[a]

Type of stimulus sentence	Type of response	Eight-year-old Blacks		Eight-year-old Whites	
		Lower	Middle	Lower	Middle
Standard English	Correct repetition	.501	.595	.584	.791
BEV	Translation	.198	.244	.287	.444
BEV	Correct repetition	.300	.298	.134	.129
Standard English	Translation	.217	.145	.075	.058
		Ten-year-old Blacks		Ten-year-old Whites	
		Lower	Middle	Lower	Middle
Standard English	Correct repetition	.716	.829	.784	.897
BEV	Translation	.293	.410	.463	.495
BEV	Correct repetition	.460	.377	.174	.217
Standard English	Translation	.195	.103	.056	.026

[a]Data from Hall and Freedle (1973)

what is implied, we will examine an interpretation first advanced by Baratz (1969). She suggests that BEV and SE are different *coding schemas*. In terms of the data just presented, we interpret Baratz's statement to mean that children who are more familiar with BEV, as has been observed to be the case for the lower SES Blacks, will tend to encode in their-term memory information corresponding to the SE code.

For example, if the incoming stimulus for a Black lower-class child is in his familiar dialect, the child does not have to do any extra work in encoding the information since it already is in the preferred, parent lect. If the child retrieves the information in the same form as it is coded in his memory, this means that he will repeat a large number of BEV grammatical structures correctly. This same Black child also receives SE sentences. By the above argument, he will tend to encode many of these SE sentences in BEV form. When it is time to retrieve them, he should thus give back many translations, since by assumption he tends to retrieve information in terms of the representation in his immediate or short-term memory.

Exactly the reverse argument holds for middle-class White children. Briefly, they will get a large proportion of standard structures correct, and will also tend to give a large proportion of translations from BEV into SE.

This is exactly what happened in the data presented here. Middle SES Blacks and lower SES Whites fall somewhere in between the two extremes, most likely because they speak a mixed lect. Indeed this statement has been corroborated in some recent work on memory and dialect with young children (see Hall, Reder, & Cole, 1975). Using a story recall technique, they found that Black children, when retelling stories, did so in a mixture of BEV and SE grammatical forms.

To summarize: When asked to recall sentences, Black children perform better than do White children in terms of percentages correct when the stimulus is given in BEV. White children perform better than do Black children when the stimulus is given in SE. Moreover, children switch from one code to the other, and Black children show superiority in this technique, which suggests that their total linguistic resources are greater than that of monolingual White children.

Having seen that children do in fact code-switch when given stimulus sentences in BEV and SE, we are faced with the question of the origin of this behavior. Our feeling is that formal schooling plays a critical role in this regard, a feeling that is supported by the following data (see Hall & Freedle, 1973, for a more technical analysis).

The data have to do with the averages of the correct recall of sentences for four groups of children (lower SES Blacks, middle SES Blacks, lower SES Whites, and middle SES Whites) at two age periods (8 and 10).

To gauge the effect of schooling on code switching given the data under discussion, we must first pose and answer the following attendant questions:

1. Is the rate of change for White children in response to SE any different from that for Black children?

2. Is the rate of change for White children in response to BEV any different from that for Black children?

3. Do Black children show a higher or lower rate measure in responding to SE as compared with BEV?

4. Do lower SES and middle SES Black children differ in their rate measures for SE?

5. Does this class difference for SE rate measures also hold for lower and middle SES White children?

6. Is there a similar rate difference for SES when White children respond to BEV?

7. Do Black children show differences similar to those of White children across SES in responding to BEV?

The answers to these questions reveal patterns of similarity as well as difference. Black children are not significantly different from White children in their rate of improvement (change) from 8 to 10 years when responding to SE sentences. Since language production as presented here involves such underlying abilities as memory, comprehension of language, etc., we interpret the finding to mean that Black children are not inferior to White children in their "learning ability." They do differ from Whites, however, in that they did not get as many SE sentences correct as did the White children at age 8. On the other hand, we find that Black children have a significantly higher rate than do White children when responding correctly to BEV sentences from 8 to 10 years. Whether or not this latter finding reflects a difference in opportunity to learn BEV among the groups or something else is not clear. But it is an especially interesting finding in light of the fact that our work reveals that Blacks also learn SE at a much higher rate than they do BEV from the 8- to 10-year period, a difference that we interpret as reflecting an ever-increasing exposure to SE as well as a steady pressure from the school setting to learn and speak SE.

When one moves from racial to SES categories the findings are quite revealing. Taking the results on Black children first, we find that whereas all children improve in their ability to use SE as reflected in the kind of task given, middle SES children improve significantly, more so than do those in the lower SES category. This probably reflects the prevailing middle-class orientation of the school's curriculum and the facility of the middle SES children to identify with it. They have, that is, a higher motivation and willingness to gain competence in SE. We speculate, moreover, that lower SES children probably have a greater sense of antagonism to SE, as well as less contact with a range of speakers of it, largely as a result of the kinds of groupings of children set up in the school as well as the school's expectation for lower SES children.

If a class or SES interpretation is true, it should be generalizable across race lines. When we examine the data for the lower- and middle-class White children in response to SE, we find that middle-class students outdistance lower SES children, although to a less significant degree than is the case among Black children. We must keep in mind that SE more closely approximates the lect of lower SES White children than that of lower SES Black children, although such an observation is not entirely borne out when we examine responses of this group of children to BEV sentences. The middle SES children show more gain than do lower SES children.

In summary, the pattern of results from the study discussed here indicates that Black children irrespective of SES level are equal to White children in their rate of improvement in SE from 8 to 10 years. Black children are superior to White children in their facility with BEV. Lower SES Black children "learn" SE more slowly than do middle-class Black children, which does not seem to be the case among White children of differing SES levels.

We feel justified in our claim that code-switching occurs in Black and White children and that it seems more prevalent among Black children. The evidence supporting our claim can be found in (1) the translation behavior of 8- and 10-year-old children from differing SES levels, and (2) the increase in the ability to repeat back SE sentences from ages 8 to 10. This second point also supports our contention that education is effective in facilitating the code-switching that we observed. We cannot close this presentation without discussing why a child might develop skill in code-switching, particularly if his parent lect is BEV. While we do not know for certain, we speculate that it has to do primarily with his perception of the negative social consequences for him of speaking a "nonstandard" lect.

The social consequences of nonstandard speech for children can affect teacher–pupil as well as peer relationships. The consequences of a teacher's attitude toward a given lect are profound. For example, it can affect her initial judgment about how smart a child is likely to be, or how we will fare as a learner, how he is grouped for instruction, and how his contributions in class are treated, etc. This in turn affects the child's attitude about himself as a school learner, his willingness to participate, his expectations about results of his participation, etc. The consequences of nonstandard speech with respect to one's standing with peers are also profound. It is often suggested that high status in peer and school settings requires opposing rules for using or not using nonstandard speech at different ages. Then it is the child's perception of the risks involved in speaking a nonstandard lect and the gains or benefits to be derived from speaking a standard one that leads him to want to learn to code-switch.

REFERENCES

Baratz, J. C. A bi-dialectal task for determining language proficiency in economically disadvantaged Negro children. *Child Development,* 1969, **40,** 889–902.

Hall, W. S., & Freedle, R. O. A developmental investigation of standard and nonstandard English among black and white children. *Human Development,* 1973, **16,** 440–464.

Hall, W. S., Reder, S., & Cole, M. Story recall in young Black and White children: Effects of racial group membership, race of experimenter, and dialect, *Developmental Psychology,* 1975, in press.

Hollingshead, A. B. & Redlich, F. C. *Social class and mental illness: A community study.* New York: Wiley, 1958.

Labov, W. *Language in the inner city: Studies in the Black English vernacular.* Philadelphia: University of Pennsylvania Press, 1973.

Mitchell-Kernan, C. I. Language behavior in a black urban community. Unpublished doctoral dissertation, University of California at Berkeley, 1969.

12

Black English in Black Folklore

Danille Taylor

There are probably as many views about Black English, what it is and from where it came, as there are about Black folklore. One of the strongest relates Black English to African roots and comes from the development of the concept of the oral tradition. African society is oral as opposed to European culture being literate in the sense of stressing the written form of communication, and the differences between these two types of cultures may foster misunderstanding between the two peoples. Black folklore is a vehicle through which Black English can be studied. The influence of the oral African tradition on Black culture can be traced through the evolution of Black folklore, its forms and vernacular, that is, Black English.

Many connotations come to mind when one mentions the word "folklore," "primitive," "uncultured," "unsophisticated," etc. On closer analysis of folklore and the "folks" from which it is derived, these impressions vanish. The folk or people that derive a folklore do not have to be confined to any class or ethnic group. Alan Dundes (1973) quite aptly explains who the folk are of any given folklore: "Any group of people who share at least one linking factor—be it occupation, religion, or ethnicity—qualify as a 'folk' [p. 1]." The development of lore by groups that have something in common reinforces their solidarity. There can be lore created by college students that all will remember and retell in future years at reunions. There can be the lore of criminals, churchgoers, bankers, computer programmers, farmers; the list can go on indefinitely. The lore is told among this select group of people for their edification or entertainment and is best understood within this select group.

Folklore is primarily an oral tradition. The fluency, complexity, and wittiness of this oral tradition is also a factor that is not determined by class or formal education. As will be illustrated later, certain components of American society which are often viewed as being the most nonverbal and the most unimaginative have created the most imaginative and animate folklore still thriving in America today. Of course, with the advent of the modern age, much of the rich folklore has been transcribed on paper for the appreciation of a larger group or for scholarly purposes. Since folklore is an oral tradition which flows with time, its transcription on paper freezes it in time. Any form that flows with time may be different tomorrow from what it is today or was yesterday. Oral traditions can either grow or die depending upon the folk and their needs. The needs of the folk can be defined as their interest in and the relevance of the themes and characters that are inscribed into a folklore. Another factor that must be considered is the art involved in transcribing and obtaining informants. This is a major consideration for anyone studying folklore, because the transcriptions may be inaccurate. The skill of being a folklorist is never mastered by all folklore collectors.

In light of the above definitions and comments on the general topic of folklore it becomes apparent that the topic of Afro-American folklore opens up another Pandora's box. Afro-Americans have a very rich culture and their folklore is just one of its manifestations. There seems to be little controversy about the richness of this folklore, but there is dispute about its origins and the reasons behind some of the forms into which it has developed. Did Afro-American folklore originate in Europe or Africa, or did it rise from the bosom of America? Each part of this question has an answer. Afro-Americans are a people of African descent who were able to sustain more than their racial origins and heritage during their captivity in America. African cultural remnants can be found in many aspects of Black life, their music being one main example. It is only logical that folklore, an oral tradition, would be sustained by an orally cultured people. The similarities found between Afro-American folklore and European folklore cannot be totally negated. These similarities can probably best be explained by the fact that African slaves were not totally isolated from Americans of European descent. The aspects that appealed to the slaves in the European-based folklore were borrowed and incorporated into their folklore. It could be said, then, that Afro-American folklore did rise from the bosom of America, but that bosom was not a vacuum.

Many of the animal tales such as the Uncle Remus stories closely correlate with African tales. The tales of these two different continents differ in small details but contain the same "folkloristic elements" (Dundes, 1973, p. 45). The animals in the Remus tales have been changed to those indigenous to the American continent. These differences in small details are what make the Remus tales Afro-American folklore as opposed to African folklore. The common link between the African folklore, the

Uncle Remus tales, and the urban lore that will be discussed here is that they are based on an oral tradition as opposed to a literary European tradition.

The controversy regarding the origins of Afro-American folklore has caused the emotions involved with racism and racial pride to interfere in the study of this foklore. The racist wants to disavow any connection between this lore and African lore, claiming that this lore is European based or sprang from a vacuum in America. There can be no culture for Afro-Americans other than the one given to them by White America. Some Blacks call for the abolition of old folklore because it is antithetical to the concept of nation-building. Other Blacks feel that the recognition of folklore makes Black people be viewed as primitive, illiterate, and ignorant by White America. These groups are reacting to the character of Uncle Remus, a backdrop created by the transcriber, a White Southern newspaperman, Joel Chandler Harris who had his own reasons for creating the character of Uncle Remus, a character not in the folklore as it was told to Blacks by Blacks. What they fail to recognize is the importance of this folklore—how the messages conveyed in the old tales helped to sustain a suppressed people. The tales are a spiritual link with the past which should not be severed. There are those, however, who do recognize Black folklore as the rich expression of the realities of the lives of Black people.

The problem of the collector versus the informant, a crucial issue, has been touched upon before. Many Blacks maintain that the White collector cannot accurately transcribe the folklore he hears from his Black informants. There are several reasons why they feel this way. The collector, because he is White, may not receive the authentic lore as told to Blacks by Blacks. The heart of the problem is the language in which the folklore is told: Black English. Any collector of Black English, be he a folklorist or a linguist, must attune his ear to the language. Not only must he be able to physically understand the language, but the vernacular *must* be correctly interpreted. Black English is a cultural language which is best understood by those that understand Black culture. This understanding for those who have not lived the Black experience is difficult at best to obtain. Having studied Black English formally, and having had it presented from, all viewpoints, the present author feels that Black English, like Black folklore and Black music, is an African-based form and that these forms must be understood in light of their African roots.

There is no doubt that Afro-Americans are of African descent, yet doubt remains about the philosophical and cultural remnants of their ancestors. African culture is an oral culture which logically could adapt itself very readily to the system in which it was placed. What is meant by "adapt" is that in a system that prevented the slaves from becoming literate, the slave's own culture, based on an oral tradition, had more chance of surviving than one based on a literary tradition. There are certain characteristics of the culturally oral man that differ drastically from the culturally literate man. These differences, some of which will be elaborated upon later, cannot help but foster misunderstanding and create gaps in communication. These gaps and misunderstandings exist to this day between speakers of Standard English and Black English.

The differences between Standard English and Black English are deeper than just lexicon and vernacular; they are differences between a literate culture and an oral culture. Communication—its meaning and the forms in which it takes place—is different in the two cultures. In a literate culture a tangible medium, the written word, takes precedence over speech, the oral word. In both cultures men seek to convey messages, but the message itself is the medium in the oral culture. Without a medium, such as the written word, the act of communication becomes more intense, emotional, and expressive. This emotionality causes the oral man to become more immersed in his immediate environment, including place, time, and audience. Awareness of these factors enables the speaker to use them effectively as tools to relay his messages. His conception of time revolves around the fleetingness of sound—the medium of his message. There is no time lag between his conception of his message and his delivery. In both cultures the speaker has time to formulate his message, but the medium for expression causes the man of the written word to detach himself intellectually from his environment, while the oral man uses his environment. When the literate man's message is received, he does not find himself confronted by his audience. The oral man must not only take content into account, but audience reaction and control as well. His sense of "collectivism" (Sidran, 1972, p. 3) is greater. His audience, being attuned emotionally to an oral culture, is more responsive to an emotional, imaginative delivery. To achieve this goal, traditionally oral speakers have heightened their sensitivity to physical attributes. For them tonal quality becomes important; thus the existence of tonal African language, languages where a tonal difference creates a new word. Rhythm, body language, and imaginative allusions are mandatory. The body and mind become the medium, and the great orator uses them to his best advantage.

Another important element in oral cultures is that since the audience responds immediately to a message the oral man must be spontaneous. If the response is unfavorable then changes must be made immediately to alter that response. The audience can also control the speaker by its reactions and responses. If the oral man were as intellectually detached from his immediate environment as the literate man, then the collectivism between speaker and audience would be lost. The message is alive, stimulating the alive imaginations of the culturally oral audience.

The African philosophy that enables the oral man to evoke not only his imagination but that of his audience has been described by Jahn (Dundes, 1973, pp. 94–95). Concepts are expressed in terms of force. There is a common stem "-ntu" which alters the meaning of words, such as human being (Muntu), thing (kintu), and place and time (hantu), to mean more than just their English translations. Kuntu is a modal force like laughter, beauty, or rhythm. Muntu is not just a human being but a "force endowed with intelligence." The "-ntu" gives all things a linking quality with a "universal force." African philosophy delves even further into the idea of forces. There is "Nommo . . . the driven power" which gives life to all things. Nommo does not control Muntu, but Muntu controls the driving force Nommo. Nommo can be "controlled or evoked through the power of words." It is not just words that can control or evoke Nommo—it is the rhythm of the spoken word that is the power.

Not only are "the implications of Jahn's analysis for American Negro folklore" immense (Dundes, 1973, p. 96), but those implications hold for Black English as well. The perspective between God and man is different in the two cultures. Man is not summoned by God, but man summons God, Nommo, through words and rhythms. Nommo is manifested in all that is; therefore, he is summoned by polyrhythms. The European concept of God and man is monotheistic and monorhythmic. The African concept enables all to become more personally involved in the forces of life. This personal participation, found not only in Afro-American music but in folklore as well, has been called "the intrusive I." Examples can be found in the expressions "my blues" and "my story." European folklore and music, however, are more objective and the third-person technique is employed.

Abrahams describes "the intrusive I" as he discovered it in the urban folklore of Blacks living in Philadelphia:

> This "intrusive I" is a convenient gambit in the narrative game. It allows the narrator two personae at the same time, his own as narrator or commentator and that of the hero. He can unite the two at will if he is artful in his narration; he can also disassociate the two if he wishes.... Even when the narrator's persona retreats from that of the hero or main character, the narrator remains, intruding as a commentator. The "I" never disappears completely, though it may recede temporarily [Abrahams, 1970, p. 58].

In Black English the speaker is communicating from an African viewpoint; he is using his language in a much different way from the literary speaker. The forces of time, place, rhythm, and God all become part of the speaker as he talks. His language reflects this fact. The very tone and narrative technique used by Afro-Americans in their folklore have derived from a traceable African source.

There are several forms of Black folklore that have been categorized by folklorists: tales, proverbs, playing the dozens, toasts, jokes, signifying, and the rhymes in children's games. While some folklorists have implied that some of these forms have African counterparts, the studies have not been comprehensive enough yet for conclusive proof. More important for the purposes of this presentation are the ties between the oral traditions, that is, how Afro-Americans have developed their African oral tradition in their captivity in America. The simplest form to cite and define is the proverb which is metaphorical in nature and uses language to its fullest extent. The meaning behind a proverb is not obvious and the listener must use his knowledge of the situation, speaker, and cultural background to understand it. There is no superfluous language in the proverb. "Don' say no mo' wid yo' mouf dan yo' back kin stan'" (Brewer, in Dundes, 1973, p. 249) is an example of a proverb. This proverb dates back to slave times when slaves discussed an escape and were caught doing so. The punishment would be whipping.

The other verbal forms—the dozens, signifying, tales, jokes, toasts, and children's rhymes—cannot be so easily compartmentalized. They are examples of the phenomenon described by Sidran (1972): "The oral culture is primarily a living, organic organization, rather than a technocratic structure, and it rails against compartmentalization [p. 18]." Several folklorists have studied these forms and upon comparing their definitions and theories it becomes apparent that there is a great deal of overlapping. A children's rhyme:

> Just before your mother died
> She called you to her side.
> She gave you a pair of drawers.
> Before your father died.
> She put'em in the sink.
> The sink began to stink.
> She put'em on the track.
> The train backed back.
> She put'em on the fence.
> Aint' seen'em since [Abrahams, in Dundes, 1973, p. 302].

is a rough representation of some of the aforementioned forms. The direct insult and subtle implications are synonymous to the dozens and signifying. The attempt to create a story within a stylized structure is the initial step in telling toasts and tales. The accuracy of the transcriber in this example and several yet to come is also a common problem. For instance, the use of the word "mother" is incorrect. "Mama" and "mammy" are the correct forms found among Black speakers in these folklore forms.

The dozens and signifying are much of the time interchangeable descriptive terms. Other names for the same forms are joning, playing, and sounding. The different names are local terms for the same phenomenon.

The tale "The Signifying Monkey" is the most commonly known reference to signifying. The interesting point about this tale is that the monkey signifies but the story is told in a tale or toast format:

"Monkey," said the Lion,
Beat to his unbooted knees,
"You and all your signifying children
Better stay up in them trees."
Which is why today
Monkey does his signifying
A-way-up out of the way [Hughes & Bontemps, 1958, p. 363].

The above ending to the toast has a moralistic tone similar to the proverb mentioned before; those that must signify had better stay in their element or be ready for a good whupping. Proverbs and toasts of this kind not only have their entertainment value but are educational too. It should be more obvious to the reader how one can become confused when approaching these forms from a literary and compartmentalized viewpoint. These forms blend together to complement and augment one another.

What is in some cases called the "clean" dozens can also be called children's rhymes, as in the example previously cited. The common element in the dozens, signifying, joning, etc., is the direct confrontation between two people. Usually there is an audience encouraging the two people on to greater heights of glory, that is, insult. When the teasing involves insults to the other person's family, usually their mother, then it is more commonly known as the "dirty" dozens:

I hate to talk about your mother (mama)
She's a good old soul.
She got a ten-ton pussy
And a rubber asshole.
She got hairs on her pussy
That sweep the floor.
She got knobs on her titties
That open the door [Abrahams, in Dundes, 1973, p. 300].

The rhyme element is still characteristic in this example as with the children's rhyme.

In signifying, the message that the speaker wants to convey is encoded in a larger framework. Signifying is very similar to the proverb in this respect, the difference being that signifying is more of a spontaneous verbal reaction to a situation and it utilizes more language, as in the following:

There was these two boys from Fort Worth, they was over in Paris, France, and with the Army, and they was standin' on the corner without much in partic'lar to do when a couple of o-fay chicks come strollin' by, you know what I mean, a couple of nice French gals—and they was very nice indeed with the exception that one of them appeared to be considerable older than the other one. like she might be the great grandmother of the other one or somethin' like that, you see. So these boys was diggin' these chicks and one of them say: "Man, let's make a move, I believe we do awright there!" And the other one say: "Well, now, similar thought occurred to me as well, but...er...uh... how is we goin decide who takes the *grandmother?* I don't want no old bitch like that!" So the other one say: "How we goin *decide?* Why man, I goin take the grandmother! I the one see these chicks first, and I gets to take my choice!" So the other one say: "Well, now you talking, You gets the grandmother, and I gets the young one—that's fine! But tell me this, boy—how comes you wants the old lady, instead of the fine young gal?" So the other one say: "Why, don't you know? Ain't you with it? She been white...LONGER! [Mitchell-Kernan, in Dundes, 1973, p. 316]."

This example can also be called a joke. It becomes an example of signifying when the situation is taken into account. In this particular instance the speaker is commenting on the absurd lengths some Black men will go to for a White woman. If a listener were not familiar with signifying he might only take it as a joke.

"Story in Harlem Slang," created by Zora Hurston (1970), illustrates how different forms of folklore can be used in a tale. This tale, written in 1942, is rich in the Black vernacular of that period. The plot is as follows: A young man in Harlem, because he has no steady woman from whom he can earn his living, must seek out women anew each day. He meets a fellow pimp and the two banter back and forth, almost exchanging blows as they deny each other's aptitude to procure great amounts of money from women. They then spot a young woman and try to entice her into taking one of them to dinner. She is not the type of woman who allows a man to manipulate her and has heard their "rap" too many times before, so she scorns them. One of the men attempts to grab her pocketbook in frustration and she becomes further enraged. For a moment violence almost erupts, but she leaves them humiliated. They then try to play the significance of the incident down, but the main character's mind wanders and he remembers the good old days down South when he always had a meal.

There are several good examples in this tale of the verbal forms previously discussed (Hurston, in Dundes, 1973, pp. 223–229, including her glossary). Jelly, the main character, signifies (a term sometimes used when expressing one's feelings and the situation): "Oh, just like de bear—nowhere. Like de bear's brother, I ain't no further. Like de bear's daughter—ain't got a quarter [p. 223]." Jelly is flat broke with no immediate prospects for obtaining any money. He regrets this confession. "Sweet Back gave him a top-superior, cut-eye look. Looked at Jelly like a showman looks at an ape. Just as far above Jelly as fried chicken is over branch water [p. 223]." Sweet Back uses body language to express his contempt for not only Jelly's economic condition but also for his confession of it. This type of body language can be found in all types of situations among speakers of Black English. The reaction that Sweet Back has to Jelly's confession would not be difficult to interpret, but not all forms of body language can be so easily interpreted by those unfamiliar with Black culture.

Sweet Back beings to tease Jelly about his misfortune. He talks about one of the women he saw Jelly with the night before. A game of the dozens begins:

> Git out my face, Jelly! Dat broad I seen you with wasn't no pe-ola. She was one of them coal-scuttle blondes with hair just close to her head as ninety-nine is to a hundred. She lookted like she had seventy-five pounds of clear bosom, guts in her feet, and she lookted like six months in front and nine months behind. Buy you a whiskey still! Dat broad couldn't make the down payment on a pair of sox."
> "Sweet Back, you trying to talk out of place." Jelly stiffened.
> "If you trying to jump salty, Jelly, that's your mammy."
> "Don't play in de family, Sweet Back. I don't play de dozens. I done told you [Hurston, 1970, p. 224]."

This passage illustrates how teasing, joning, signifying, etc., can lead not only to the dirty dozens but to a fight as well. Jelly has been forced to cover up his confession of hard times with exaggerations about his women. He tries to imply that the confession is a joke, but Sweet Back does not let him get away with this trick because he knows the truth and states it in the above passage. Jelly is backed into a wall and the situation has the potential of becoming dangerous. Sweet Back can tell the truth is beginning to hit home and he confidently throws out the reference to Jelly's mother. If an audience had been present it would have probably encouraged them to the point where a fight would have been unavoidable. A fight only takes place in these situations when one party is not able to keep up the verbal duel. If a fight had erupted, then the vanquished would have said "mo wid you' mouf dan you' back can stand."

When the young woman appears in the narrative, the two men try "rapping" to her, each trying to outdo the other. "Rapping" is a personalized style of talking initiated usually by men to get to know a woman to whom they are attracted:

> "Big stars falling!" Jelly said out loud when she was within hearing distance. "It must be just before day!"
> "Yeah, man!" Sweet Back agreed. "Must be a recess in Heaven—pretty angel like that out on the ground." The girl drew abreast of them, reeling and rocking her hips.
> "I'd walk clear to Diddy-Wah-Diddy to get a chance to speak to a pretty lil' ground-angel like that," Jelly went on.
> "Aw, man, you ain't willing to go very far. Me, I'd go slap to Ginny-Gall, where they eat cow-rump, skin and all. [Hurston, 1970, p. 225]."

Rapping is a spontaneous art which is accompanied by a sincere and innocent mask. Though the young woman knows that she will not go along with any of their talk she gives them the signals to continue their endeavors. If she had not wanted to hear their compliments she would not have stopped, particularly in the enticing manner that she does. She wants to join in the game. The aggressive type of behavior needed in the verbal battles of Black folklore is not confined to just the male sex. She is quick with her tongue as she throws back responses to their raps. Her responses can be summed up in one expression she uses: "I'm just like the cemetery—I'm not putting out, I'm taking in! Dig? [p. 226]." She has won the verbal battle.

This story is told in prose form, as it was created by Zora Hurston, but it embodies the vivid imaginative language of Black English. The narrative is just as imaginative and colorful as the dialogue that we have examined:

> Wait till I light up my coal-pot and I'll tell you about this Zigabio called Jelly. Well, all right now. He was a sealskin brown and papa-tree-top-tall. Skinny in the hips and solid built for speed. He was born with this rough-dried hair, but when he laid on the grease and pressed it down overnight with his stocking-cap, it looked just like that righteous moss, and had so many waves you got seasick from looking. Solid, man, solid [Hurston, 1970, p. 222].

This narrative is set up in such a way that the narrator could intrude if she wanted to; the "intrusive I." Zora Hurston was the most accomplished and skilled folklorist of her day. As is obvious from this story, she was so familiar and comfortable with her material that she was able to create her own folklore. She—the writer—does not intrude as the transcriber as Joel Chandler Harris did in the Uncle Remus tales.

Afro-American folklore has evolved to meet the needs of urban Blacks, yet it still retains its African origins. Most of the vocabulary of Black English can be found in Black folklore. In the course of our research we have learned about Black English as a language, but there has been little discussion of the vocabulary of this language.

By using Hurston's tale and the glossary found at the end of it as our dictionary of Black vernacular of the 1940's, we will show how Black English is a growing and changing language. Several sources published by White authors on American slang since and prior to the 1940's illustrate how for the most part the vernacular of Black English is unknown to most of White America. These sources are *The Dictionary of American Slang* (Wentworth & Flexner, 1960), *An American Dictionary of Slang* (Weingarten, 1954) and *Dictionary of American Slang* (1934) by Weseen. The sources devoted solely to Afro-American vernacular by Black authors are the Hurston story and glossary, Clarence Major's *Dic-*

tionary of Afro-American Slang (1970), and the author's own familiarity with the vernacular.

No source that we have had at our disposal has been complete, inclusive of White and Black expressions, even in respect to their time. *The Dictionary of American Slang* (1960) by Wentworth and Flexner was far more complete with respect to Black vernacular than anticipated. On the other hand, Major's *Dictionary of Afro-American Slang* was very disappointing due to some unfortunate omissions. This is the only book readily available in print entirely devoted to Black vernacular and this area needs further documentation. A discussion of how these sources faired with respect to 1940's Black vernacular will follow the discussion on the vernacular itself.

First, a distinction must be made between the term "slang" as used by mainstream America and Black vernacular. With the increase of Black awareness in the 1960's, much of the vocabulary used by Black Americans has been understood not merely to be pet phrases or slang but words and idiomatic phrases which are the very life of a much larger structure known as Black English. The distinction between formal and informal Black English must also be made. Formal Black English uses the vernacular more commonly called slang. When a speaker of Black English speaks in Standard English he may not change his syntax and lexicon, but he may change his vernacular, a phenomenon common to speakers changing languages. Slang is a vernacular that is only used by speakers of Standard English in informal speech.

The vernacular of Black English is subject to a considerable amount of change because it is part of an oral language which itself is vulnerable to the changing needs of its speakers. The best example of this is the difference between Northern urban Black English and Southern rural Black English. Where the pace of life is swift, as in the Northern urban centers, the language changes quickly. Terms found in use today may be passé tomorrow. Another factor that is speeding the changes found in the vernacular is the great amount of exposure that Black English is receiving. White America has its ear on Black America. Some Black expressions are readily adapted by Standard English speakers. Nothing will make a Black expression become passé faster than for it to become popular in White speech. An example is the expression "Right-On." It has become so popular in Standard English that a major pen manufacturer has adapted it to use in their advertising: "Write-On." You do not hear "Right-On" very much anymore among speakers of Black English.

The best transcribers of urban Black English would have to be those that are so tuned to the twists and turns of the language that they are not thrown off by changes. They can hear a new word or expression and with minimal effort know its meaning. To do this the transcriber has to be sensitive to urban Black culture. Not only must he be able to understand the new term but he must be able to incorporate it into his own speech.

On closer inspection of Black English's vocabulary, the words begin to fit into categories expressive of the Black experience. There are words that apply only to Black people and those that apply only to Whites. There are adjectives that apply only to Blacks or others that can be applied to anyone. There are verbal phrases that can be found in conversations and there are nouns that are substitute terms for places. There are two subgroups within these general categories—words that are sexual inferences and terms referring to music. Examples of all of these categories can be found in the Hurston (1942) story and glossary. Some expressions have withstood the test of time while others have not and still others have changed in meaning since the 1940's. Some Black expressions have been used in the vernacular of White America for a long time, others have appeared there only recently. It has not been assumed by this author that all of the phrases from the Hurston source are of Black origin, only that they are used, primarily in their given definitions, by Blacks in the United States. The vocabulary to be discussed in this work are terms referring to Black people.

Terms cited by Hurston as substitutes for a Black person are "conk buster, dark black, eight rock, handkerchief head, jig, Monkey chaser, 'My People, My People,' cuffee, pancake, park ape, Russian, and Zigaboo [Hurston, 1942, pp. 227–229]." Four of the most commonly known ones *not found* in her work are Negro, Afro-American, colored, and Black. These four terms are the ones used in the larger American framework to describe the descendants of Africans now in America. The most commonly used in Black English as opposed to Standard English are Black and colored. These two in-group expressions (used among speakers of Black English) are strongly related to the revolution of the other two terms—Afro-American and Negro. During the period when "Negro" was predominantly used in Standard English, "colored" was the in-group expression. Negro was a term chosen *for* Blacks, not *by* Blacks. Colored has a banal, nondescript connotation as if Blacks have no culture or roots. Both words reflect a lack of self-determination, control, and self-respect. (A Negro was Black, but only if one understood Spanish.) With the advent of the 1960's Blacks began to see themselves in a different light; they had roots, a motherland, a distinct culture—they were Afro-Americans. However, this is a rather long and awkward word to use in everyday speech so the in-group expression became Black. Blacks had attained a new awakened pride and awareness of their Blackness. There was no longer any need to be ashamed of being Black. These four terms are formal self-descriptions so, true to the Black oral tradition, more imaginative terms have been created.

The terms used by Hurston are in-group expressions. There are those that are derogatory in nature and those that carry no particular value judgment in themselves. The context of the sentence, tone, and body language used with the words can make them negative or positive in meaning. Handkerchief head is still in use today though mainly by older people and it has a definite negative meaning. There is a difference between a handkerchief head and a pancake as defined by Hurston. A pancake is a totally humble person whereas a handkerchief head or an Uncle Tom, a common term today, may be a braggert around Blacks but humble around Whites.

Two in-group expressions for the race of Blacks found in the glossary are "Aunt Hagar" and "My People, My People." "Aunt Hagar" has gone out of use for the most part but "My People, My People," a "sad satiric expression in the Negro language; sad when a Negro comments on the backwardness of some of his race; at other times, used for satiric or comic effect [Hurston, 1973, p. 228]," is still in use. "Aunt Hagar" and "My People, My People" imply a sense of unity and family, a kinship that is essential for the survival of Blacks in America.

"Jig," "cuffee" (an original African word), and "Zigaboo" are interchangeable and are without particular value judgment. They are substitute words for a Black person and are in-group terms. They are words (with the exception of cuffee) whose origins have been lost but which were frequently used in the vernacular of Black English during the 1940's. Because of lack of use they have drifted out of the spoken language and new words have taken their place in popularity.

"Nigger" is the prime example of a term which has increased in frequency but is only acceptable as an in-group expression. It is a word that has all of the negative connotations of what it is to be Black in America. Yet ironically it is now used heavily by Blacks and has come to signify a sense of "street" kinship. The negative meaning of the word is still in use but it can only be used as a self-incrimination like "My People, My People," and not in a Black–White confrontation. When used negatively, it is a warning of rising disgust or anger. The 1960's brought new introspective vision to Blacks. No longer were they afraid to use the good and bad terms of their race.

Two other words used to describe Blacks in the glossary are "monkey chaser" and "Russian." A monkey chaser is a derogatory word for a West Indian Black. It might still be in use in communities where there is conflict between West Indian Blacks and American Blacks. In many neighborhoods where second generation West Indians live and have blended into the mainstream of the general Black population, the term has died out. It derived from the antagonism of people of the same race who were, on the surface, culturally different. In an oppressed group and in a system where one group must be superior to another, this type of debasement will take place. The exotic jungle environment of the islands where monkeys are supposed to be is the background for the idea of a "monkey chaser." A "Russian" is a Black person who recently left the South and "rushed up here [p. 228]." Again, it is a term used to emphasize the difference between the native city dweller and a newcomer. Since the North no longer holds the allure as the promised land, Black migration from the South has slowed down since the 1940's. A term that is now used in the place of "Russian" is "country." Such a person still sticks out like a sore thumb because he is not hip to city ways. The term, however, is not as negative in meaning as Russian. There can even be pride in being country because it is now realized that being citified and hip is not always desirable. Stability and wisdom might even be typical of someone who is country.

There are also terms that refer only to Black men and those that refer only to Black women. There was a term "Brother in Black" in the glossary which has evolved and been shortened to "Brother" or "Bro." His female counterpart is "Sister" or "Sis." Another similar term in use today is "Blood." These expressions signify the common blood and ancestry of Blacks in America, an idea heavily emphasized in the 1960's when the need for community and unity were realized. If someone is confronting another person with behavior that is contrary to nation-building or is anti-Black the term Brother can be said with satirical overtones. A "homeboy" is an affectionate term used to describe someone who is from your home, a Brother. "Skillets," used in the 1940's, probably referred to the black color of iron skillets and would not be used in a complimentary manner. "Ace," "cat," and "stud"—all modern terms—are also used as synonyms for Black men. An "ace" is a close friend. A "cat" and "stud" are more hip men with stud having strong sexual overtones.

Men who spend a large portion of their time looking at and discussing women have developed an elaborate set of descriptive terms for females. Derogatory terms for a woman in the glossary are "coal scuttle blond, black woman, mammy, and Granny Grunt." "Coal scuttle blond" seems to refer to the catastrophic attempts of some women to be as "beautiful" as a blond, the epitome of whiteness, by dying their hair. "Mammy" stirs up ties to the "house nigger" woman who scuffled around after "Miss Ann." An "Aunt Jemimah" is a present-day equivalent, and if used in reference to one's mother or woman, it could be grounds for a fight. It is used in the children's rhyme "Ain't-cha-Mammy on the pancake box?" Said quickly it sounds like "Aunt Jemimah on the pancake box?" "Granny Grunt," a term still in use, refers to a sagacious, mythical character. The Black woman of the 1940's was not a very prized possession among a large group who thought white was "beautiful." Men who described light-skinned women in a complimentary way might call them a "pe-ola." A man's girlfriend that was considered to be a bit too young for him might be called "pigmeat" in the 1940's. He, like a pig, slobbers and grovels over her tender young meat.

Modern terms for a young good-looking woman are "fox" and "hammer." Fox may refer to the keen mind and sleek body of a woman, a compliment since more than just physical attributes are being admired. A hammer refers to a woman who is physically very well endowed and who knows it. Neutral terms used by men for women today are "broad" and "chick." Affectionate terms used to describe a man's special woman, a woman totally equipped with all of the positive attributes of the species, are "my main drag," "main squeeze," and "my lady." There is less emphasis today, if any, on a woman's color. The proverb "The blacker the berry, the sweeter the juice" is taken to heart today. Negative terms such as "bitch," "whore," "wench," etc., when used in reference to a man's woman, are grounds for a serious "ass-whuppin."

The adjectives found in Hurston's glossary which were used by Blacks to describe themselves revolve around their African racial characteristics. The reader must remember that Hurston's story was written in the 1940's when racial characteristics were a source of shame for many Blacks. The Black Power movement of the 1960's erased much of the shame that Black people felt for themselves, but even today remnants of this shame remain throughout the Black community. It takes more than a few summers to erase the repressive attitudes built up over almost four hundred years of oppression. Terms used to describe some of these African characteristics are "bad hair, naps, tight head, liver-lip, and gator-faced." "Bad hair," "naps," and "tight head" refer to the tightly curled hair of Afro-Americans. A contemporary term used to describe those that tried to rid themselves of these curls is "fried head," a derogatory term. "Righteous mass" or "grass" and "made hair" were terms used to describe good hair, good hair being similar to the straight hair of Whites. Usually this good hair effect could only be achieved by using a hot comb on the hair. "Liver-lip" and "gator-faced" are terms of exaggeration used to insult someone. "Chochannah lips" and "gorilla faced" are modern expressions that are synonymous with the aforementioned ones. "A "park ape" was a 1940's expression making the age-old reference between Blacks and apes. "Jar head," "hammer head," and "peanut head" today refer to some of the more unusual conformations in head shape. These expressions were mainly used when Blacks wore their hair very short so that the shape of their head was very noticeable. Afros have saved many a child from being teased about the shape of his head. One of the more imaginative expressions found in Hurston's glossary referring to skin color is "eight rock," the eight ball in billiards. The slurs on physical characteristics can be found today in confrontations between two Black people.

It is interesting that among the books that claim to be volumes of American slang, none of them included all twelve terms that were listed by Hurston as being equivalent to Negro. When Weseen's book was published in 1934, not one of these terms was included. Weingarten (1954) includes one word in his book—"jig." Wentworth (1960) had not only the word "jig" but also the words from which this term derived, "zigaboo" and "jigaboo." In his volume, "handkerchief head," "cuffee" (an original African word), "pancake," and "Russian" all had their correct definitions. Major (1970) has four of the words—"handkerchief head," "cuffee," "pancake," and "zigaboo."

There are many words used in Black and White vernacular which are phonetically similar but which have different interpretations. An example is the term "conk buster." Hurston (1942, p. 23) defines it as "cheap liquor; also an intellectual Negro." Major defines it as "anything that proved mentally difficult; also sometimes referred to what drugs or liquor did to the mind." The only term comparable to this phrase found in the dictionaries by the White authors is "conk." Wentworth and Weseen define it as head or a hit on the head, Weingarten only as a hit on the head. Major (1970, p. 46) defines "conk" as a "pomade for the hair; the human head itself." With all of these diverse meanings it is understandable why a Standard English speaker or a person that is not familiar with Black English, upon hearing the word "conk buster," might misinterpret a speaker of Black English. The term conk has become more specific in its definition today to mean a man who has had a lye process applied to his hair to make it straight.

The overall trend seems to be that either Black vernacular was not a conscious part of the language of mainstream America or it was consciously left out of documents of American vernacular. By 1960 most of the expressions of Black America that had been incorporated into the informal speech of White America were recognized as being of Black origin. By 1970, while some Black expressions had been documented in dictionaries of White slang, only one Black author dedicated an entire work to the vernacular's documentation. More of these types of work are needed.

It should be obvious that the vernacular of Black English is not one of a nonverbal people. The spontaneity, wittiness, fluidity, and mental dexterity required of urban Black English speakers can be matched with any component of American society. In Black communities, Blacks exercise their minds through their folklore forms. Through these forms their minds and tongues are sharpened so that they can successfully adapt to the rigors of being Black in America. The verbal games could be vicious but then life is too. The person who is most respected is not the one who fights first, but the one who can use his mind to outtalk his opponent. A cool level head is required to do this, to evoke Nommo. As H. Rap Brown said, he got *his education* in the streets (Brown, in Dundes, 1973, p. 353).

REFERENCES

Abrahams, R. *Deep down in the jungle*. Chicago: Aldine, 1970.

Brewer, J. M. *American Negro folklore*. Chicago: Quadrangle, 1968.

Dillard, J. L. *Black English*. New York, Random House, 1973.

Dundes, A. *Mother wit and the laughing barrel*. Englewood Cliffs, New Jersey: Prentice-Hall, 1973.

Herskovitz, M. *The myth of the Negro Past*. Boston: Beacon Press, 1958.

Hughes, L., & Bontemps, A. *Book of Negro folklore*. New York: Dodd, Meade, 1958.

Hurston, Z. *Mules and men*. New York: Harper & Row, 1970.

Lester, J. *Black folklore*. New York: Grove Press, 1969.

Major, C. *Dictionary of Afro-American slang*. New York: International Publ., 1970.

Sidran, B. *Blacktalk*. New York: Holt, Rinehart & Winston, 1972.

Spalding, H. *Encyclopedia of Black folklore and humor*. Middle Village, New York: Jonathan David Publ., 1972.

Weseen, M. *Dictionary of American slang*. New York: Crowell, 1934.

Weingarten, J. *An American dictionary of slang and colloquial speech*. New York: 1954.

Wentworth, H., & Flexner, S. *Dictionary of American slang*. New York: Crowell, 1960.

Part IV
IMPLICATIONS

13

Linguistic Relativity:
Any Relevance to Black English?

John B. Carroll

Educational Testing Service[1]

Does the language one speaks influence the way one thinks? Is any particular language, or form of language, in some way inferior to another, in the sense that it is less adequate for expressing complex logical thought?

These are highly general questions that have received the attention of linguists, psychologists, and philosophers for many years. If they have affirmative answers—and it is not at all certain that they do—one might begin to wonder whether Black English influences Black thinking in some way or whether Black English is less adequate than, say, "Standard English" for expressing logical thought. What we want to do in this presentation is to consider the arguments that have been brought forward on the question of the influence of language on thought, and the possible relevance of these arguments for thinking about the status of Black English.[2]

It's clear that there is some kind of intimate connection between language and thought. Communicating our thoughts to one another without some form of language is hardly conceivable. We tend to formulate our

---

[1] From Fall 1974, Department of Psychology, University of North Carolina at Chapel Hill.

[2] I use the term Black English as if Black English were some *one* form of language. Of course, there are many varieties of Black English, and not all Blacks speak Black English. But the question of what Black English is or may be is taken up elsewhere in this volume; I hope I may be excused, therefore, for omitting a discussion of the problems in defining it.

thoughts in language. A lot of our thinking is done with the concepts that language provides words for. When we learn a new word, phrase, or slogan, something seems to happen to our thinking, or even to our tendencies to act.

Sometimes learning a new word, like *jealousy*, simply provides a name for a concept that, even before learning the word, we already have an idea or at least a "gut feeling" about. Some people would claim that even animals—such as dogs—can feel jealousy, and certainly young children can be jealous well before they learn a word for this feeling. All the same, learning the word focuses attention on the idea named by the word. A child who has just learned the word jealousy is probably more conscious of *being* jealous when he has that feeling.

Some words introduce us to special scientific concepts. Take the case of the word *gravitation*. Now, everyone has always been subject to the force of gravitation—except an astronaut in orbit, say, but it was only within the last few hundred years that man arrived at a scientific concept of gravitation and something about its laws. When a person learns the word gravitation, and something about its meaning, he is in effect learning something about our present scientific concept of the universe and, in this sense, learning the word influences his thinking.

Other words introduce one to concepts in the social sphere. Take the case of the phrase *civil rights*—a phrase that probably didn't even come into existence or popularity until the nineteenth century. It was the name of a new social concept—or a new application and extension of a concept that goes back perhaps a couple of thousand years (assuming that the Greeks and Romans had some vague idea of civil rights, at least for select citizens). Without knowing that phrase, a person might easily be unaware that his civil rights had been abridged; knowing the phrase and its meaning, he might be more likely to take action to protect his civil rights.

We can agree, then, that knowing the words of a language makes an individual more aware of the concepts that can guide his thinking and action. In this way, language influences thought. In general, the more concepts one knows and has words for, the more precise his thinking can be.

Some languages have richer vocabularies than others. Languages of major civilizations like English, Russian, or French have literally hundreds of thousands of words in their vocabularies, while languages of indigenous tribes and cultures in various parts of the world have far fewer words. One might think that limitations of vocabulary in these latter languages would put a limit on the complexity of thought that they could express.

Such a conclusion, however, would be erroneous. It ignores several facts. First, the differences in vocabulary richness are largely due to the fact that the vocabularies of languages like English, Russian, and French contain many scientific and technical terms that have been added as a result of the march of civilization. Also, these languages contain many words borrowed or derived from other languages; for example, English contains many words derived from Latin, Greek, and other languages. Second, people tend to underestimate the vocabulary richness of languages of "primitive" or aboriginal groups. Actually, such languages contain a more or less complete array of terms for all sorts of objects, events, and human thoughts and emotions. As far as linguists have been able to determine, all languages are about equally able to communicate highly complex forms of logical thought. Even languages of aboriginal groups are able to assimilate terms for scientific concepts. Navaho has developed a highly refined vocabulary for modern medical concepts. Swahili has been able to add terms and expressions for all the aspects of modern political and social life. In Malaysia and Indonesia, academies and language commissions are busy inventing and standardizing terms in their language to accommodate the concepts needed in contemporary civilization.

What about Black English in this respect? Does Black English have a vocabulary that is less rich than that of Standard English? Unless one takes a very narrow view of what Black English is, the answer is no. As a dialect of English, Black English shares with Standard English, or *can* share with it a great part of the Standard English vocabulary. Words and phrases like *jealousy, gravitation,* and *civil rights* are as much a part of Black English as they are of Standard English, or any other form of English. It may be true that not all users of Black English know all these words, but it's also true that not all users of Standard English know these words. Any speaker of a language acquires its vocabulary in gradual stages—as the result of increasing exposure to the vocabulary, whether in the home, the community, or the school. People who speak Black English as their native dialect can, and do, learn and use words like jealousy and gravitation, right along with thousands of other words that are also found in Standard English. Most of these words are used in Black English in much the same way that they are used in Standard English. Of course, there also are words that are found *only* in Black English, or that have developed special meanings in Black English: words like *soul, chick,* and *bread.* This is only natural: all dialects of English that are used by special groups in particular parts of the world have developed their special vocabularies, idioms, and slang, to talk about things and ideas that are especially important to them or to express attitudes different from those of other groups.

The general conclusion up to now, then, is this: as far as richness of vocabulary is concerned, all languages are equally capable of expressing thought and ideas, and it cannot be said that any one language or dialect is superior or inferior to another in this respect. But each language and each dialect develops vocabulary for expressing the concepts that are especially important in some way in the cultures of the groups using those languages and dialects.

THE "WHORFIAN" HYPOTHESIS
OF LINGUISTIC RELATIVITY

In a remarkable series of articles, originally published in the late 1930's but made available as a collection (Whorf, 1956), Benjamin Lee Whorf (1897–1941) raised the question of whether different languages might possibly reflect different "world views" or views of reality—not so much in their vocabularies, but in the deeper layers of their linguistic structures and grammars. He tended to believe that they do. His view has been called the doctrine of *linguistic relativity* because it proposes that our perception and understanding of the world is relative to the language we speak, i.e., depends on it.

By profession, Whorf was a chemical engineer who worked for a fire insurance company, but he developed a great personal interest in languages and was able to spend considerable time pursuing this interest. During the last ten years of his life, he became a student and close associate of the well-known American linguist Edward Sapir, a professor at Yale. Mostly through Sapir's encouragement, he studied various American Indian languages, becoming impressed with the marvelously subtle ways in which their structures and grammars seemed to reflect ways of perceiving and thinking about things that were different from the ways in which "standard average European" languages like English, French, and German seemed to view these matters.

In Whorf's own words, his hypothesis was as follows:

> The background linguistic system (in other words, the grammar) of each language is not merely a reproducing instrument for voicing ideas but rather is itself the shaper of ideas, the program and guide for the individual's mental activity, for his analysis of impressions, for his synthesis of his mental stock in trade. Formulation of ideas is not an independent process, strictly rational in the old sense, but is part of a particular grammar and differs, from slightly to greatly, as between different grammars. We dissect nature along lines laid down by our native languages.... We cut nature up, organize it into concepts, and ascribe significance as we do, largely because we are parties to an agreement to organize it in this way—an agreement that holds throughout our speech community and is codified in the patterns of our language ... [Whorf, 1956, pp. 212 ff.].

Unfortunately, however, Whorf never put forth a formal *testable* form of his hypothesis, that is, a statement of it that would allow experimental verification of whether the form of a language grammar does in fact have the kinds of influence on thinking that Whorf claimed. Later on, we will discuss attempts that some scientists have made to test the Whorfian hypothesis.

Whorf's own evidence for his hypothesis came from more or less informal observations about various languages and their grammars, with occasional attempts to correlate his observations with data about the cultures of the peoples speaking those languages.

Perhaps the most quoted example is Whorf's assertion that the Eskimo language contains words for many different kinds of snow—"falling snow, snow on the ground, snow packed hard like ice, slushy snow, wind-driven snow," etc., whereas English contains only one "all-inclusive" word: *snow*. "To an Eskimo," Whorf (1956) writes, "this all-inclusive word would be almost unthinkable; he would say that falling snow, slushy snow, and so on, are sensuously and operationally different, different things to contend with; he uses different words for them and for other kinds of snow [p. 216]." Whorf failed to document exactly what Eskimo words he had in mind, and experts in the Eskimo language have raised doubts about the validity of Whorf's observations. Furthermore, one can point out that English does have various words relating to snow and freezing rain: sleet, hail, rime, frost, etc., and English-speaking ski enthusiasts have developed a whole vocabulary to deal with different qualities of snow fields. Perhaps the precision of vocabulary is simply a matter of what things are important for a person to distinguish.

The example about words for snow in Eskimo, however, is only one of many that Whorf gave to illustrate his ideas. A more subtle and striking example is one from Shawnee. In this American Indian language, the sentences for "I push his head back" and "I drop it in water and it floats (bobs back)" are highly similar, whereas they are, of course, quite different in English. In Shawnee, both sentences contain as a central element of the verb the root /kwašk/ which conveys the meaning "condition of force and reaction, pressure back, recoil." Thus, pushing back someone's head is perceived as involving not only the initial force of pushing, but also the resistance and recoil offered by the head. When an object is dropped in water and bobs back, there is also, according to the Shawnee sentence, a semantic element of reaction and recoil—a physical idea that would not readily be perceived by the speaker of English.

At another point Whorf contrasts the kinds of grammatical classifications of concepts made by Hopi and English. He starts by pointing out that in English, there is a general tendency to classify "long-lasting events" like *man* and *house* as nouns, whereas "short-lasting events" like *strike, turn,* and *run* are codified as verbs. English is not very careful, however, to classify ideas in this way, for some long-lasting events are verbs, like *keep, adhere, extend, dwell,* etc., and some short-lasting events are nouns, like *fist, lightning, spark, noise,* etc. In contrast, he asserts, the Hopi language is very careful to separate short-lasting events from long-lasting ones. "In the Hopi language, 'lightning, wave, flame, meteor, puff of smoke, pulsation' are verbs—events of necessarily brief duration cannot be anything but verbs. 'Cloud' and 'storm' are at about the lower limit of duration for nouns. Hopi, you see, actually has a classification of events (or linguistic isolates) by duration type, something strange to our modes of thought [p. 215]."

From these and other examples, Whorf proposes that the Hopi language is actually *superior* to English for expressing ideas of modern physics— for example, vibratory and wave phenomena.

In an article entitled "The Relation of Habitual Thought and Behavior to Language," originally published in 1941 (Whorf, 1956, pp. 134–159), Whorf attempted to show parallels between Hopi language structure and Hopi culture and behavior. First, however, he pointed out examples of influences of language on thought in English. In his fire-prevention work, he had observed that people tended to be careful about not smoking around *full* gasoline drums, but not to be so careful around *empty* gasoline drums. The word empty, he thought, misled people into ignoring the explosive vapors that empty gasoline drums might contain. "Such examples, which could be greatly multiplied, will suffice to show how the cue to a certain line of behavior is often given by the analogies of the linguistic formula in which the situation is spoken of, and by which to some degree it is analyzed, classified, and allotted its place in that world which is to a large extent unconsciously built up on the language habits of the group [Whorf, 1956, p. 137]."

Turning to Hopi, one of the questions that Whorf asked was, "Are there traceable affinities between (a) cultural and behavioral norms and (b) large-scale linguistic patterns?" His conclusion was highly affirmative. One obvious trait that he observed in Hopi culture was its emphasis on *preparation,* that is, announcing and getting ready for events well beforehand, preparing for public ceremonies, practicing rituals, praying for desired results in the future, and so on, in special ways and with special attention. This trait he found reflected in the Hopi language in its treatment of concepts of time. To the Hopi, a period of time, like a day, cannot be pluralized or considered in the plural. Days are always counted ordinally, the first day, the second day, etc., so that in Hopi it is impossible to say "They stayed ten days"; rather, this meaning is conveyed by saying something meaning "They stayed until the eleventh day." Time is something that develops and grows, rather than going in cycles (as it does in English), according to Whorf. Ordinal counting of periods of time means to the Hopi that successive appearances of the *same* thing are involved, and (at least according to Whorf) this view of time affects the way the Hopi deal with the future, "by working within a present situation which is expected to carry impresses, both obvious and occult, forward into the future event of interest [p. 148]." Thus, preparing for events in the future involves concentrated "thought power" and "persistence and constant insistent repetition" of thoughts about the future.

If Whorf had ever turned his attention to Black English (if, indeed, linguistic analyses of the dialect had been available then), he might well have been intrigued with certain phenomena involving the copula *be*. According to some analyses, the difference between *He sick* and *He be sick*, or between *They working* and *They be working* is one of emphasizing the temporary versus permanent or long-lasting aspect of the attribute. Thus, *they working* means "they are working right now" while *they be working* means "they've been working for some time, and will be for some time to come." Fasold (1969), however, claims that the use of *be* often emphasizes the *intermittent* nature of the activity, so that *they be working* means "They work every so often." I leave the reader to speculate what kind of cultural difference, if any, might correspond to the Black English way of "cutting up reality."

STUDIES AND CRITIQUES OF THE LINGUISTIC RELATIVITY HYPOTHESIS

Because Whorf's techniques were merely inferential, the "Whorfian hypothesis" has never been generally accepted or confirmed. Eric Lenneberg (1953) pointed out that Whorf's examples are unconvincing because they do no more than illustrate various arbitrary, metaphorical ways of expressing ideas that are common to all languages. If a Hopi linguist were to look at English the way Whorf looked at Hopi, he might express astonishment at the English word *breakfast* and conclude that speakers of English always think of a breakfast as "breaking a fast." In other words, Lenneberg felt that Whorf was reading too much into the analysis of language forms, inferring different mental states, whereas in actuality the mental states might be much the same across languages.

In 1953, a 5-day conference on the Whorfian hypothesis was held in Chicago, involving a number of distinguished linguists, anthropologists, and psychologists. The proceedings of the conference were reported in a volume edited by Hoijer (1954). While a wide variety of points of view were expressed, in reading this volume one cannot escape the conclusion that the tone was essentially skeptical. Not only Whorf's reasoning, but even his linguistic facts came under question. Franklin Fearing, a psychologist who attended the conference, argued that if anything, the relation between language and thought is likely to be that *thought influences language,* rather than the other way around. He argued this from evidence that even before they learn language, children attain a great many general concepts of reality—of space, time, and the general shape and behavior of the environment. Language encodes these general concepts, and if different languages encode them in different ways, the differences are more apparent than real. Nevertheless, a few of the conferees—in particular, Hoijer (an anthropologist) and Hockett (a linguist)—felt that there was enough promise in the Whorfian hypothesis to justify considering it seriously and doing further research based on it.

During the summers of 1955 and 1956, a team of researchers under the present writer attempted to find evidence for or against the Whorfian hypothesis in a series of experiments conducted among various language groups in the American Southwest, mostly groups of American Indians. The basic idea of this research effort was to find instances in which one could trace a definite correlation between language structure and certain forms of nonlinguistic behavior. It was decided, however, not to try to investigate the world views of the groups on any grand philosophical scale; rather, the goal was to study various fairly simple forms of behavior such as the sorting and classification of objects in instances where the linguistic categorizations seemed to differ across languages.

For example, in the Hopi language there is a verb which means "to close an opening" which is applied whenever a distinct hole, aperture, or opening is covered or closed up. It can be applied, for example, to closing the lid of a box, or to covering an open box with a cloth. I prepared a set of pictures depicting these actions and one other (covering a sewing machine with a cloth), and asked both English speakers and Hopi speakers to select which two of the three pictures "went together." The Hopis showed more tendency to put together the two "closing" pictures, whereas the English speakers had a greater tendency to put together the two pictures of "covering." It seemed that the Hopi verb directed the perceptions of the Hopi speakers, whereas the English concept of "cover" (which can be applied regardless of whether there is an opening to be covered) guided the sortings of the English speakers.

An even more dramatic example of an apparent influence of language on behavior was obtained among the Navahos. In Navaho, certain concepts of handling (*pick up, give, take,* etc.) require the use of different verb forms depending on the form or shape characteristics of the object being handled. Navaho-speaking children learn these forms very early. Now, it has been observed for a long time that at very early ages, say age 3, English-speaking (and also French-speaking) children tend to sort objects by color rather than form; only at later ages does classification by form become dominant. We found that young Navaho-speaking children matched for age with other Navaho children who spoke English rather than Navaho had a greater tendency to sort objects by form than the non-Navaho-speaking children. It was tempting to speculate that this was a result of the characteristics of the Navaho language. It may well have been; the trouble was that we also found that middle-class White children in Boston used form characteristics in sorting about as much as the Navaho-speaking children, perhaps as a result of the increased use of toys and puzzles involving spatial forms in the play activities of such children.

These and a few other findings tended to support some weak version of the Whorfian hypothesis. Insofar as languages differ in the ways they encode objective experiences, language users tend to sort out and distinguish experiences differently according to the categories provided by their respective languages, and these cognitions will tend to have certain effects on behavior when that behavior depends on the verbal codes provided by language. The effects, however, are very small and do not mean that people's minds are locked into the categories provided by their language, for they can always perceive other ways of categorizing things and events.

When we tried to explore further possible consequences of a Whorfian hypothesis, the results were generally negative. For example, we used Osgood's semantic differential technique to see whether the basic "semantic" dimensions found in Western cultures would also be observed in speakers of Indian languages; the general results (Suci, 1960) were that the semantic dimensions were universal. In another experiment, an attempt was made to see whether specific types of Hopi verbs would have any influence on the efficiency of communication between Hopi speakers. It happens that Hopi, like a number of other languages, has different verbs for different modes of carrying—carrying on one's back, carrying in one's hands, carrying in a basket, etc. It was thought, therefore, that Hopi speakers would be more accurate in describing pictures of such activities in Hopi than when they described them in English. Actually, no differences were found, although it still remains to be seen whether monolingual English speakers would be just as accurate.

The general conclusion of all these studies was that while the lexicon and grammar of a language might have certain effects on behavior, or at least be reflected in behavior, the effects were small and not of any far-reaching importance (Carroll, 1963). Mental operations seem to be largely independent of the language in which they take place, although they may undergo certain transformations as a bilingual individual passes from one language to another. A truly bilingual individual would be a person who has learned to manage these transformations. For example, an English–Spanish bilingual would learn to manage the fact that in English there is only one basic verb *to be,* whereas in Spanish there is one verb *(ser)* to express generally "permanent" states of being and another verb *(estar)* to convey more or less "temporary" states of being. The difference, in Spanish, is merely a conventional one, and the absence of the difference in English does not mean that speakers of English cannot distinguish between permanent and temporary states; it is simply that he is not *required* to distinguish between them when he speaks.

We might return for a moment to the observation that Black English seems to have different usages of the verb *to be* from Standard English. If the meanings of *they working* and *they be working* are different in Black English, whereas Standard English does not require making a distinction between continuous and intermittent activity, it is unlikely that speakers of Black English are more aware of such a distinction than speakers of Standard English; Standard English might still find means of conveying the distinction, saying "they are working all the time" in one case and "they are working every so often" in the other. It is unlikely that the linguistic differences between Black English and Standard English in the usage of the verb *to be* reflect differences in "world view." And a speaker of Black English learning Standard English is unlikely to notice any "gap" in Standard English whereby the distinction between continuous and intermittent activity is difficult to convey. Nevertheless, these remarks are speculative; perhaps speakers of Black English would have a different view of this matter.

Besides the studies cited above, there have been many other studies that have sought to test the validity of the Whorfian hypothesis, beginning with a well-known experimental investigation by Brown and Lenneberg (1954). Brown and Lenneberg, using only English-speaking subjects, showed that the "codability" of a stimulus (a color), that is, the extent to which people could agree on a name for the stimulus, was correlated with a subject's success in remembering that color in a recognition memory task. Thus, highly nameable colors were remembered and recognized better than colors which subjects found hard to name distinctly. But this experiment and others like it (e.g., Lantz & Stefflre, 1964) cannot be considered to be a true test of the Whorfian hypothesis, for it merely shows that in trying to remember things, people rely on verbal codes when they are available, and have difficulty when those codes are less available. It says nothing about the way people actually perceive colors and nothing about whether verbal codes influence the perception of colors. If the Whorfian hypothesis were true, the availability of a verbal code might influence color perception. In a recent study, Heider and Olivier (1972) were able to compare the visual color perceptions of speakers of English with those of members of a Stone Age tribe in New Guinea (the Dani) whose language contains only two color terms. They found no evidence that the color terminologies of the two languages had any effect on the way in which color perceptions were structured in memory. Thus, the expectations from a strong form of the Whorfian hypothesis were not confirmed.

It should be carefully noted, in any case, that Whorf never claimed or alleged that the languages of indigenous groups—such as American Indian tribes—were in any way inferior to the languages of "civilized" groups like English or other "standard average European" languages. In fact, if anything, Whorf tended to believe that languages of American Indians were in certain ways superior to "standard average European" languages, in that the latter forced their speakers into certain restricted molds of thought, such as always perceiving situations in terms of actors, actions, and objects, and failing to notice subtle distinctions between different modes of action, different time relations, etc. There is serious doubt that speakers of standard average European languages like English are really constrained in their modes of thought, however, in the sense that those modes of thought are strictly determined by the grammars of their languages. We now believe that it is more likely that the categories of thought are universal among mankind, and are universally reflected in all languages and dialects. If so, these categories of thought are just as well reflected in Black English as they are in any other form of English, or in any other form of language, for that matter.

REFERENCES

Brown, R., & Lenneberg, E. A study in language and cognition. *Journal of Abnormal and Social Psychology,* 1954, **49,** 454–462.

Carroll, J. B. Linguistic relativity, contrastive linguistics, and language learning. *International Review of Applied Linguistics,* 1963, **1,** 1–20.

Fasold, R. W. Tense and the form *be* in Black English. *Language,* 1969, **45,** 763–776.

Heider, E. R., & Olivier, D. C. The structure of the color space in naming and memory for two languages. *Cognitive Psychology,* 1972, 3, 337–354.

Hoijer, H. (Ed.) *Language in culture: Conference on the interrelations of language and other aspects of culture.* Chicago: University of Chicago Press, 1954.

Lantz, D., & Stefflre, V. Language and cognition revisited. *Journal of Abnormal and Social Psychology,* 1964, **69,** 472–481.

Lenneberg, E. Cognition in ethnolinguistics. *Language,* 1953, **29,** 463–471.

Suci, G. J. A comparison of semantic structures in American Southwest culture groups. *Journal of Abnormal and Social Psychology,* 1960, **61,** 25–30.

Whorf, B. L. *Language, thought, and reality: Selected writings of Benjamin Lee Whorf.* Edited and with an introduction by J. B. Carroll. Cambridge, Massachusetts: MIT Press, 1956.

14

The Cognitive Deficit–Difference Controversy: A Black Sociopolitical Perspective

M. Eugene Wiggins

Federal City College

We learned long ago that through language communication man has the basic capacity to grasp and organize his culture and his world, and to relate it to the complexity of the universe in which he lives. Although group behavioral differences suggest that the phonological, syntactic, and semantic composition of languages are culturally stratified, this stratification in no way suggests a dichotomy between man and language, indeed, it is an intellectual struggle to conceive of man void of language, and language void of man's cardinal need for it. It is far simpler to observe the remarkably inseparable bond that so clearly exists between the two, and to declare the natural and universal character of their coexistence.

We can support this hypothesis in the observation that every child, whoever he is, wherever he may be (given the right to normal development), will inherit an undisputed claim to language acquisition during the early years of life. In spite of the complex nature of language, we know that children will seize the substance of its linguistic properties and in time will expose its code with a very systematic performance. While the acquisition of language appears to most of us as rather rudimentary in its workings, to the many scholars who have had to wrestle with an understanding of its intricately complex nature, its uniquely human trait, the magnitude of acquiring language is phenomenal.

Granting the fundamental premises governing the inherent nature of language and man, and their natural coexistence, we are, nonetheless, here to perpetuate the controversial deliberations that focus upon the application of these commonly noted assertions to the linguistic style of Black people. It is as though abruptly and without the furnishing of warning, we have unexpectedly come face to face with the staggering awareness that Black people are human after all. This would appear so given the existence of these controversial proceedings for more than a decade now. Of course, we all know, fundamentally, that the persistent survival of such gatherings are solely reflective of how enormously difficult it is for this society to acknowledge human qualities in Black people. Having pointed out that truism, I can predict the uprise of opposing voices. But screams of refutation are not necessarily compatible with an appeal for honesty. Any issue that involves Black people is always a political and controversial one, and the nucleus of that controversy is ever central to the question of whether Black people are really people—except when their behavior bears a striking correspondence to a White, often middle-class style; for America has traditionally matched equality with homogeneity, and the repelling consequence for Blacks in assuming the daring posture of heterogeneity has always been linked to discussions that focused upon organic ills of Black behavior. For why else then, has the current cognitive deficit–difference dispute maintained so similar a pose to the age-old dispute of heredity, intelligence, and Black people? Certainly, the shape of the arguments form an obviously political figure on the subject of what constitutes normal, appropriate behavior. I cannot, for example, suggest any other reason why educators and psychologists, many of them bearing the mark of experts and scholars in their respective disciplines, chose not to consider the theory of cultural and linguistic universals, allegedly common to all people, when they began looking at the behavior of Black children during the early 1960's. They were cognizant then, as well as they are now, that they were observing children who by the very nature of their existence were not the same as White children, of whatever economic footing. And they knew, equally well, the sociopolitical significance of continuing the tradition that pointed toward the Black child (indeed Black people in general) as basically inferior stock, linguistically and intellectually. One need not go through any kind of intellectual toil to make note of this particularly obvious verity. Its roots are as ancient in performance as the institution of racism, and its vines as durable as the tenacious belief in which they are manifested. I do not now and I never have acknowledged the age-old promise of objective and scientific observation when researchers, particularly White researchers, attempt to translate the meaning behind Black behavior. And, having made that point, let me delve into the specifics of my argument by reviewing the developments that occurred in the 1960's with respect to the linguistic facility of Black children dwelling in low-income communities.

THE CURRENT ORIGIN
OF THE COGNITIVE DEFICIT–DIFFERENCE DISPUTE

One might recall that the dispute actually began with the late President Lyndon B. Johnson's "War On Poverty" when the awarding of federal grants for the purpose of investigating the lack of academic achievement on the part of Black children in public education was at a premium. White researchers, allegedly searching for an understanding of why so many Black children failed in school, focused their attention, among other things, upon the language the children used. Their approach was somewhat different from the earlier nonexperimental observations of "thick lips, lazy tongues, and flat noses." The racism would have been too obvious. Instead, these researchers, having accumulated mounds of data on the acquisition of language among White middle-class children, and having designed a host of test instruments from these data, proceeded to invade school buildings situated in central cities throughout the country in efforts to pursue objective scientific experiments in the study of the language performance of Black children. Predictably, when they rushed the interpretations of their results to education journals and publishing companies, once again the Black community became the target of negative adjectives that described its population as a sickened form of hearty White behavior. Black children, they implied, failed to grasp the nature of their language and their world, something so commonly found in every other group of children, a phenomenon all others manage to do with relative ease (Deutsch, 1965; John, 1963; Raph, 1967; Bereiter, 1965; Bereiter & Englemann, 1966). But these children were different, for some reason, and that difference seemed to be manifested not in the legitimacy of cultural and linguistic stratification, but in the lacking of their intellectual capacity to form a language and a culture that reflect the substance of their inheritance. Volumes of ink were spilled on the theory that Black children are unable to speak clearly, that they cannot discriminate auditorally, that they cannot conceptualize, that Black mothers do not know how to be mothers, and that Black fathers are not in the home. In effect, the Black community was atrociously void of stimulating any type of linguistic and intellectual growth. Black people, particularly the poor, were a culturally deprived lot, not worthy of even the slightest hint that they were culturally and linguistically different. Labels such as the "culturally deprived" (later changed to the "culturally disadvantaged") had a seemingly natural appeal to the fancy of educators. Hence, the portrait was pointed, the tradition was saved and framed, and the intended grossness of its style suspended to the wall alongside multitudes of portraits, centuries old, that portrayed what White America perceived to be the inferior character of Black Americans. The performance had been presented many times before. Only this time the fallacy was executed under the theme of "educating the deprived."

A classic example of this repulsive portrait so deeply couched under the frame of education can be seen in a booklet published by Head-Start and distributed to teachers in the program. Labov (1970) reports that the booklet begins with the following remarks:

> You'll notice that these children who come to class are not the same as other children in many ways. They don't play a great deal, they just sort of stand around, and they don't talk a great deal, as a matter of fact, you'll notice they're just quiet, they ... don't say much, and as a matter of fact, you'll notice they also don't laugh very much.... Furthermore, in their lives, they've had very little reason to laugh.... You have an opportunity to do something truly great. You will give these children, for the first time in their lives, a knowledge of how to play. You will give these children, for the first time in their lives, an opportunity to laugh, you will give them the first reason they've ever had to laugh [pp. 2–3].

Meanwhile, many Black parents, unemployed or underpaid, grappling in the gut of poverty, having been advised of the academic grandeur of mass instruction programs that emerged out of the cognitive deficit theories, sent their children to school pleased that the system would work better for their children than it had for them.

Interestingly, during the early period of "deprivation" claims, linguists, strong on their theory on linguistic relativism, stood mute. Although it is not clear why, one might suspect that linguists, for the most part, did not deal in any depth with Black dialects of English prior to 1960, except for the works of Lorenzo Turner (1949) and Melville Herskovits (1941), whose works became far more popular during the 1960's than when they were initially published. Scholars in this discipline had travelled and observed linguistic stratification throughout the world and had written admirably about the languages and life-styles of people in the most remote places. Yet, here in their country, when the alarm sounded on Black people and "deprivation," they remained noticeably silent. Stewart (1964) lends further insight into the nature of this silence:

> There are probably a number of reasons for this neglect, and as a first step it might be useful to review some of these. First, there has been the general attitude, common even among some linguists, that nonstandard speech is less worthy of study than varieties of speech with high prestige and social acceptability. As this relates to the speech of Negroes, it has been reinforced by a commendable desire to emphasize the potential of the Negro to be identical to

white Americans, and accordingly to de-emphasize any current behavioral patterns which might not seem to contribute directly to that goal. Where attention
has been paid to nonstandard Negro speech, much of it has unfortunately been
in the form of amateurish and often racistic speculation by early "authorities,"
and this has undoubtedly discouraged many reputable linguists from specializing
in the area. Lastly, respect for the feelings of Negroes themselves has probably
played a part in discouraging the study of Negro speech. For, as is quite understandable, many Negroes (particularly educated ones) are somewhat sensitive
about any public focus on distinctively Negro behavior, particularly if it happens
to be that of lower class Negroes. In some cases, this attitude may stem from
a belief that such studies, where unmatched by comparable ones of the behavior
of educated Negroes, might well encourage old stereotypes about the American
Negro by giving an incomplete picture of the cultural range which he represents.
In other cases, the same attitude may betray a feeling of insecurity in individuals who themselves have made an incomplete transition from a lower class,
nonstandard speech background, and who may accordingly feel threatened by
any evidence of the proximity of behavior which they have worked very hard
to leave behind [pp. 10–19].

When, finally, the linguist spoke up and began to refute the cognitive
deficit theorists, the debates became heated and controversial. Linguists
argued with fervor that their colleagues were confused between the acquisition of language and the acquisition of Standard English, that Black
children from low-income families are linguistically different, not deficient, that they have a language but the linguistic rules of the language
differ from that of Standard English and that what one hears from these
children is a nonstandard form of English. That there would appear to
be some confusion on the part of educators and psychologists between
language acquisition and the acquisition of a middle-class dialect seemed
true enough in honor of the linguist's position, but the linguist clearly
failed to comprehend that the labels "cultural deprivation" and "linguistic deprivation" ultimately reflected on the age-old tradition of viewing
Black behavior from a social pathology mold. It hardly touches the
periphery to point to the problem as simply a matter of confusion in
understanding the difference between the acquisition of Standard English
and the acquisition of language. I find it inconceivable to believe, given
their academic expertise, that the cognitive deficit theorists were confused. Certainly, they were no more confused than those who had described Black behavior before them. Central to the workings of education
is the negative slant toward those who stand aside from what is deemed
proper and positive and in the interest of this country's tradition, and
to thrust forward the labels of political elements that strive gallantly
under the umbrella of education. Except as a slave market force, Black
people have never been deemed compatible with the interest of this country, particularly with respect to education. Consequently, it should come
as no surprise that Black children from low-income families do not

achieve as well in school as their middle- and upper-income counterparts. Educators have always looked at the "average" child in such a way that suggested he was a White child. Ethnic and cultural differences, cognitively and linguistically, have been traditionally ignored. Education as it exists in this country has never been designed to educate poor people, least of all Black people, and it has always been the child from the White middle-class elite who was really expected to carry on the "American ideal." To say, then, that the issue is one of confusion in the understanding of language acquisition is far from penetrating the nature of the controversy. It would seem feasible to question whether the arguments have anything at all to do with linguistics and education. And if one accepts the invitation to step beyond the bickering among researchers and academicians, one is forced to acknowledge the fact that more likely than not the core of the issue focuses upon a people's need to survive in an oppressed situation; more specifically, a Black people's need to survive in a sociopolitical climate where those in power view that need within the strictest limits. For indeed the real issue is always Black people, and much of what has been said and written about Black people and language has nothing at all to do with the linguistics of the matter, but has all to do with speakers of the language and how those speakers are expected to function in a society that reasons, through its power and control, that its Black members approach nothing short of White behavioral norms.

THE "BEST APPROACH" CONTROVERSY

The arguments have focused upon what method works best in teaching Black children to speak Standard English and what method works best in teaching them to read for the purpose of improving their economic status. For example, while the linguist has argued his position well, it is, obviously, the validity of his very position that places him at such a great disadvantage. His stand for the appreciation of linguistic differences, particularly in reference to Black children, and his push for bidialectalism as opposed to eradication are not going to bear the mark of popularity in the American school system. Indeed, it reeks with the radical audacity to lend credibility to a mode of behavior that the fathers of education long ago ruled deplorable. On the other hand, advocates of the cognitive deficit theory stand brilliantly in the minds of educators as the authorities on the subject of educating Black children from low-income families; since the theory is quite deeply entrenched in the question of Black intellect. Accordingly, linguistics and education have nothing to do with the subject.

Proceeding further into the matter, it would appear that one could present several specific reasons why cognitive deficit theorists such as

Sigfried Englemann head the list of so-called experts in compensatory education for Black children. First, Englemann has an instruction program which, allegedly, is purposefully designed to develop cognitive, linguistic, and reading skills in Black children during the preschool years.[1] It does not matter whether the program really does this. What matters is that he and his associates designed a program that catered to the conventional doubts of public educators in their attitude about the scholastic capabilities of Black children. Further, to add a dose of potency to the treatment, the authors included in that package a guaranteed cure for the ills of the Black child who, they argued, does not understand the meaning of words such as *not* and *under*. Educators, then, were gifted not with an assemblage of controversial rhetoric and confrontations, but with *the* cure—to be seen, to be held, and, indeed, to be administered. Certainly, this better enabled them to live more comfortably with their hidden negativisms manifested in their frustrations and failures in teaching these children.

Linguistic materials, on the other hand, have been primarily concerned with instruction by implication rather than by application. This by itself is particularly defeating. As any teacher of children knows, the tendency is to favor materials in hand rather than become attracted to the implications of materials through rhetorical vigor. Also, linguistic materials have not focused upon the preschool ages when the "cognitive deficiency syndrome" is supposedly more evident. In the early 1960's, for example, large amounts of money were invested in preschool programs as witnessed in such programs as Head Start. This interest and money were captured in the Bereiter–Englemann Program (Distar) designed specifically for early childhood education and adopted as the primary instruction lesson in many Head Start programs.

Furthermore, linguists generally have been at odds with respect to the most effective methodological approach to teach Black children Standard English and reading. Consequently, in terms of the actual development of materials of whatever method, nothing close to an instruction program of the intensity of Englemann's has been designed by the linguist. This lack of a detailed instruction program places the linguist at a great disadvantage in promoting his theories—aside from the fact, as I have mentioned, that the linguist had no materials to fit the emphasis on early childhood compensatory education. Englemann (1971) was well aware of this when he raised the question, "Does the linguistic position imply any kind of instruction? The answer is no!":

[1] Englemann claims that his program is not designed just for poor Black children, but poor White children as well. Yet, his experiments in the application of his materials have been almost exclusively with Black children.

What kind of programs can Labov suggest by virtue of his theory and his evidence? For every reading approach that he suggests, another linguist can suggest a different approach. For every language program that he proposes another linguist can propose a different program. Yet, all of the linguists work from the same theory, the same evidence. Why is such inconsistency possible? Simply because linguistic theory does not imply instruction. It does not imply what should be taught in a dialect. It does not imply that the program should be one of linguistic patterns or paragraph reading. It does not imply what kind of reinforcers should be used, even though some who have been lured by the linguistic approach seem to think that approaches that change dialects are criminal, unmotivating and dangerous [p. 146].

In short, Englemann moved very quickly to promote the cause of behavioral change through instruction rather than behavioral acceptance, a notion which any number of educators across the country would gladly support, particularly with respect to Black children. Consequently, his design has a striking appeal to the system's political position which is the imposition of prescriptive, arbitrary norms set up by White America to which people are expected to conform in order to serve the ends of the defining class.

Lest someone willfully misinterprets my point, I am not presenting the case against the use of a standard dialect. Indeed, for Blacks who desire this end it is their choice and it certainly has been the choice of many Blacks for many years. However, the notion that learning to speak a particular linguistic code such as Standard English will achieve for Blacks a lift in their economic and political plight is unmistakably deceiving, as language is not now and never has been the contributing agent of oppression. Terms such as "cognitive deficient" came into vogue only during a period when the education system was hard pressed to explain its failure in educating Black children. Before then no one concerned themselves with why the children were not achieving in school. Certainly, terms such as "culturally disadvantaged," "Standard English," and "Nonstandard English" were not suggested. Consequently, these labels had to be promoted to disguise the system's failures. Hence, the finger was slanted toward the child and his community and the system's participants were better able to falsely appraise themselves autonomous of the conditions that prevented Black children from, say, learning to read. In sum, the problem was the child; all fared well with the school. Therefore, the arguments for the need of Blacks to speak a standard dialect represent, simply, another route that White America has taken in justifying and sheltering the centuries of injustices that have been handed down to the Black man, on the one hand, and in diverting his attention from the real issues, on the other. More specifically, they reflect an institution that says, in effect, that the decisions for and about Black people shall be dutifully determined by Whites for the perpetuation of America's political control over Blacks.

Meanwhile, the linguist awkwardly struggles with the belief that the issue is really linguistic—or educational.

Furthermore, let us suppose for a moment that on the basis of their theories, the linguists did have some consistent type of instruction program. Would it be feasible to assume that educators would leap to it as quickly and as readily as they have to the program of Englemann and his associates? Granted, a most unlikely occurrence.

Why? Because the contemptuous fancy of cultural and linguistic differences in support of Black communication in public schools, U.S.A., is about as popular, attitudinally, as integrated housing is socially.

For example, if one can agree with Baratz's (1969) idea that through the use of "transition readers" the Black child should be taught to read first in his own dialect followed by teaching him to read in standard English, one might conclude that theoretically such readers would reflect an attempt to function within the framework of accepting Black communication as an integral part of a Black cultural reality. On the other hand, the posture of Englemann's Distar program rejects Black speech (indeed Black intelligence) as an integral part of a White mental reality. Hence, from a sociopolitical perspective, the Distar program hums the tune of the White American power structure and therefore becomes the program. Consequently, when the "transition readers" approach the schoolhouse steps, Distar, or its likes, will be blocking the entrance.

LESSONS FROM THE PAST
AND PERSPECTIVES FOR THE FUTURE

What conclusions, then, might one make—from a Black perspective—about this controversy which is so deeply entrenched in the sociopolitical temper of education. Actually, the cognitive deficit–difference controversy in its practical methodological application over the best method to teach Black children to acquire adequate skills in the use of Standard English is, for the most part, academic; that is, in terms of the economic, sociopolitical, and educational lacking of Blacks in this country, the question of linguistic competency in Standard English has little if anything to do with whether Blacks succeed in school or whether Blacks are able to gain a certain status of employability. Yet, in the past decade, Blacks have been smothered with what is standard and what is nonstandard, although neither school has bothered to examine the consequences of political and economic power which defines what is standard and what is nonstandard; we have been overwhelmed with the question of language for the sake of employability, although historically language has never been closely correlated with employability for Blacks; we have been lectured to on how we should be educated and how we should not be educated, the assumption being that there has always been serious intent to educate us to begin with; we have been taught what actions represent human-like behavior and what actions do not, although given the history of our struggle in this country we have been viewed outside the arena of humanness. In sum, we have been well indoctrinated on how we can best remain oppressed, and how we can best think that we are not oppressed. The cognitive deficit–difference polemicists failed notoriously, either consciously or unconsciously, to attend to the full impact of racial discrimination in this country and its ruthless effects on the survival of people in an oppressed situation. Indeed, both schools of thought present similarly strong position statements that the Black child's language is one of his greatest handicaps. While the philosophical perspectives differ greatly, both end up suggesting that what is needed are special training techniques to enhance the child's linguistic and reading skills in Standard English either for the purpose of changing his behavior or helping him to become bidialectal for reasons of employability, or both, depending upon one's interpretation of the arguments. In any event, one might see no difference except in approach between what the two groups are arguing about. In short, what one really sees is a collection of academicians and scientists, mainly White, giving lip service and bickering among themselves about how Black people should best struggle with their poverty; as if by some spell of magic, learning to speak Standard English will relieve Blacks of the burden of racism and of economic and political deprivation and will immediately thrust them into the ranks of economic and political significance.

Both schools of thought have willingly invited many Black scholars in communication to side with them on their issues and have therefore succeeded in diverting their attention from the struggle of Black determination so that now Blacks are beginning to bicker among themselves about whether we speak correctly or not, a classic example of exhausting one's energy in trivia. Bidialectalism is one's choice. However, the notion of compulsory bidialectalism as a means of employability is ridiculous since it serves to camouflage the real issue that Blacks are not employed in certain jobs because of color and no other reason. Least of all does language have anything to do with it. As Baraka (Jones, 1966) points out, "Africans never had any idea that learning 'good English' and wearing shoes had anything to do with the validity of their lives on earth."

It is no more valid to assume that bidialectalism will affect the soaring trend in unemployment among Blacks than it is to assume that the institution of racism would crumble to bits were Blacks to suddenly take command of a middle-class dialect. Certainly, this can be seen in the fact that there exists in this country any number of White electricians, plumbers, and construction workers who are consistently employed and paid good salaries accompanied by good unionized fringe benefits, and who speak a variety of English that in no way lends itself to "good English." Yet, even for Blacks who are capable of performing these skills and whose dialect may be no more removed from "good English" than their White counterparts, getting hired is done on a token basis, if they are hired at all. On the other hand, Blacks who seek office jobs or jobs that demand daily contact with the public (i.e., bank tellers, telephone operators) quite often switch or soon learn to switch dialects with no formal training at all. Given the economic demands of the situation, Blacks have historically switched in their linguistic behavior with little or no difficulty. Being hired provided the motivation, not the inverse where learning the dialect provided the job.

THE ROLE OF THE BLACK SCHOLAR
IN COMMUNICATIONS

Accordingly, Black scholars in communication do not need to spend the excellence of their minds and misguide their expertise by arguing with or against White people over whether Black communication is legitimate or not. We know now as we have long known that it is, so why exhaust our energies at that level? We have, for example, become entrapped in defense of our legitimacy, actively perpetuating barren quarrels in conferences that surrender endlessly to the apartheid of Black intellectual suspect and uncertainty. Our reactions have been overwhelmed with the dire need to prove to our White counterparts the bona fide nature of our existence. White researchers come forth with all kinds of interpretations about how Black folks live and what Black folks need, while Black participants hurl forth all kinds of defensive philosophies to refute their suggestions—and quite often, each other.

Our initiatives should be in continuing among ourselves with respect to viable directions in which we must proceed relative to Black survival. Least of all should we continue to follow the models of White social scientists. We must look more carefully at the issues that we want to research and especially examine more carefully the interpretation of the data that emerge from such research. For example, the Black community is in desperate need of information with respect to the sociopolitical dimensions of Black communication. As one scopes the many routes to oppression, language usage not aside, one does not have to go through exhaustive research to conclude that many Blacks generally observe their own means of communication in the most negative fashion imaginable, which obviously is a direct reflection on how many Blacks view themselves. There is, after all, a thin line—if any line at all—between bad language and bad people. White America has been overwhelmingly successful in creating and promoting this monstrous and vicious animal of self-hatred. Debating with White people—and each other—only continues to remove us from the very people we spend so much time defending. The risk, it is feared, is that we make ourselves vulnerable to the same kinds of procedures used by White researchers in eliciting data in superficial situations and coming to faulty conclusions in interpreting such data with no in depth information on how language is actually used in the community. It is apparently this kind of risk that erroneously led Grier and Cobbs (1971) to the awesome conclusion that young Black boys who engage in the "dozens ritual" feel hostility for their mothers, on the one hand, and that Black men who indiscriminately exchange the word "motherfucker" are lost, hopeless isolates from society, on the other. Williams (1974) makes the point very well:

It appears quite obvious that if Blacks are to understand themselves and what their lives have meant and mean today, they will have to form the questions and do the research. The Black communicationist must leave Whites to the block . . . and move on into the heart of the Black community to understand what is being said, what the words mean, and what changes when the way one talks changes [p. 165].

It is also this kind of risk that during the 1960's led many Black scholars into the amen corner of White social scientists whose insulting idea is to treat the cancer of poverty and discrimination with a band-aid of language instruction programs.

Our specific challenge, then, is to address ourselves to the development of the Black community with an emergence of perspectives focused upon the promotion of self-determination, self-worth, pride, and dignity. I am reminded here that such expressions have assumed a rather stale position in the lives of Blacks, but it is not because of their definition that this has happened, but because of how men have interpreted those definitions; more specifically, in many instances, how Whites have defined them for Blacks. But as Lester (1968) points out, "Black consciousness is an essential part of speaking and defining for ourselves. It is the foundation of Black power." We must join hands with Black scholars in the areas of education, community organization, psychology, political science, economics, sociology, and religion. It is not a question of such absurd notions as Standard English for the sake of employability, or, more specifically, how to come to grips with the best, most rapid method of making instant black duplicates of white models. More sensibly, it is a matter of developing sound economic and sociopolitical principles viable to Black survival which would lead toward sound educational strategies that would be determined from a multidisciplinarian approach. Communication portrays a dynamic role in the total spectrum. Blacks need to gain the realization that Black communication is as distinctively Afro-American as Black skin, that respect for one's speech, whatever it is, is also respect for oneself, and that to veto that fact yields nothing less than an adverse response to one's view of oneself, a syndrome that has too long haunted the Black community.

More importantly, perhaps, is the role of definition in terms of how people come to grips with their world. For example, Black communication is not intended here to mean, simply, final consonant deletion, the absence of the copula or third person singular-s deletion, or rapping or playing the dozens. Indeed, Black speech encompasses the whole process of communication in terms of its style, vocabulary, rhythm, intonation, and nonverbal features, all of which are manifested in a state of existence and survival and which demand a kind of environmental experience unique to the organization of one's world. It does not involve just a linguistic description with no invitation to the physical disposition of its users. It is, after all, its users who are enforcing its existence, most obviously in response to the profound nature of how, for the moment, and related to their history, they perceive their world. As Fanon (1967) points out:

> To speak means to be in a position to use a certain syntax, to grasp the morphology of this or that language, but it means above all to assume a culture, to support the weight of civilization.... A man who has a language consequently possesses the world expressed and implied by the language.... Mastery of language affords remarkable power [pp. 17–18].

In summary, then, Blacks in communication must now begin to make the critical move. I suggest that we begin with a kind of political instrument that pushes us into the act of defining strategies and goals ranging from religion to politics to education. I suggest this as a beginning because the concept of definition as a political reality is entrenched in Blacks defining for themselves as opposed to letting others define for them. As Lester (1968) points out: "Politics demands a certain rhetoric; it does not demand moral action to fit the rhetoric." For example, Lyndon Johnson, Lester points out, redefined the Civil Rights Movement when he uttered the words "We shall overcome," and his picture now adorns the cover of the music sheet rather than Martin Luther King's. Accordingly, Blacks should be aware of social scientists who would like to believe that there is in fact a real dichotomy between education and politics, as Baratz (1970) suggests.

Once Blacks became aware of the significance of the power of definition as the essence of the total Black struggle, we will no longer look to Whites to determine the validity of our lives on earth. We will have traveled long beyond.

REFERENCES

Baratz, J. Teaching reading in a Negro school. In J. Baratz & R. Shuy (Eds.), *Teaching black children to read,* Washington, D.C.: Center for Applied Linguistics, 1969.

Baratz, J. Should Black children learn White dialect? *Journal of the American Speech & Hearing Association,* 1970, **12**, 415–417.

Bereiter, C. Academic instruction and preschool children. In R. Corbin & M. Crosby (Eds.), *Language programs for the disadvantaged.* Champaign, Illinois: National Council of Teachers of English, 1965.

Bereiter, C., & Englemann, S. *Teaching disadvantaged children in preschool.* Englewood Cliffs, N.J.: Prentice-Hall, 1966.

Deutsch, M. The role of social class in language development and cognition. *American Journal of Orthopsychiatry,* 1965, **35**, 78–88.

Englemann, S. The inadequacies of the linguistic approach in teaching situations. *Sociolinguistics: A crossdisciplinary perspective.* Washington, D.C.: Center for Applied Linguistics, 1971. Pp. 141–151.

Fanon, F. *Black skin, white masks.* New York: Grove Press, 1967.

Grier, W., & Cobb, P. *The Jesus bag.* New York: McGraw-Hill, 1971.

Herskovits, M. *The myth of the Negro past.* New York: Harper, 1941.

John, V. The intellectual development of slum children: some preliminary findings. *American Journal of Orthopsychiatry,* 1963, **33**, 813–822.

Jones, L. *Home: Social essays.* New York: William Morrow, 1966.

Labov, W. Systematically misleading data from test questions. Unpublished manuscript of the Colloquium Sponsored by the School of Social Work and the Department of Linguistics, The University of Michigan, April, 1970.

Lester, J. *Look out, Whitey! Black Power's gon' get your mama!* New York: Grove Press, 1968.

Raph, J. Language and speech deficits in culturally disadvantaged children: Implications for the speech clinician. *Journal of Speech and Hearing Disorders,* 1967, **32**, 203–217.

Stewart, W. Urban Negro speech: Sociolinguistic factors affecting English teaching. In R. Shuy (Ed.), *Social dialects and language learning.* Champaign, Illinois: National Council of Teachers of English, 1964. Pp. 10–19.

Turner, L. *Africanism in the Gullah dialect.* Chicago: University of Chicago Press, 1949.

Williams, R. The struggle to know, the struggle to survive. In J. Daniel (Ed.), *Black communication: Dimensions of research and instruction.* New York: Speech Communication Association, 1974. P. 165.

15

Black People and Black English: Attitudes and Deeducation in a Biased Macroculture

Ann Covington

Federal City College

Sometime ago I conducted a Black English seminar for parents. For this seminar the major complaint of the handbook used was the lack of information concerning the people who were quoted. The parents felt that without some background information concerning the sources they could not know how much value to place on what was being said. You might have similar questions about me. And although you might not believe a scintilla of what I say, you should have a visceral feeling for what I have to say. We are all products of our environment and our perceptions are colored by our experience.

I grew up in the 1930's in a small Midwestern town. Out of the population of 20,000 there were at the most 500 Blacks. We all lived "across the tracks" in a neighborhood consisting of Blacks and immigrants. (The term "ghetto" had not yet been co-opted from the Jews living in Nazi Germany or elsewhere in Europe.) Economic status or educational background did not determine where you lived. This was determined by race. The Blacks formed social groupings based on aspirations and social or religious values, not incomes.

We did not have major educational problems because there were so few of us. Our schooling came as a by-product of the desire of White parents to educate their children. We were educated because Whites had to educate their own. There would rarely be more than one Black child in a classroom. With only one high school and three elementary schools in town, the boundaries were so broad that they included all socio-economic groups.

Nevertheless we were not in Mecca. We knew that we were Black and, more fundamentally, we were aware of the fallout of a racist society. We were demeaned in many ways. The social disenfranchisement was manifested in signs: "no Jews, no niggers, no dogs allowed," in the burning of crosses in front of my parents' home before they found a haven across the tracks, and in the fact that as children we knew that certain jobs were open only to White children. It made no difference what variety of English we spoke (just as it did not make a difference in Nazi Germany that many Jews spoke flawless German without an accent when the pogroms started). I maintain that language style did not make a crucial difference in the 1930's and does not make the crucial difference today.

Growing up as a product of a Black family with high aspirations and living in a predominantly White environment, I learned very early that the malignant, satanic impulses of the macroculture were directed toward the race, not the language. In fact, the language was never called into question. It did not have to be since that was the period of overt racism.

Later, as a speech pathologist I spent over ten years working in the public schools of Michigan. This time was divided among 100% White schools, 100% Black schools, mixed schools, schools in low socioeconomic areas, and schools in high socioeconomic areas. I have observed firsthand the differences in the educational processes in various schools. I have been in schools where I have observed the "de-education process" and I have been in schools where education was a viable experience. Deeducation of course, was observed in the Black poor schools and education at its best in the White middle-class schools. I have found that we can definitely equate the quality of education with socioeconomic status. I do not impugn all of the teachers, but I do impugn the society for allowing such a demeaning system to exist.

For the past five years I have been involved in education at the university level. This has resulted in an intensification of my interest in Black English.

A major finding in my dissertation, Teacher Attitudes toward Black English: Effects on Student Achievement (1972) was the difference in perception among teachers and linguists about what constituted Black English and want constituted Standard English. Many of the students that the linguists classified as Black English speakers were perceived by the teachers as Standard English speakers.

What is Black English? I personally embrace the concept of Black English espoused by Black psychologists, social workers, linguists, and speech pathologists at the 1973 Conference on Cognitive and Language Development of the Black Child held in St. Louis, Missouri. The concept, referred to as Ebonics, includes under the rubric of Black English that speech spoken by Black people that is recognizably Black. It might be recognizably Black because of phonology, morphology, syntax, phrasing, intonation, vocalics, or something yet to be identified. The popular way of looking at language is on a continuum from Black (Nonstandard) to Standard, a straight-line approach. The ends of the line are brought together in Ebonics, looking at language in a circular way with emphasis on how something is said, when it is said, and to whom it is said.

The concept of Black English as a form of Nonstandard White English was negated by the group. This negation was based on the fact that a linguistic system cannot be considered nonstandard before an exact determination of what is "standard." The standard versus nonstandard dichotomy overlooks the purpose of language. More generally, language consists of arbitrary signs and symbols used by a social group to interact verbally with one another. When one examines a language, this is the framework in which it should be examined. Does a language fulfill its purpose? Does it enable a social group to interact verbally? Does it meet the needs of the populace by conveying their ideas, concepts, and values. If it does these things it must be considered standard, and it can be considered nonstandard only if one takes it into the comparative arena.

Comparisons are made by the "elitist" members of society, the scholars, or the prestigious few. Their system, be it language or life-style, becomes the norm or the standard. Whatever differs from that standard becomes nonstandard. Ebonics does not fall into that trap. It does not allow one group to dictate how another group will look at our language or life-style. Ebonics does not allow one group to look at another in a comparative sense because the norms of outsiders are inapplicable.

Equally, or more importantly, it was felt by the St. Louis group that a straight-line approach is not the way to look at language. Looking at language in a circular sense allows one to determine whether language is fulfilling its role as a vehicle of communication. It allows one to see how it is used, when, where, and for what.

Presently Black culture is being described and analyzed more by Whites than Blacks. Consequently, a predominance of works on the street culture of Northern urban Blacks, which is something frequently found exotic is now available. One is led to believe that Black culture is synonymous with street culture; however, every Black person knows differently. Only a person from the outside, a person who does not know, a person using his norms as the standard, could write some of the "garbage" that appears in the literature today. For example, "Deutsch has studied such children with techniques of the experimental psychologists, and he finds them to have inferior visual discrimination, inferior judgment concerning time, number and other basic concepts. He finds that this inferiority is not due to physical defects of eyes, ears, and brain, but is due to inferior habits of hearing, seeing and thinking. Presumably, the family environment of these children did not teach them to pay attention to what was being said around them or to the visual scene [Beck & Saxe, 1965, p. viii]."

But Black people are realizing more and more that they have the power to define their behaviors and life-styles as much as other racial and ethnic groups. In the past they may have questioned or even laughed at the way they were referred to by Whites in the literature. However, their top priority was not in refuting but in surviving. Today with more and more Blacks entering the academic arena, Black language and culture are being studied by people who are intimately a part of it. In the future you will see more refutations in literature, and you will begin to see a language and culture described to which you can relate.

I have a group of students at Federal City College who are doing a pilot study on Black culture. They are filming scenes from the Black experience as totally as a pilot will permit. The film is to be shown to a number of Black audiences representing members of different age, sex, and socioeconomic statuses. At each showing a questionnaire will be distributed among the audience to ascertain how they define Black culture. From this survey, the pilot, and the subsequent analysis will come some definitive statements taken from a Black perspective based on hard data rather than opinion. Our anticipation for the future is to have data collected by people who have an intimate knowledge of not only the culture, but the language also.

Quite frequently one who is at a loss in trying to define Black English is not at a loss in recognizing it. How many times have you heard someone speak on the telephone and immediately knew the person was Black? You might not be able to pinpoint how you knew, but you knew. Your response to the person might be based on your attitudes toward Blacks or Black English. It is hard to separate the two. Just as all Blacks are not recognizably Black, so the speaking pattern of some Blacks is not recognizably Black and would not fit under the popular rubrics of Black English. Perhaps you have had occasion to make an appointment to see a house or have an interview for a job only to find the job taken or the house no longer available when you arrived. This might happen when speech is not recognizably Black but the individual is. When the race of a person is identified with his speech, weeding out is done at that level; if not, it is done at the next level. In other words, you would have.been saved a trip if the person on the other end of the telephone had known you were Black. If what you want is not open to Black people, you are not going to get it regardless of how you talk.

I make this point to show that it is the Blackness that people react to negatively, not necessarily the linguistic system. In our enlightened society today, when we do not want to appear "racist" or "prejudiced," we can articulate about a linguistic system that is "not up to par" and exclude on that basis. If we are more subtle, liberal, or smart, we can turn everything around and make it appear that we are really concerned. We establish compensatory language programs for 3-year-old Black children so that they will be able to get jobs. This is very interesting especially since we have linguists telling us that all languages are legitimate, that all language meets the needs of the particular social group, that you do not put a value judgment on language, etc. BUT Black children need compensatory language programs so that they can operate in the macroculture. It's that big BUT that bothers me.

I have been looking at some of these preschoolers who would be candidates for language intervention programs either because they are Black or because they are poor or both. These are children who are destined not to read or to read far below level. I have found that when they attend preschool and have positive, accepting teachers who are not trying to force them into a mold, they start reading at three or four. A very good example of this is the Anacostia Preschool Program in Washington, D.C. I asked the teachers how they could account for the children reading: Was it the approach that they were using? Were the children extremely bright, or exactly what did they feel was transpiring? They felt that it was the attitude of the teacher, and they were concerned about what would happen to the children when they reached kindergarten and became part of the de-education process. What the teachers told me supports the self-fulfilling prophecy. If you expect someone to succeed, your expectations are transmitted to that person, either verbally, or nonverbally, and he responds accordingly. The converse is also true, and it is the converse that we see happening so frequently. It is the converse that is probably in large part responsible for the de-education process itself.

I have observed Black children as young as 20 months who have a sight vocabulary of ten words. They are starting to read even though they are not aware of it. A positive approach would be to recognize what they have, let them know you recognize it, and proceed from there rather than assume that they are "handicapped." However, it is customary to begin with the assumption that they are culturally disadvantaged or socially deprived because they come from homes where books were not available and parents did not read or talk to them.

Interestingly enough, shortly after visiting the Anacostia Preschool Program, I attended a meeting with a special education specialist who was White and who had assessed the Anacostia children. When asked if they had handicapping conditions and, if so, what they were, his response was that they were socially deprived. My immediate reaction was "It's good he's the specialist and not the teacher." If he had been the teacher, I'm certain that the deeducation process would have started immediately and the self-fulfilling prophecy as described by Rosenthal and Jacobson (1968) would now be nearing fruition.

I cannot stress too much my feelings that positive attitudes and acceptance are crucial in the educational process. It would seem to me that if a teacher really felt strongly about young Black children learning to speak "Standard English," the ideal way to bring it about would be to show that child respect, love, and acceptance and to use the speech pattern you would like the child to learn. We all know that young children are very imitative beings and they are quick to emulate people they admire. They will imitate the way the Teacher walks, talks, acts, etc. If they like the teacher, they want to be like the teacher. Young children are very perceptive, much more so than we often think. Again, going back to Anacostia, I asked the teachers about code-switching behavior. They reported that at the age of three the children were already switching their speech patterns, and that the speech they heard at school was different from that which the child used at home or at the playground.

The Anacostia Preschool Program was conceived by parents. They found the funding, interviewed staff members, and had the final say-so on who would be hired. The director, teachers, and parents worked as a unit, each realizing his role and objectives. I'm certain that this kind of involvement, along with the tone set by the director, has led to the results noted. Frequently, the role of the parent is overlooked in the educational process or parents are included in a process without being given the background information they need to function at maximum as members of the team. Educators assume that they know what is best for children and the best way to bring it about, quite often, without consultation with parents. Should a child be forced to speak Standard English? Should Standard English be taught as a second language? These are questions that plague educators. They would have a much easier job and a better chance of reaching their educational objectives if they consulted with enlightened and informed parents.

While at the Learning Research and Development Center at the University of Pittsburgh, I, in concert with Alphonso Washington, conducted a series of parent seminars entitled Black English: Educational Implications. The seminars ran for a period of ten weeks during which time the parents were made aware of the difference–deficit theory, philosophies behind Head-Start programs, language-intervention programs, teaching Standard English as a second language, and concepts and theories regarding Black English. We felt that in order for parents to serve as informed members of a team or agents of change, they needed this information. Some of the sessions ran from 8 p.m. to 3 a.m. because parents became so involved with the issues. Guest speakers were invited so that parents could hear several sides of a question. They were quite impressed with the legitimacy of Black English and considered it liberating. Comments were made concerning their reluctance to speak up at PTA meetings even though they knew that they had something "dynamite" to say because they felt people would react negatively to how they said what they had to say. They talked in terms of their limitations with regard to "school learning," but not education.

After the seminar they were requested to make changes in recommendations for the handbook *Black English: Educational Implications* (Covington & Washington, 1972, unpublished). They also made recommendations as to what they wanted for their children. They were totally against language-intervention programs, textbooks written in Black English, teaching Standard English as a second language, and anything that would suggest that their children were disadvantaged. They recommended (1) that teachers speak Standard English in instruction; (2) that their children use the same textbooks as White children and that the textbooks be revised to be more representative of a pluralistic culture; (3) that their children not be reprimanded for speaking Black English in schools; and (4) that standards in written work be the same for all children. During the course of the seminar, they made frequent trips to the schools to ascertain what was happening with their children. They were appalled with the literature and how they had been described in the literature and they wondered how an "educated person" could use such euphemisms as "nonverbal, culturally disadvantaged, and socially deprived."

Earlier I mentioned the nature of what we find in the literature. This information is seriously questioned by Black people from varying social economic levels and educational backgrounds. It is extremely important that studies from a Black perspective be included in the literature.

I feel that if the study of Black English is going to make a meaningful and productive difference, it is going to do so at the level of the public school teacher, with his outlook and attitudes, especially with his interpersonal relationship with young Black children. A positive self-image is very important for everyone. This should be enhanced rather than destroyed when the child enters the educational system.

It has been stated that attitudes form the basis of all language and communications. If this statement is true, and it seems likely that it is, definite steps should be taken to change negative attitudes that might affect the education of Black children. As part of a project at the Center for Applied Linguistics in Washington, D.C. (Taylor & Hayes, 1971), a Language Attitude Scale was developed. One purpose of the scale was to solicit data on what teachers thought about Black English. The scale was presented to teachers before and after a course in social dialects. They found that the professed attitudes were altered significantly following the course. As a result of their findings, they suggested that such courses should be required for teaching certification.

Questions on the Likert-type scale covered four content categories: (1) structure of Black English; (2) consequences of using and accepting Black English; (3) philosophies concerning use and acceptance of Black English; and (4) cognitive and intellectual abilities of speakers of Black English. The scoring was as follows: five points for strong disagreement with a positive statement; four points for moderate disagreement with a positive statement; three points for neither agreement nor disagreement; two points for moderate agreement with a negative statement; and one point for strong agreement with a negative statement.

I have been concerned with the way people respond to the items on the Language Attitude Scale and have used a modified version as frequently as possible. By being one of the first speakers in the Princeton Black English Seminars, I had the opportunity to assess the attitudes of the Princeton students and also to use the scale as a take-off point in discussing educational implications of Black English.

The scale was presented to the 15 students at the onset of the class. They were requested not to sign the form. After it was completed it was collected and discussed. Some of the items, and justifiably so, were found to be ambiguous by the students. These were so noted.

Even though they were not given a definition of Black English, their perceptions of Black English were basically the same as other groups. As I noted earlier, a Black person might not be able to give a precise definition of the language, but he is aware of what it is all about and of negative attitudes toward it. This was exemplified when the students gave examples of what had happened to them when they spoke the language. They talked in terms of being corrected by their parents, of switching behavior, of speaking "proper," and of the intimate nature of the language. Implicit in this awareness is the knowledge that it can be used and is used to exclude outsiders or nonmembers of the racial group. The group had positive feelings toward the language and those feelings were manifested in their discussion as well as in their responses to the questionnaire.

All 15 students strongly disagreed with Item 10 which stated, "Black English is an inferior language system." The 14 students who responded to Item 4, "It would be detrimental to our country's welfare if the use of Black English became socially acceptable," all strongly disagreed with the statement.

The mean score of the Princeton students was 1.5. The range was 1.0 to 2.2. The mean indicates a very positive attitude toward Black English. In fact, the students' mean score was a little more positive than that of other student groups. They exemplified the kind of positive attitude that we need to see more of in teachers and people who are training to be teachers. The group at Princeton was certainly not at all typical because people who attend such courses when they are not required obviously have some interest in and concern for the subject matter.

If we are going to make a difference in the education of Black children we must strive to change attitudes. We must move from the euphemisms, including culturally deprived, culturally disadvantaged, culturally different, and socially disadvantaged. Special compensatory programs have been designed to educate these children. When one examines some of these programs and the definitions of the terms, it becomes evident that the problems in education are perceived as resulting from a deficit in the home or environment. This becomes particularly dangerous because it diverts attention from the source of the problem to the child. We must address ourselves to language and attitudes toward language since language has become the theoretical base for compensatory educational programs.

The failure of compensatory educational programs has now become a rallying point for the genetic inferiority theorists. They do not look at the programs and whether or not they were designed to work, but prefer instead to blame the child, and not only the child but the entire race. According to them, there is something inherent in being Black that makes one inferior; and since this is the case, why even try to educate them, especially in the sense that White children are educated.

Joseph White (1970) stated:

The White educational psychologist looking at the Black home does not see the familiar White cultural trappings and seeing some that he does not understand, the tendency of the psychologist has been to assume that the child is deprived in some way. As a psychologist, he thus enters the observational net of the Black home with a deficit or weakness hypothesis, so that his recommended programs are based upon some concepts of enrichment for the child ... It is enrichment defined by the dominant culture—from Headstart to Upward Bound to language enrichment programs, etc. Somehow the analysis is always corrective; implied is always some deficit that the child brings to the situation from his home. This analysis has pre-psychological origins and it is a clear carry-over from slavery and reconstruction days—that there is something inferior about the Black child and, therefore, the Black man.

REFERENCES

Beck, J. M., & Saxe, R. *Teaching the culturally disadvantaged pupil.* Springfield, Illinois: Charles C Thomas, 1965. Introduction by R. J. Haverhurst.

Covington, A. *Teacher attitudes toward Black English: Effects on student achievement.* Unpublished doctoral dissertation, The University of Pittsburgh, 1972.

Covington, A., & Washington, A. *Black English: Educational implications. A handbook for parents.* Unpublished, 1972.

Rosenthal, R., & Jacobson, L. *Pygmalion in the classroom.* New York: Holt, Rinehart & Winston, 1968.

Taylor, O., & Hayes, A. *Five interrelated studies to increase the effectiveness of English language instruction in schools.* Washington, D.C.: Center for Applied Linguistics, 1971.

White, J. Guidelines for black psychologists. *The Black Scholar,* 1970, **5**(1), 52–57.

16

Levels of Sociolinguistic Bias in Testing

Walt Wolfram

Federal City College and Center for Applied Linguistics

INTRODUCTION

At no other time in the history of American education has the general role of testing been called into such serious question. The importance that mainstream American society places on testing should be obvious to anyone with even the slightest sense of recall. In fact, it seems that standardized tests could be added to the small list of inevitables in this society, such as taxes and death. Before we entered elementary school, we were probably given a battery of tests to determine our readiness for school. Throughout our elementary and secondary school education, standardized tests were given at specified intervals in order to evaluate our educational achievement. Our preparedness for college was further evaluated on the basis of the Scholastic Aptitude Test, and our potential for graduate study was measured in the Graduate Record Examination. As if this were not sufficient, our capabilities for certain types of employment may have been determined on the basis of a standardized test such as the Civil Service Entrance Examination.

Admittedly, test scores are difficult to resist, given their widespread use by all types of agencies. Their importance in any particular agency is simply a reflection of the role that they are assigned in the larger society. Standardized tests are used as instruments which produce objectified quantitative information of one type or another. Quantifiable scores do show significant distinctions between various groups of individuals in our society, so that an appeal to an objectifiable parameter of measurement can become an important type of principled basis for evaluating a group or an individual's performance. And, when we find that there is a high convergence of validity, it appears that there is considerable basis for the use of tests.

Despite the traditional rationale for testing, there is a growing feeling that tests may also do some disservice to those who are classified on the basis of their use. Obviously, when we have a test revealing significant differences between various groups in the population, we have demonstrated something. But the uneasy question constantly recurring is whether these tests show what they are specifically designed to show. "Objective" quantitative results in no way guarantee the validity of the test in terms of what it was designed to test. Although there are various matters of validity that have been raised with reference to standardized testing, perhaps the most recurrent of these relates to their application across various cultural groups. In particular, these questions have arisen in terms of application to nonmainstream groups. Most prominently, but not exclusively, these concern their application to working-class Blacks, different groups of Spanish speakers, and poor rural Whites. Although we shall be concerned primarily with the matter of testing for working-class Blacks because of the focus of this volume, the questions raised here are really appropriate for all nonmainstream groups. In many instances, we find that the distribution of these groups is proportionately lower when compared with the "mainstream" population. The findings of such scores have raised several different questions concerning the tests. One is the question of whether higher test scores from high SES groups reflect genuine superiority of one type or another. Or, do high scores result from an environmental setting which promulgates certain nurtured advantages? Or, do the differential scores reflect a bias in the test materials and not any important difference in capabilities at all? Recent research in testing indicates the last question is becoming increasingly important in the consideration of any type of test application across different cultural and social groups in American society.

Although we might look at the general question of test bias utilizing solely psychometric methods, our concern here will be with the particular vantage point of sociolinguistics. From this perspective, we are interested in how language diversity in the context of society may be used to the advantage of certain groups as opposed to others. On the basis of our research into language variety in American English, we know that there are considerable differences in language systems and language uses which correlate with social status and ethnic group membership. Our knowledge of these differences, which is much more complete in some areas than in others, may serve as a basis for understanding certain types of potential sociolinguistic interference in testing. Most standardized testing is based on certain types of assumptions about the language of the test and the language of the testee, and this is where we feel that the expertise of the linguist and sociolinguist can have significant bearing. Where a particular subtest deals with linguistic aptitude as such, the import of linguistic diversity is obvious, but where the test deals with other content areas and language is used only as a vehicle to tap these areas, the considerations of linguistic diversity may not be apparent. Nonetheless, I think it can be shown that there are certain assumptions about the testing situation or the language of the test which may be just as problematical, if not as quantifiable, as the case of a language test which specifically involves language differences in the test items.

What I would like to do here is to set forth the various aspects of what I consider to be a sociolinguistic vantage point on testing. From this perspective, it appears that there are three different aspects of potential sociolinguistic bias which must be considered: (1) interference from the social occasion of testing, (2) interference from the linguistic tasks involved in testing, and (3) interference from linguistic items *per se*. Obviously, there are aspects of these three levels which invariably overlap. Yet, for the sake of convenience, it seems reasonable to discuss these three areas separately.

TESTING AS A SOCIAL OCCASION

Testing, like other types of behavior, necessarily involves the realization of a social occasion. The testing process is not devoid of cultural context regardless of how standardized the testing procedure may actually be. Although most standardized tests assume the neutrality of the testing situation as a social occasion, Roth (1970) correctly points out that it is unreasonable to expect that a tester can maintain a strictly standardized procedure while probing the subject's unstandardized background knowledge. Unfortunately, most theories of testing explicitly assume that the test takes place in a noncontextual social setting with a noncontextual cognitive orientation (Makay, 1970, p. 227). Testing is "social" in several ways. First of all, it is social in the sense that it involves interaction between the test administrator and the testee. Second, it involves a particular division of labor which is found in the testing enterprise. And finally, it is social in the sense that it operates on the output of socialization leading up to the actual situation. Subjects do not approach such a social task with totally neutral feelings or equivalent socialization processes.

Test construction involves elaborate plans for the manipulation of the subject's behavior, and these are based on two assumptions (Makay, 1970). There is, first of all, an assumption that the test designer has a viable, though implicit model of the subject's acts which can be used as a guide for his own actions in constructing the test. According to Makay (1970):

> The model must support the researcher's need to manipulate the grounds of the subject's behavior, hence the model must formulate those grounds as though they were available to the researcher. In this sense, the demands of control force upon the researcher a behavioralistic model of the actor—the grounds are external to the actor [p. 11].

Second, it is assumed that the researcher knows the ways in which the properties of situations might influence the behavior of subjects. Based on this assumption, the test designer attempts to place these properties under his control through the standardization of procedures.

Makay (1970) has summarized the critical problem in these assumptions rather succintly:

> If their conditions are met, then there is no need to proceed, the human sciences are complete. If they are not met, the researcher's theoretical knowledge of the subject's acts and the structure of the situations must, in principle, be incomplete. Thus the theory cannot suffice as a basis for his actions. The assumptions are not met perfectly. The main reason for their incompleteness is that the subject himself is an environment of his actions and the subject as environment cannot be manipulated from the outside [p. 11].

But in order to promote the orderly interpretation of data that are derived from the test situation, the researcher has no other alternative but to presume that the subject can enter and remain in the experimental frame constructed for the test. In other words, he must assume that the subject can play the researcher's game. And if he cannot bring the subject into the experimental frame, then there is no objectifiable way in which the abilities of the subject which the tester wants to measure can be tapped.

The basic issue here, then, concerns the assumption of the "sameness" of the environment and the irrelevance of potentially different socialization processes which may create this particular situation. From a sociolinguistic viewpoint, the question at this point is determining the extent to which potentially different historical backgrounds may be individualistic or cultural. To a certain extent, we cannot completely dismiss the individual aspects which may result in different perceptions of the social occasion. There seems to be some evidence that certain individuals from all SES groups may be adversely affected by the judgmental and competitive conditions which characterize the testing situation. But we must go one step further in noting that there is also a sense in which our conception of culture forces us to look at the systematic cross-cultural aspects of the testing situation. For a number of reasons, we are led to believe that the testing situation is biased in favor of particular SES and ethnic groups. In the case of minority peoples, there is an awareness that tests have been used traditionally as a vehicle of discrimination. To deny that these perceptions can affect how an individual from these groups approaches the test situation seems to be totally unrealistic. Expectations of success and failure can play an essential role in the actual outcome of the test.

There is also a sense in which it appears that middle-class cultural groups have particular types of socialization processes which may simulate the type of expectations found in bureaucratic testing. For one, there is some evidence that the middle classes are considerably more informed about what is taking place in various educational and governmental agencies—those agencies which are responsible for establishing various educational and social goals that are measured through testing. In an effort to prepare children for success in terms of these bureaucratic agencies, this knowledge may lead to both direct and indirect socialization in the process of test-taking. On the other hand, there has been a traditional lack of involvement by lower classes in such bureaucratic institutions and the role of testing in measuring the achievement of certain goals thus remains outside of their general interests; it thus stands to reason that important aspects in the socialization process of test-taking may not take place.

Since I have become concerned with the socialization processes which may prepare children for testing, I have become particularly interested in observing certain types of vocabulary acquisition which might lead to an advantage in performing word definition tasks in testing. A recent train ride provided me with a particularly interesting anecdote in contrasting styles of definition. Across from me sat an obviously middle-class mother and her 4-year-old child. As the conductor walked through the train to collect the tickets, the youngster asked who the man in the uniform was. She was given a fairly succinct definition of a conductor as a man who collects tickets and helps passengers to and from the train. The mother concluded her definition with the remark "We call him a conductor." As an added tidbit, the child was told that the people who ride trains are called "passengers." To top it off, the child was instructed to tell the teacher in her nursery school about conductors and passengers when she reported her trip. Unless my associations with middle-class parents betray me, I don't think that this type of situation is particularly atypical. With such a socialization process behind her, I would predict that such a child will be well equipped to perform some of the definition tasks to be required of her in later word definition tests (many of which take the form "A conductor is . . ."). On the other hand, I have observed similar situations on the train where an obviously working-class mother would be asked a similar question by her child. A response like "He just wants the ticket" or some analogous statement was given as the definition. To a certain extent, both children will end up with a working definition of the man with the blue uniform who collects the tickets on the train. But the process of labeling as it correlates with the definition of a conductor, the extra definition of "passenger," the tidbit about remembering the label, and the definitions would all seem to indicate different styles of definition socialization. In the one case, the label was clearly correlated with the definition while the other simply gave an appropriate contextual reference.

While I am not ready to make a general statement about differing styles of word definition as they correlate with social class on the basis of selected anecdotes, I think we must be ready to admit that certain socialization processes with respect to language usage may place particular groups at an advantage when it comes to utilizing their prior experience in test performance.

To the reader who feels that the case has been overstated concerning the role of the social occasion involved in testing, let me simply quote from the instructions of a fairly typical test guide. As it turns out, these "hints for taking tests" come from a brochure on taking aptitude tests, published by the U.S. Department of Labor, but they really could have come from any number of test instructions:

1. Get ready for the test by taking other tests on your own.
2. Don't let the thought of taking a test throw you, but being a little nervous won't hurt you.
3. Arrive early, rested, and prepared to take the test.
4. Ask questions until you understand what you are supposed to do.
5. Some parts of the test may be easier than others. Don't let the hard parts keep you from doing well on the easier parts.
6. Keep time limits in mind when you take a test.
7. Don't be afraid to answer when you aren't sure you are right but don't guess wildly.
8. Work as fast as you can but try not to make mistakes. Some tests have short time limits [U.S. Department of Labor, 1968, back cover].

All of the above "hints" are really concerned with socialization process involved in test-taking. Hint 1 deals with the development of test-taking as a type of social activity into which one should become enculturated by exposure to the process of test-taking itself. Our chances of success on any given test are enhanced by having been exposed to previous test-type activities, whether they be other tests, preparatory test activities, or other socialization processes which simulate the types of activities

called for in tests. When we look at Hints 2 and 3, we find this socialization process extended to operating under competitive and judgmental
pressures. This, of course, presumes that the test-taker has reason to believe that the competitive situation might work to his advantage. But
what if there is a history of using such competitive situations as the basis
for the exclusion of certain groups? There seems to be some solid sociological basis for the popular dictum that "success breeds success and
failure, failure." Hints 4 and 6 deal with the assumption that the tester
can enter and remain in the experimental frame constructed for the test.
As we mentioned before, there is no objectifiable way in which the abilities of the subject can be tapped apart from this assumption. But if the
subject cannot or will not enter into this frame, then we are left with an
unjustified assumption about the neutrality of the occasion. Finally,
Hints 5, 7, and 8 deal with particular types of orientation procedures
which tell how we are to assess different variables in the test. Hint 5 deals
with a "coping" task in which the tester should know he can compensate
for the difficult parts by concentrating on the easier sections. Hint 7 deals
with an assessment of the role of guessing as opposed to only answering
questions of which the test-taker is certain. And hint 8 deals with an
understanding of how the relation of time should be dealt with in respect
to accuracy. Now the interesting paradox found in the hints for test-
taking is that a number of them are theoretically part of the assumptions
about the neutrality of the testing situation at the same time that they
are admitted as contributing factors to success or failure in a test. If
it is admitted that these hints may change how a person scores in a test,
which most constructors will do, then the assumption about neutrality
of the social occasion built into the test cannot be valid.

The way in which some test-takers rush to the nearest bookstore to
obtain a manual that will specifically help them prepare for various tests
readily attests to the role of socialization in testing. For the individual
who knows where to get such manuals (which may, in part, be part of
the more general socialization process) it doesn't take long to come up
with an excerpt like the following:

Used correctly, your "self-tutor" will show you what to expect and will give
you a speedy brush-up on the subjects peculiar to your exam. Some of these
are subjects not taught in schools at all. Even if your study time is very
limited, you should:

— Become familiar with the type of examination you will meet.
— Improve your general examination taking skill.
— Improve your skill in analyzing and answering questions involving reason-
  ing, judgment, comparison, and evaluation.
— Improve your speed and skill in reading and understanding what you read—
  an important part of your ability to learn and an important part of most tests.

— Prepare yourself in the particular fields which measure your learning.

This book will tell you exactly what to study by presenting in full every type of question you will get on the actual test. You'll do better merely by familiarizing yourself with them [Turner, *Practice for the Armed Forces Tests,* 1973, p. 9].

While we may allow for a certain amount of merchandizing that is inevitably a part of such manuals, I am not aware of any legal suits that have cited these manuals for false advertising. It is little wonder, then, that some educators have strongly supported Raspberry's contention that

...test-taking is a distinct, important and learnable skill in itself ... the public schools ought to teach test-taking as a routine course, beginning in elementary school [*The Washington Post,* September 4, 1974].

Although we have not looked systematically at the social values to be found in tests, we would be remiss to close this section on testing as a social occasion without mentioning something about the assumed values found in the testing situation. That there are particular value orientations which are assumed in testing seems to be fairly obvious in many types of standardized tests. Intelligence tests which contain items like why promises should be kept, what one should do if he finds an addressed stamped envelope on the street, and why it is better to give to an organized charity than the poor themselves call for a fairly obvious value orientation which matches the overt moral ideals of the society of the test designers. In a sense, then, the intelligent person is the one who can play the game and give back these ideals, regardless of how he may actually feel or behave. What is often missed, however, is the sort of value assumptions to be found in tasks which seem to be more neutral on the surface. As Labov (1970) has pointed out, even the most seemingly innocuous task of getting a young child to talk about something he is interested in is laden with value assumptions. Labov points out that among the other sorts of problems which may be involved in the types of social occasions that surround such tasks, the child must accept an orientation in which value may be placed on talking about the obvious, the goodness of talking just for the sake of talking, and that the child will not be penalized for what he says. The tester accepts these assumptions and therefore expects the child to accept them. But the child may have good reason not to accept them. All suspicions that children have do not come from the overt advice that their parents have given them about accepting candy from strangers. There may be very good reasons found in a child's background for not wanting to accept M & M's to talk "just to be talking." Any differences in the value orientations of the test designer and test-taker can again throw off our assumptions about the neutrality of testing as a social occasion.

TASK BIAS

Once we have recognized the potential interference that may be contained in any test as a social occasion, we move to the notion that testing makes certain types of assumptions concerning the specific tasks involved in test-taking. The standardization process of testing requires not only that the test be uniformly administered, but that the test materials be understood and interpreted uniformly by the subjects taking the test. The assumption that there is one correct answer is based on the constructor's faith that he and the testees share a common symbolic background in which objects have only one meaning which is apparent to all. From this perspective, meaning is not negotiated and built up over the course of the interaction, but is assumed to share a commonness by the way in which the task is arranged.

All tests, no matter what the focus of the particular subject matter, must start with the assumption that the testee comprehends the instructions (whether written or oral). These instructions are dependent upon linguistic comprehension of some type, so that tests which do not deal with language at all are still based on certain assumptions about language. If the testee cannot comprehend the task involved, he can hardly be expected to respond in an appropriate manner. From a linguistic standpoint, this involves the comprehension of sentence meanings, including the presuppositions and implications of questioning.

Tests require that the testee perceive the stimulus and possible answers in a way which matches that of the test constructor. In the construction of the test, the researcher must assume that a search back and forth between the stimulus and the possible answers will take place and that THE correct answer will somehow unambiguously emerge from the environment into the subject's mind. Obtaining correct answers, then, depends on the appropriate identification of a frame of reference on the part of the subject with the frame of reference the test constructor had in mind when he designed the test. Presumably, there is a search for a legitimate frame of reference which will be "obvious" to the testee. Once the tester presumes that the task being given the testee is "obvious," the constraints perceived by the subject become central in assessing the subject's performance. Ultimately, the notion of obviousness is based on the belief that the subject's perspective converts the information available into the instructions and knowledge that are somehow consonant with the researcher's conception of the activity. The obviousness of the instructions and questions, then, becomes a point at which we must investigate the possible discrepancy between the interpetations of the test designer and testee. The first claim that I would like to make is that not all presumed obvious information is in fact necessarily obvious. In some cases, the appeal to obviousness is based on an inability to design the task in such a way that completely precludes any other but the intended interpretation. However straightforward the task may appear to the test designer, we must admit that we can never eliminate all the possibilities for ambiguity in the task. Logically, it is impossible to exclude all possibilities since it presumes that the test designer is omniscient. Given the limitations of linguistic and real world knowledge, we must resort to the notion of sufficiency with respect to the task. Although there may exist psychometric means of "validating" procedures, there is no assurance of total sufficiency. This is so because we are still left with the variety of reasons why a subject does not get all the correct answers. We know, of course, that there are a number of reasons why an individual may not obtain the "correct" response. From our vantage point, it becomes crucial to know exactly why a subject or group of subjects did not come up with the correct response. A subject may give an incorrect response because he is unfamiliar with the vocabulary, or he may obtain the incorrect answer because he interpreted the question in terms of his own common sense, or because his presuppositions did not match those of the test designer. In terms of potential task interference, it becomes important to identify exactly why the answer is considered inappropriate by the test designer but not by certain test-takers. One type of investigation of this is an analysis of errors using an individual posttest interview approach and/or a massive examination of error patterns that correlate with membership in socially and linguistically defined groups. However, another investigative approach is available that makes use of the test material itself as data. From a sociolinguistic perspective, it becomes possible to identify some of the potential ways in which the task as presented may interfere with the identification of correct responses. We are here concerned not so much with the stated protocol in test administration, but with the subtleties of task which may interfere with the assumption of "obviousness."

Different groups may share a desire to succeed in their performance on a test, but simply interpret the protocol of "obvious" instructions differently. Take, for example, the simple instructions to repeat something. The first problem we must recognize is that the instructions to repeat allow for more than one interpretation. One interpretation calls for verbatim repetition, whereas the other allows for similarity in communicative content through paraphrase.[1] The second problem lies in the

[1] The differing interpretations of instructions to repeat are best illustrated through the difficulties that I have sometimes encountered in the classroom. On various occasions, I have been asked to repeat a statement during the course of a lecture. In some cases, I have repeated the statement verbatim, only to be informed that

assumption that the test-taker can extract from his real life uses of repetition (which are drastically different) and remain in the experimental frame where repetition is an end in itself. Interestingly enough, an informal survey of lower-class Black children's performance on a sentence repetition task showed two types of departures in the performance of the task (King, 1972).[2] One was a tendency to relate to certain language uses outside the context of the specified experimental frame which called for verbatim repetition. Thus, asked to repeat a sentence like "Is the car in the garage?" while being shown a picture of a car in the garage, many children chose to answer by giving the information relevant to the question rather than simply repeating the question. This, of course, is a reasonable way to respond to a question—outside the specialized testing situation. The other problem involved a tendency to give more detail than the verbatim repetition called for in the response. In essence, many of the stimuli were paraphrased rather than repeated verbatim. From the children's perspective, the paraphrase had to be interpreted as an attempt to succeed at the task, but from the test designer's perspective, the task was not followed as prescribed. Strict verbatim was the avenue for success in this task, not detailed recapitulation. But suppose the child's experience suggests that positive value should be placed on those types of language uses which might involve a paraphrase or caricature of what a first party has said rather than verbatim recall. Without concluding that this is actually the case in working-class Black culture, one can see how interpretations of this sort would lead to serious misunderstandings of the "simple" instructions to repeat.

Task interference is not restricted to the subtleties of unintended response patterns that may have been allowed in the designing of the test. It may also occur on a more broad level as reflected in the choice of a general method for obtaining the desired information. The choice of one method vis-à-vis another may be a serious source of potential task bias. The information which the testee can give may be the same, but one method may tap this information to a much greater extent than another method. I'm reminded here of a classroom of students who disagree as to the type of test they would prefer the teacher to construct. The information the students have to give back is the same regardless of the method, but the different students feel that different methods are to their

---

the student had heard the statement, but did not understand it; therefore, the student was asking for a repeat with the hope that I would understand it to include a paraphrase. In other cases, I have understood the request to repeat as a call for a paraphrase, only to be told that the student understood the statement and simply wanted a verbatim repetition for his lecture notes.

[2] The actual study was more concerned with predicting the dialect differences which would systematically occur in the repetition of Standard English sentences, but the recurrent problems became difficult to ignore, at least in an informal evaluation.

greatest advantage in giving back the information. Consider the notion of "word knowledge" as an illustration. Word knowledge may be obtained in a number of different ways. Synonymy is just one of the ways. The notion of word synonymy as such involves a task which is fairly restricted to the testing situation and certain types of educated writing styles (as reflected by distribution and use of thesauri). This, however, is not to say that the notion of word knowledge is not found outside of these situations. There is ample evidence that all individuals can give approximate definitions or uses of words, but it does not necessarily involve the notion of "word replaceability." As Meier (1973) puts it:

> A synonym is only one approach to "word definition" and involves a quite abstract notion about the replaceability of one word for another. It pressed for a "meaning," children (and adults) generally give a story example that describes the word or context which uses it appropriately [p. 10].

Similarly, antonymy is just one method of getting at the notion of word meaning or relationship. First, the notion of opposition may in fact imply different relationships than those which the test designer has in mind when he illustrated the notion with an "obvious" example of antonymy. Meier points out that the notion of opposite may, in fact, quite legitimately be interpreted as something which is "very different." By this interpretation items like "tall" and "far" might be considered opposites, just as surely as "tall" and "short." Failure to obtain the "correct" notion of antonymy might then be interpreted not as a result of the incapability to get the right answer, but as a result of focus on a different relationship. The assumed neutrality of tasks must indeed be questioned as it relates to different individuals and different social groups. Middle-class children, because of their familiarity with specific tasks as they are employed to get certain types of information, would appear to hold a serious advantage over their working-class counterparts in playing the test game. Given the fact that testing tasks involve a particular type of extraction from real-life language tasks, the only way success can be assured is to ensure similar familiarities with the tasks for all social groups.

By the same token that potentially misleading tasks must be looked at closely from our vantage point, we must scrutinize situations in which right answers may be arrived at for the wrong reason. Certain types of conditioned responses or styles may, in fact, serve as a basis for short-cutting the assumed process and ending up with the right answer. And in some cases, the test designer may actually build in this expectation and thus penalize the child who works through the logical process implied by the question. Following Meier (1972), this situation can be as potentially class related:

Middle-class children, because of their familiarity with certain key phrases and styles (conditioned responses), short-cut the process and succeed in producing "right" answers even though they do not carry out the logical thought implied by the question. They get it "right" for the "wrong" reason. The bright lower-class child, who cannot fall back upon the lifetime of familiarity with certain language, picture, or word association patterns, is dependent upon real mental ingenuity to make the necessary "logical" connections. As a result, even if he has equal reading skill and utilizes greater intelligence in his effort to think through the particular question on the test, he is found to answer wrong more frequently [p. 7].

From a sociolinguistic viewpoint, the type of tasks which are peculiar to testing are important because they may not adequately provide the testee the opportunity to reveal what in fact he really knows. In some cases, this is true of the choice of tasks regardless of the social class of the testee; in other cases the task may be much more clearly differentiated on the basis of the social classes due to the selective orientation of different classes to particular types of tasks involved in test-taking.

Task interference, in reference to general activities called for by certain tests, is only one part of the problem. Individual items themselves call for various tasks in terms of understanding and producing a correct response, not all of which have any apparent connection with the skill which the test purports to assess. Linguists, ordinary language philosophers, and psychologists have isolated a class of such factors involved in the meaning of sentences. There is a hidden part of the meaning that involves more than is stated on the surface, more than can be arrived at by adding the dictionary meanings of each word or even by adding the relationships between the words assigned by various types of sentence structures. This brings two kinds of problems to bear on assessing test results:

1. A failure to grasp the hidden meaning can lead to a wrong answer whose wrongness is unrelated to the skill the item is intended to test.

2. A failure to accept the assumption that certain parts of the hidden meaning are true can lead to an inability to answer an item since it is judged to be nonsensical, false, or inappropriate. The hidden part of the meaning falls into three categories: presuppositions, entailments, and conversational factors. Peg Griffin (personal communication) has provided me with the following description of each by example.

Upon encountering a sentence like (1), an English speaker immediately understands that sentences (2) and (3) have to be true if (1) is true:

(1)   All John's children have curly hair.
(2)   John has children.
(3)   Some of John's children have curly hair.

If (2) is not true, then (1) is just nonsense; if (3) is not true, then sentence (1) is false. However, in the ordinary negative of sentence (1), then

(4)   All of John's children don't have curly hair.

Sentence (2) must be true unless the sentence is to be nonsense just as above with (1), but with Sentence (3) there is a difference: Sentence (3) can be false and (4) can still be true. Sentences like (2) are termed presuppositions in relation to sentences like (1) and (4); sentences like (3) are entailments of sentences like (1).

Sentence (3) can also display the third category, conversational factors. If a person encounters Sentence (3) from a source that is "normal," i.e., not a pathological liar or a player in a game, he deduces that Sentence (1) is not true, even though (1) itself has not been encountered. He reasons that if the utterer of Sentence (3) knows that (1) is the case, the utterer of (3) would be uncooperative if he were to say less than is necessary. But, being cooperative, the reader or listener also knows, is a basic principle of language use. Therefore, he deduces that either Sentence (1) is false or the utterer of (3) does not believe he had enough evidence to utter (1). In either case, it would be wrong for the listener to assume either that all of John's children have curly hair, or that any particular one of John's children must have curly hair.

Applying this kind of information to a test item whose content is totally unrelated to language, we find that someone whom we might term linguistically adept and who assumes the test is following the cooperative principle may easily rule out the correct answer. Consider, for example, the following test item:

> When measuring an unknown audio volume with a sound level meter, the proper precaution to take is to start with the
>
> A. highest range and go down.
> B. lowest range and go up.
> C. middle range and go down.
> D. middle range and go up.[3]

Answers A and B include an unnecessary conjunction, since to *start* at a *highest* or *lowest* range leaves only one way to go in each instance. If the test is following the cooperative principle, the only need for the conjunction would be in answers C and D. Thus, on the basis of ingrained conversational factors, answers A and B are ruled out. The test-taker,

---

[3] The above question is taken from the Armed Forces Vocational Aptitude Battery, but the measuring instrument and the object measured have been changed due to matters of confidentiality. The syntax and the question format, however, are unchanged.

using his knowledge that *start* neither presupposes nor entails that the activity will be finished during any specific step, and perhaps having some additional knowledge about sound level meters, might choose C as the best answer, since *start* would not rule out *going up* the range as another possible step to gauging the voltage. Either C or D could be understood to include the other. In this case, the correct answer, B, can be ruled out by a knowledge of language. At the very least, the test-taker's knowledge of language could be involved in a conflict with his knowledge of a sound level meter. Conversational factors of the type shown here involving inferences can be viewed as large-scale presuppositions that a language user applies to situations of language use. If they do not hold, the situation and task do not make sense.

LINGUISTIC ITEMS

The third aspect of test interference involves the actual differences in linguistic items of tests and the linguistic items which a given speaker may have as a part of his linguistic system. The basis for this sort of investigation is found in the descriptive linguistic accounts of various linguistic systems as they contrast with the linguistic items found in tests. In a sense, this is what is done in what has traditionally been considered under the rubric of CONTRASTIVE LINGUISTICS. In contrastive linguistics, the descriptive accounts of two linguistic systems are placed side by side in order to observe where the patterns of the languages are similar and where they are different. These accounts may consider different levels of language systems including the way phonological, syntactical, or semantic systems are organized. In contrastive studies as they are applied to differing languages or dialects, these comparisons then serve as a basis for predicting where the speaker of Language Variety A will encounter difficulty when confronted with Language Variety B. Although all predicted interference will not, of course, be realized for one reason or another, the comparison can anticipate many of the patterns or items which will in fact interfere.[4]

---

[4] There seem to be several different types of reasons why certain predicted items may not occur. One reason is that many of the features which differentiate social dialects are differences in frequency distributions rather than categorical differences. Another is the fact that an individual speaker may not be characterized by all the features found in the types of general descriptions that linguists make of non-mainstream varieties. Still another may relate to an individual's ability to switch to more Standard English-type responses because of the formality of test situations. The relationship of predicted and realized linguistic interference in tests is currently being investigated by Wiggins (in press).

On the basis of a contrastive analysis of Standard English and any particular nonmainstream variety, we may predict what types of interference we would expect a test to hold for the speaker of that nonmainstream variety. This can be done for language tests dealing with any particular level of linguistic organization, although our descriptive information on some levels (e.g., phonological) is more complete than it is for other levels (e.g., lexicon).

Direct Interference of Linguistic Items

The aspects of potential bias on these levels can readily be seen by looking at several different language development tests. There are many different types of tests currently used to evaluate language development among preschool and kindergarten children. The significance of these tests should not be underestimated, for in many instances they have been used as the basis for the establishment of extensive language intervention programs. In other cases, children are recommended for extended periods of speech therapy on the basis of such tests.

Aspects of language development typically dealt with in diagnostic tests include articulatory development, auditory discrimination, grammatical development, and vocabulary acquisition. In some school districts, a battery of tests covering these areas are routinely given to every child in order to determine whether the child is progressing "normally" in his language development. Children with language disabilities are then referred to speech therapists for individual attention. The purpose, then, is to diagnose speech pathologies. The fact that disproportionate numbers of children from particular dialect areas are considered to have speech pathologies should immediately raise suspicion about the application of these tests.

Articulation testing is one of the areas in which dialect bias is most readily apparent. Typically, the articulation test consists of the examiner showing a series of pictures to the child. The child is told to name the item in the picture. In each item, the examiner is looking for the production of certain sounds in particular positions. For example, in an item such as *run,* he may be examining the production of the initial *r* and the final *n.* As it turns out, in most of these tests articulatory development is measured solely in terms of Standard English norms. Thus, in a commonly used articulation test such as the Templin-Darley Test of Articulation, sounds such as the diphthong *ay* in *pie, th* in *teeth, r* in *car, st* cluster in *nest,* and *th* in *there* are all considered diagnostic in determining the level of articulatory development. If the prescribed sound is not produced, it is scored as a "misarticulation," "substitution," or "omission."

On the basis of our description of phonological features of social dialects found in works by Labov (1972) and Wolfram and Fasold (1974), we know that each of the above-cited items may have a realization different from the one prescribed in the test. Some of these, such as the correspondence of *f* for final *th* in *teeth* or the final *s* for *st* in *nest* are regular realizations in certain socially stigmatized dialects; others, however, may be considered to be a part of certain regional standards, such as the monophthongization of *ay* in *pie*, or the absence of *r* in *car*. In the diagnostic form of this articulation test, there are a total of 176 sounds which are tested. For over 70 of these items, we expect realizations which might legitimately differ from the expected norm based on a social or regional dialect pattern. This is over one-third of all the items in the test. Now suppose an 8-year-old speaker of Vernacular Black English produces all the sounds correctly except for the items which may be different in his own dialect. (This is, of course, a hypothetical situation since the child would probably not be expected to give all Vernacular Black English forms for all items, given the inherently variable nature of some of the items as mentioned in Footnote 4. On the other hand, we could not realistically expect him to get correct responses on all the other items.) When his score is compared with the expected norms for various age levels, we find that the 8-year-old falls beneath the norm (i.e., mean) for the 4-year-old. Even if we realistically allow for only half of the potentially biased items to be realized in their dialectally divergent form, the child would still fall below the mean for the 5-year-old. It is no wonder, then, that disproportionate numbers of children from nonmainstream-speaking linguistic environments are erroneously classified as having retarded articulation development.

Similar types of problems can be predicted for language-based auditory discrimination tests. Items for auditory discrimination tests are typically based on Standard English norms without any provision for other dialects. The problems in these tests can be readily illustrated by looking at one of the popular tests given to determine the development of sound discrimination skills, namely, the Wepman Auditory Discrimination Test. The test is based essentially on the principle of MINIMAL WORD PAIRS. In this format, word pairs are orally presented to the subject. Some of the pairs differ by one sound (the minimal word pair) while others are produced identically. The examiner speaks aloud the word pairs to the subject, who is instructed to respond whether the pairs sound the same or different. For example, the subject may be given the items *zone–zone*, to which he is expected to respond that they are the same, and *pit–pet*, to which he is expected to respond that they are different. Unfortunately, some of the items which are minimal word pairs in one dialect are homophonous in other dialects. For example, items such as *pin–pen*, *wreath–reef, lave–lathe,* and *sheaf–sheath* are all supposed to be perceived as different. But based on the rules which have been described for various social and regional dialects all of the above illustrations would be considered homophonous.

At this point, one may suggest that even if children do not make certain phonological distinctions between words, they still should be able to perceive the difference produced by the tester. But this is not necessarily the case, since we edit items to correspond to our own sound system. Because of this editing process, it is much more difficult to perceive distinctions we ordinarily do not make. This difficulty can be easily illustrated by the perception problems encountered by English speakers learning the Spanish sound system. When asked to distinguish between *p* and *b* in Spanish, they typically have problems initially because they perceive the sounds in terms of the English system. In Spanish, *p* and *b* are just distinguished by voicing, but in English, *p* is usually also distinguished from *b* by aspiration [p^h]. In many instances, it is this aspiration which is the most important identifying characteristic. Without the aspiration as a cue, introductory students want to assign Spanish *p* to *b*, although the native Spanish speaker would have no difficulty hearing the distinction. The problem for the introductory Spanish student is not primarily one of auditory discrimination, but the tendency to filter the sounds through his own system of contrasts. A similar type of filtering process can be expected by the speaker of a dialect where he does not ordinarily expect contrasts between sounds.

Developmental tests for grammatical ability do not fare much better than those designed to measure various aspects of phonology. The validity of such tests in measuring ANY child's actual grammatical maturity is quite questionable. In many instances, the variables which are used to measure grammatical development simply do not match the variables which research on language acquisition point out as diagnostic for various stages of acquisition. But if the validity of these tests is questionable for Standard English-speaking children, the problems are compounded for the speaker of a nonstandard dialect. In most conventional grammatical tests, only a Standard English grammatical form is accepted as a correct response. Again we can best exemplify this point by looking at an actual test, the Illinois Test of Psycholinguistic Abilities (ITPA). ITPA consists of a battery of tests to measure various aspects of language development. One of the subtests dealing directly with grammar is called "grammatic closure." In this section, the child is asked to supply a missing word in a sentence as the tester points to a picture. For example, the examiner shows a picture of two beds to a child. He points to the first and says, "Here is a bed." Then he points to the two beds and says, "Here are two_____." The child is expected to respond with the form *beds* if he has acquired the grammatical category of pluralization. All of the expected forms must be in Standard English in order to be accepted as a correct response. Thus, the child who responds with *hisself* for *himself,* *mans* or *mens* for *men,* and *hanged up* for *hung up* must be scored as incorrect. Of the total of 33 actual items in this part of the test, 27 of them may legitimately have different dialect forms according to the rules formulated in Wolfram and Fasold (1974). Obviously, any child who does not speak Standard English cannot expect to score well in this area. Ultimately, such responses are interpreted erroneously as indicative of delayed grammatical development and in need of remediation.

Finally, we should mention something about vocabulary tests even though we have less information on lexical differences in different social dialects of American English.

There are a number of different ways in which vocabulary tests can be directly biased against various dialects of English. In some cases, culture-specific vocabulary items are used, that is, the word is outside the experience of the testee. For example, the use of the term *tobaggan* may clearly be outside the experience of certain social or regional groups. It is also possible that an item may be within the experience of a given subculture, but it is known by a different term. A child, for example, may not be familiar with the term *spectacles,* but he may be quite familiar with this item when referred to as *glasses* or *eyeglasses.* In a tabulation of potentially culture-specific items in the Peabody Picture Vocabulary Test, one of the main standards for measuring vocabulary development in young children, Roberts (1970, p. 21) notes that 13 of the first 50 items (26%) are potentially culture-specific to speakers of Standard English. Nonstandard speakers can hardly expect to compete with middle-class Standard English speakers given this sort of potential bias. In addition to the above types of bias, there exists the possibility that a child may be familiar with a term, only to be thrown off by the particular pronunciation of the item as given by the examiner. Thus, if *wasp* is pronounced something like *wahsp* by the examiner while the child would normally produce it something like *waws,* the child may not be sufficiently sophisticated to overcome the variation. We must remember that in an artificial testing situation, the extralinguistic and linguistic contexts that normally could be appealed to for comprehension are often absent.

Nondirect Interference of Linguistic Items

In the preceding section, we have dealt only with the prediction of fairly straightforward linguistic bias as related to speakers of nonmainstream varieties. Two further points need to be mentioned, however. First of all, we must note that the absence of direct interference of the type discussed above does not necessarily mean that there exists no bias related to linguistic forms and items. The use of language items in a test may potentially result in difficulties for the test-taker regardless of the content area if his language is not isomorphic with the language of the test. Although the prediction of specifically interferring items on a test dealing with a content area other than language may be somewhat more difficult due to the other factors which may result in a right or wrong answer, the potential bias remains, nonetheless. Second, we must point out that although our discussion of language differences in tests and spoken language has focused on nonmainstream speakers, this should not be understood to imply that there is complete isomorphy between the language of tests and the spoken language of even the most mainstream Standard English speaker. There is a sense in which the language of most tests does not really match the ordinary language patterns of practically all test-takers because language patterns used in testing represent a style of language which is somewhat different from natural conversation.

The style of speech typically used in testing is what we might designate the "formal standard." Formal standardization in language is based on the written language of established writers, which automatically limits it to the most formal style of older, highly educated speech. As a result, the standardized form of any language is nearly always conservative to the point of obsolescence. It also refers to what is prescribed for a language by the grammar and usage books, dictionaries, orthoepical guides, and in some instances, language academies. As it turns out, these formal codes are drawn up such that no one, or almost no one, actually speaks the formal standard language. Consider again the illustration we gave earlier in which the question was stated *When measuring an unknown volume with a sound level meter, the proper precaution is to start with the* . . . . Both the vocabulary and the syntactical arrangement of the units would be unexpected in natural conversation. The first clause in normal conversation might be expected to come out like *When you want to measure the volume* . . . including an overt use of impersonal *you*, the statement that this is a desirable act to undertake as indicated in *want to*, and an elimination of the vocabulary item *unknown* since it is presumed that one only measures things which he does not already know. We can further point out the notion of a question in this item as it is stylistically defined in terms of a testing situation. The example given above was introduced along with other items in the test as a question. But the item takes the form of a sentence completion task which probably would not be defined as a question in natural conversation.

At this point, we are only illustrating the discrepancy of the language style of testing and the language style of ordinary conversation for the speaker of any dialect of English. But viewing discrepancy for the non-standard speaker we see an extension of the continuum considerably beyond that of the standard speaker, since the natural conversation of the nonstandard speaker is considerably more diverse from formal Standard English than it is for the informal Standard English speaker. Representing this discrepancy in terms of a continuum, we may illustrate this simply as follows:

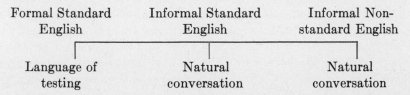

Justification for this type of continuum rests upon a basic fact about the discipline of linguistics and a basic assumption of sociolinguistics. Linguists of whatever theoretical persuasion recognize that a grammar must be adequate to describe the competence of the speaker–hearer as a unit; that is, there are no proposals for grammars that could account only for the ability to produce communication exclusive of or in contradiction (of) the ability to understand or vice versa. Empirical and theoretical concerns motivate this stance. Sociolinguists, observing the heterogeneity of a speech community, add to this the basic notion that the speaker–hearer competence is asymmetrical, that is, a description of speaking competence is a subset of a description of understanding. These two notions allow us to posit a continuum as a model with the entire speaker–hearer unit placed on the continuum with adjacency relationships between pairs of speakers and/or groups of speakers established by means of the contact of each overlapping unit even when the judgment depends on factors present only in the larger understanding competence. Furthermore, sociolinguists have consistently observed a relationship between social class and stylistic factors such that the more formal style of a given lower social class is closer to the language of a higher social class than is the less formal style, and the less formal style of a given higher class is closer to the language of a lower social class than is the more formal style. This last notion allows us to posit that the character and direction of the continuum is, in its essential features, as is suggested here.

On the basis of this sort of continuum, we may suggest a reasonable hypothesis of language interference in testing which may apply to direct and indirect interference: *The more distant the speaking style of natural conversation is from the language of testing, the more potential linguistic interference there will be for the testee.*[5] In terms of this hypothesis, we may predict that those items which accentuate the formal Standard English may be found to have an effect on all testees confronted with the language style of testing. But since the distance between formal Standard English and informal Nonstandard English is greater than that between formal Standard English and informal Standard English, the more serious interference will be caused for the nonstandard speaker.

CONCLUSION

If nothing else, I hope that this presentation will point out some of the relevant questions that must be asked about tests from a sociolinguistic perspective. If we are dealing with a language test, we must begin by asking what aspect of language the test claims to be testing. Following our familiarization with what the test claims to be testing, we must ask what aspect of language the test is actually testing. All tests which consistently differentiate groups of individuals measure something, but it may not necessarily measure what is set out to measure. Some current tests may be rather effective tools for measuring certain linguistic abilities, but they may not be the abilities which the test was designed to measure. If appropriate, we must ask what specific problems the test may pose for a speaker of a nonmainstream variety. This question must deal not only with the predicted responses which will differ from the Standard English norm, but the assumptions of the test as a social occasion as well. In light of these matters, then, we must ask how the scores should be interpreted for both the mainstream and the nonmainstream speaker. With reference to nonlanguage tests, we are still confronted with the social occasion, the language of directions, and how language is used as a vehicle to tap the information that is desired. All of these are considerations in viewing any test from the vantage point of sociolinguistics.

Although there have been some promising insights already gained about the nature of testing from this perspective [e.g., Cicourel (1970), Roberts (1970), and Meier (1973)], we have only begun to tap the potential contributions that must be made on all three of the levels which I have discussed here. If we can recognize and do something about the levels of sociolinguistic bias I have set forth, then perhaps we can start talking about applied sociolinguistics in a nontrivial way. And chances are that, in the process, we will discover some important theoretical principles about the nature of language in society.

[5] For an illustration of the application of the continuum principle to a nonlanguage test, see Griffin, Wolfram, and Taylor (1974). The problem of prediction in such a continuum is, of course, the matter of discrete quantification.

ACKNOWLEDGMENTS

Many discussions with Reg Griffin have aided me immeasurably in formulating the ideas expressed in this contribution.

REFERENCES

Cicourel, A. V. *Language and school performance*. Ford Foundation, Division of Public Education, final research report, 1970.

Griffin, P., Wolfram, W., & Taylor, O. A sociolinguistic analysis of the Armed Services vocational aptitude battery. Unpublished final report, Arlington, Virginia: Center for Applied Linguistics, 1974.

King, P. An Analysis of the northwestern syntax screening test for lower class black children in Prince George's County. Unpublished master's thesis, Howard University, 1972.

Labov, W. Systematically misleading data from test questions. Paper presented at University of Michigan Colloquium, Ann Arbor, Michigan, 1970.

Labov, W. *Language in the inner city: Studies in the Black English vernacular* Philadelphia: University of Pennsylvania Press, 1972.

Makay, R. Standardized tests: Objective/objectified measures of "competence." In A. Cicourel, *Language and school performance*. Ford Foundation, Division of Public Education, final research report, 1970.

Meier, D. *Reading failure and the tests*. New York: Workshop Center for Open Education, 1973.

Raspberry, W. *The Washington Post*, September 4, 1974, p. 23.

Roberts, E. An evaluation of standardized tests as tools for the measurement of language development. In *Language research Report*, No. 1, Cambridge: Language Research Foundation, 1970.

Roth, D. R. Intelligence testing as a social activity. In A. Cicourel, *Language and school performance*. Ford Foundation, Division of Public Education, final research report, 1970.

Turner, D. R. *Practice for the Armed Forces tests*. New York: Arco, 1973.

U.S. Department of Labor. *Doing your best on aptitude tests*. Washington, D.C.: U.S. Government Printing Office, 1968.

Ward, M. C. *Them children: A study in language learning*. New York: Holt, Rinehart, and Winston, 1971.

Wiggins, M. E. Predictive bias analysis in the administering of the Templin–Darley Test of Articulation to eight-year-old speakers of Black English. Unpublished doctoral dissertation, University of Pittsburgh, forthcoming.

Wolfram, W., & Fasold, R. *The study of social dialects in American English*. Englewood Cliffs, New Jersey: Prentice-Hall, 1974.

Biographical Sketches

JOHN B. CARROLL is Professor of Psychology and Director of the L. L. Thurstone Psychometric Laboratory at the University of North Carolina. He had recently been a Senior Research Psychologist at the Educational Testing Service. His teaching career at Harvard spanned some eighteen years, from 1949 to 1967.

Receiving his doctorate in Psychology from Minnesota in 1941, he has a continued interest in language, authoring two books, *The Study of Language* (1953) and *Language & Thought* (1964) and editing the well-known *Language, Thought and Reality: Collected Writings of B. L. Whorf* (1956). He is the recipient of several awards and honors, has served as President of Division 15 of the American Psychological Association and the Psychonomic Society and helped to found the National Academy of Education.

ANN COVINGTON is an Associate Professor and Chairwoman of the Speech and Hearing Program at Federal City College. After serving as a consultant for the Detroit Public School System, she spent two years teaching English as a second language in Ethiopia as a member of the Peace Corps.

She received her doctorate in Communication from the University of Pittsburgh prior to coming to Federal City College in 1972. In addition to her academic duties, she is an active member of a number of national agencies that deal with communication problems or public services such as the American Speech and Hearing Association, Board of Directors of

United Cerebral Palsy, National Council for Black Child Development and the Gerontological Society.

ERNEST DUNN is Associate Professor and Chairman of the Departments of African and Afro-American Studies in Livingston College, Rutgers University. Dr. Dunn received his Bachelor of Arts degree from Wesleyan University, his Bachelor of Divinity from Hartford Seminary Foundation and his masters and doctoral degrees from Michigan State University. His major interests include African literature and folklore, Black English, language teaching and curriculum development, and Descriptive Linguistics. He has done fieldwork in Africa and taught African languages in the Peace Corps training program at Michigan State University. He was also Language Coordinator for that program at Boston University. Professor Dunn has published a number of articles on African and Afro-American linguistics.

ROY FREEDLE is a Senior Research Psychologist at the Educational Testing Service. He received a doctorate in Experimental Psychology at Columbia University in 1964, and does research in psycholinguistics. He has coedited a book on the subject with John Carroll, *Language Comprehension and The Acquisition of Knowledge* (1972) and has co-authored a book with another of our contributors, William Hall, entitled *Culture and Language: An Essay on The Black American Experience* (1975).

ANGELA GILLIAM is an Associate Professor of Anthropology at the State University of New York, College at Old Westbury. She received her Bachelor of Arts degree from the University of California at Los Angeles in 1958, in Latin American Studies, and did graduate work in Ethnology and Applied Anthropology at the National School of Anthropology and History, Mexico City. Fluent in English, Spanish, Portuguese and French, Ms. Gilliam is currently writing her dissertation on *Language Attitudes and Ethno-Class in Salvador, Bahia, and São Paulo,* based on field work conducted in Brazil. She has published several articles relating to African language in the Americas, and is currently translating the last works of Brazilian poet, Solano Trindade.

WILLIAM S. HALL received his doctorate in Clinical Psychology at the University of Chicago in 1968. Since then he has taught at Princeton University where he was a Jonathan Dickinson Bicentennial Preceptor, and at Vassar College. He is the Chairman of the Committee on Research for the Association of Black Psychologists. At present, his research interests are on language acquisition and usage, particularly by Black Americans, and he carries out this work as an Associate Professor and the Director of the Institute on Comparative Development at Rockefeller University.

DEDORAH SEARS HARRISON is currently a Ford Foundation Fellow and is writing her doctoral dissertation in psycholinguistics in the Department of Psychology at Princeton University. A native of Kansas City, she was a University Scholar at New York University, from which she obtained her bachelor's degree in Psychology in 1971. In the fall of 1975, she will assume the duties of an Assistant Professor of Psychology at the University of Kansas and will teach courses on psycholinguistics and cognitive psychology.

WILLIAM G. MOULTON, a Professor of Linguistics at Princeton University since 1960, received his doctorate in Germanic Linguistics at Yale University in 1941. He has been a President of the Linguistic Society of America and has authored three books: *Swiss German Dialect and Romance Patois* (1941), *The Sounds of English and German* (1962), *A Linguistic Guide to Language Learning* (1966, 1972). A specialist in Swiss German dialects, Professor Moulton has been particularly interested in phonology, and has held Fulbright, American Council of Learned Societies, and Guggenheim Fellowships for study in Switzerland and the Netherlands.

VERLEY O'NEAL is now a graduate student in Educational Psychology at Stanford University. A native of New Orleans, Louisiana, he majored in Psychology at Princeton University, specializing in psycholinguistics. He was a student member of the seminar, and his senior thesis served as the basis for his chapter. He completed his studies and graduated from Princeton in June, 1974.

KLAUS RIEGEL received his doctorate from the Universität Hamburg in 1958, and is a German–American English bilingual. He is currently Professor of Psychology and Chairman of the Program in Psycholinguistics at the University of Michigan with which he has been associated since 1959. Professor Riegel is also Editor of the journal, *Human Development*, and has research interests in psycholinguistics and gerontology. He is a past President of the Gerontological Society.

GILBERT SPRAUVE comes from the Virgin Islands and, after completing his doctorate in Linguistics at Princeton University in 1974, returned to his post of Assistant Professor of Modern Language at the College of the Virgin Islands.

He received bachelor's degrees in French from Brooklyn College and in Hispanic Studies from the University of Puerto Rico (both in 1960) as well as a master's in Linguistics from the University of Southern California (1965). He is interested in West Indian creoles and spent a Fulbright year (1968–1969) on St. Lucia and the Dominica Islands collecting curriculum materials for a patois class held at the College of the Virgin Islands.

DANILLE TAYLOR is now a free-lance writer and a credit analyst for the Philadelphia National Bank, and studies evenings at the Wharton School. She was a student member of the seminar, majored in English at Princeton and graduated in June, 1974, with a certificate from the Afro-American Studies Program. Her senior thesis was entitled, "Black Novels, 1920–1930," involving both thematic and historical analyses of Black writers during that decade.

TOM TRABASSO is a Professor of Psychology at Princeton University, where he teaches courses in language, thought, cognition, and cognitive development. He received his doctorate in Experimental Psychology from Michigan State University in 1961, did postdoctoral research at Stanford University and taught at the University of California, Los Angeles, prior to coming to Princeton. He has coauthored a book with Gordon H. Bower, *Attention in Learning* (1967) and has been an Editor of *Cognitive Psychology*.

ELIZABETH TRAUGOTT was born in Great Britain and received her bachelor of arts degree in English Language at Oxford University in 1960, and a doctorate in the same subject at the University of California, Berkeley, in 1964. She became an Associate Professor in Linguistics at Stanford University in 1970, after teaching at Berkeley. She is author of the book, *A History of English Syntax* (1972), and was a Visiting Associate Professor at Princeton during the time the seminar was held in the fall of 1973.

IVAN VAN SERTIMA, born in Guyana, studied at the University of London. He is presently an Assistant Professor at Douglas College, Rutgers University, where he teaches courses in Third World literatures and the African presence in American cultures. Formerly with the Guyana Information Service and the Central Office of Information in London, Ivan Van Sertima has extensive broadcasting experience with the British Broadcasting Corporation and has also broadcast for the Canadian Broadcasting Corporation and West German Radio.

The author of numerous short stories and special studies, he has written a collection of poetry, *River and the Wall, Caribbean Writers (Critical Essays)*, and has also compiled *A Swahili Dictionary of Legal Terms*. He is presently working on a book on African contacts with the Americas in pre-Columbian times, which is to be published by Random House in the fall of 1975.

EUGENE WIGGINS is an Assistant Professor in Speech and Communication at Federal City College where he also coordinates the Speech and Hearing Clinic. He received his bachelor of science degree in Speech Pathology at the Hampton Institute in 1963, and his masters in the same field in 1969, from the University of Michigan. In addition to his teaching and administrative duties at Federal City College, he is working on a doctorate in Speech Pathology at the University of Pittsburgh.

RONALD WILLIAMS is now the Provost as well as a Professor of Communication Sciences at Federal City College. He has been an active contributor to research, reviews and practice in the areas of speech and language since receiving his doctorate in Phonetics and Psycholinguistics at Ohio State University in 1969, and prior study leading to bachelor of arts and master's degrees at Western Reserve University.

A Fellow of the American Speech and Hearing Association, he has edited a book with Orlando Taylor, *Blacks and Their Word: Linguistics to Criticism*, which will be published soon by the Indiana University Press.

WALTER WOLFRAM received his doctorate in Linguistics from the Hartford Seminary Foundation in 1969. At present, he holds the positions of Professor of Communication Sciences at Federal City College and Senior Researcher at the Center for Applied Linguistics. His interest centers in sociolinguistics and he has done a number of studies on speech by minority members in American society. He has written four books: *Field Techniques in An Urban Language Study* (with R. W. Shuy and W. K. Riley, 1968), *A Sociolinguistic Description of Detroit Negro Speech* (1969), *Sociolinguistic Aspects of Assimilation: Puerto Rican English in New York City* (1973), and *The Study of Social Dialects in The United States* (with R. W. Fasold, 1974). In addition, he coedited, with N. H. Clarke, *Black-White Speech Relations* (1971).

Author Index

Subject Index